Monetary uncertainty

ୠୠ Bank Mendes Gans nv 1883-1983

Eduard J. Bomhoff

Monetary uncertainty

1983
North-Holland
Amsterdam - New York - Oxford

© ELSEVIER SCIENCE PUBLISHERS B.V., 1983

ISBN 0 444 86734 1

Publishers :

ELSEVIER SCIENCE PUBLISHERS B.V.
P.O. BOX 1991
1000 BZ AMSTERDAM
THE NETHERLANDS

Sole distributors for the U.S.A. and Canada :

ELSEVIER SCIENCE PUBLISHING COMPANY, INC.
52 VANDERBILT AVENUE
NEW YORK, N.Y. 10017

LIBRARY OF CONGRESS CATALOGING IN PUBLICATION DATA

Bomhoff, Eduard J., 1944-
Monetary uncertainty

Includes index
1. Money.
2. Uncertainty.
3. Title
HG221.B57483 1983   332.4   83-14047
ISBN 0-444-86734-1

BOOK DESIGN AND ILLUSTRATION HANS DEN HOLLANDER

PRINTED SSN NIJMEGEN

Foreword

It is at our request that Professor Dr. E.J. Bomhoff has written this book on 'Monetary Uncertainty' in honour of the 100 years anniversary of the Bank in August, 1983.

Our many friends and relations here and abroad will, we feel sure, be pleased with the offering of this study on a current topic from the hand of an expert such as Professor Bomhoff of the Erasmus University in Rotterdam.

We consider ourselves fortunate to have found Drs. L. Metzemaekers, former Managing Editor of 'Het Financieel Dagblad', willing to introduce this book with an account of our Bank's history. In this he gives an oversight of the 100 years of the Bank, seen within the framework of the economic developments in the world during this period.

The publication of 'Monetary Uncertainty' will, we expect, contribute to a better insight into monetary developments in the Western world.

August 1983
Management Bank Mendes Gans nv.

History of Mendes Gans

I The Financial World of Amsterdam Circa 1880

The history of the Bank Mendes Gans goes back to the year 1883, when the Amsterdam born Julius Gans founded a stockbrokerage office under the name Gans and Company. It is clear from his first business stationary that he acted as an agent or correspondent for the Parisian firm F.L. Huilier and the London house Pinto and Oppenheim. This indicated that the 'securities, drafts and coupons' he traded in, according to the same source, were mainly of foreign origin, as was customary at the time on the Dutch Stock Exchange.

Gans operated chiefly at the Amsterdam Stock Exchange, which had a different function in the 80's of the last century than it would have later. When Julius Gans, in 1883, became a member of the 'Society for the Stock Exchange', this society had been founded only seven years before with the aim of bringing law and order to the trade in stocks at the Amsterdam Stock Exchange. It originated from the 'General Exchange Committee' and the 'Securities Society' dating back to 1857. The need for law and order was, indeed, great. In 1860, a group of 127 stockbrokers asked the Amsterdam City Council for measures to maintain order. The Commodities Exchange and the Stock Exchange had been housed in the Exchange building of Hendrick de Keyser on the Rokin since the 17th century, which due to decay had to be torn down in 1835. In its place came the 'Exchange with the Columns' on the Dam Square on the site where eventually the store the Bijenkorf would rise. Anyone could visit the Stock Exchange for a fee of twenty-five cents. One can imagine the bustle and noise, upon reading that on Mondays, the average number of visits was 5,000 and on other days, an average of 3,000.

The Stock Exchange flourished and went through an enormous expansion period at the expense of the commodity trade, which was not very active in the 80's of the last century. Although Amsterdam was very important as a commodities market in 17th century Europe, during Napoleon's reign, and as a result of the 'continental system', the important commodity markets were moved to London. Moreover, many commodity dealers crossed over to stock trading so that from 1860, more than a quarter of the available space in the Exchange building was occupied by it. Professional dealers, speculators and the plain curious crowded in the corner of the building where the stock trade took place. In 1830, the government was requested to bar non-participants, but this was thought of as a breach of trade freedom. Stocks were seen as normal goods which everyone could freely offer. 'Buying and selling stocks is not a profession in itself; everyone is free to practise it', according to a ministerial verdict from 1861. In 1871, the Amsterdam Chamber of Commerce was still of that same opinion.

However, around the middle of the 19th century, the stock trade concentrated on professional practice with the exclusion of adventurers and speculators. Moreover, a specialisation took place, in connection with changes in the structure of the aforementioned international commodities trade. The trade in drafts and securities, which before had been a side activity to the Commodity Exchange, developed into an independent trade.

As a result, the need for individual space, rules of admission, and regulations for the notation of price quotations grew. In 1876, from this triple need originated the 'Society for the Stock Exchange'. It was 1913 when the Stock Exchange acquired its own building on the Beursplein (the Stock Exchange Square), the site of the former, well known, 'Bible' hotel. This put a definite halt to the frequent riots, which previously resulted in the police being called in, and which gave a bad reputation to stock trading.

The Society did not immediately succeed in this. Only gradually, and over several years would it succeed in professionalising, setting down procedures for, and technically equipping the trade according to the technological developments of its time with the installation of the telephone and the telegraph as a means of communication and information.

It was still rather chaotic at the Stock Exchange at the time Julius Gans started his stock brokerage office. The Exchange was then an attraction for Dutch, as well as foreign tourists who regularly disturbed the peace. The Amsterdam police acted with great reluctance and were empowered to act by the mayor only under exceptional circumstances. This often resulted in the professional dealers taking matters into their own hands to restore order. Thus it was possible that 'a group of people from the stocktrading corner of the Exchange' was forced to bodily remove four 'Zeeuwse landlieden' (Zeeland farmers) on August 24, 1884. It wasn't until 1913, when the Stock Exchange occupied its own building, that these disturbances were put to an end. The Society had, by then, firmly instituted professional trade, organised the noting of the price quotations, and restricted admittance to its own members who had to fulfill specific requirements set down by the Board of Directors. Only stockbrokers and securitiesbrokers who could prove they were in trade as a profession (and practised that profession in Amsterdam), as well as banks situated in Amsterdam, could become members of the Society and participate in the trade at the Exchange. This territorial requirement, which was maintained until after the First World War, gave an advantage to the professional traders and banks in Amsterdam over those in the provinces and contributed greatly to Amsterdam becoming the financial center of the Netherlands, as it had been the center for commodity trade in the 17th and 18th centuries.

The flourishing stock trade was, in fact, a split off from the commodity trade. The latter lost much of its importance because of the French occupation and, after that, the nationalistic system in the Dutch East Indies, which made the trade in tropical produce a state monopoly and gave exclusive rights to the Dutch Trading Company, founded by King William I. The stock trade then divested itself of the commodity trade, which would never again regain its international importance. When nationalism was finally abolished under the influence of liberal politics after 1850 and the trade in tropical produce again became private trade, Amsterdam became the founding site of many Netherlands-Indian Companies. But the international importance of the produce trade was limited, and far inferior to the one in London.

The independent trade in stock was primarily aimed at foreign countries when Gans started his stockbrokers office. Foreign funds were in great demand by Dutch investors. In 1890, they had approximately DFL. 3 billion in foreign currencies. Only ten percent of the stocks traded in Amsterdam were Dutch and were mainly government loans and traditional funds from commerce and shipping.

The Netherlands was then at the beginning of its Industrial Revolution, which started seventy-five years later here than in the surrounding European countries. In England, this process had started more than a century earlier. The Dutch economy became associated with the modern international economic structure only at the outbreak of World War One. The Stock Exchange initially contributed little or nothing to the industrialisation of its own country. It was not yet functioning as a market for capital for the burgeoning industry. It was primarily a market for individual investors, who were interested in an capital income and who did not want to invest their money in risky industrial shares. Historians of Dutch economy all agree that the beginning industralisation could not be served at the Amsterdam Exchange. There was more faith in foreign stocks and bonds. Not until the period between 1895 and 1914 did interest in industrial investments increase significantly and grow by 200-300 % per year, whereas in the preceding period the growth rate was only 30-60%. This growth concentrated primarily on new branches of industry and on the capital goods industry. Notable is, too, that banks shied away from this investment activity for quite a long time. Banks restricted themselves to the traditional sections of commerce and shipping, thereby indirectly contributing to a healthy investment climate.

In 1914, only ten percent of the national quotations at the Exchange were for industrial enterprises. Then the Dutch investor, who had built up his wealth under pre-industrial circumstances, started to become interested in the rising Dutch industry. The first Dutch industrial fund was noted in 1896.

It was not uncommon to have mutual financial interests between companies and industrial sectors. Cotton weavers had an interest in spinning mills, and ship owners in ship yards. Furthermore, family wealth was used for the foundation of new industries. The most well known, but not exceptional example, was the foundation of Philips in 1891, based on accumulated capital from the banking house of Zaltbommel. provision of capital was also supported by profit surplus.

The importance of foreign funds for the Amsterdam Exchange can be seen from the table below concerning the amounts of traded funds.

Year	Foreign Funds	Dutch East Indian	State Funds	Banks	Tram E Railways
1880	222	11	10	5	28
1885	281	17	21	9	43
1890	368	55	29	12	49
1895	485	92	31	16	48
1900	531	165	46	26	49
1905	596	190	58	43	62
1910	727	201	81	51	66
1914	840	265	109	66	68

(Notations from foreign funds, Dutch East Indian, Dutch State funds, banks and trams and Railways between 1880 and 1914, quoted from Prof. Dr. Johan de Vries: 'A Century Full of Stocks' page 87. The figures indicate the total funds. In 1880, a total of sixty-six Dutch funds were noted. This number was increased to 691 funds in 1914. In contrast there were 840 foreign funds and 265 Dutch East Indian.)

II The Stockbrokerage office of Gans and Co.

Gans and Co. was one of many stockbrokerage offices founded in the last quarter of the previous century. Although it was not one of the really big offices of its time, it did belong to the group which was very internationally oriented, not only as far as the origins of its traded funds were concerned, but also its client base.

It is not certain where the founding capital originated. From later information it is clear, however, that the contribution by Gans himself was DFL. 20.000. Another participant was a certain J. A. Mesritz for DFL. 5,000; both reserved the right 'to bring more capital into the partnership'. There was a company, therefore, but nothing is known about the partner Mesritz. His position at Gans and Co is not clear. We only know that there was a partnership contract between both parties. The name of Mesritz was not mentioned in the name of the company. Possibly the partnership was not entered into on the same day as the founding of the company, which took place in May 1883, although it did occur in the same year.

In a letter dated August 6, 1883, Gans was nominated as a member of the Society for the Stock Exchange, which had been founded seven years before. According to the articles of the statutes, a new member had to be nominated by ten members. In Gans' case these included Messrs. L. Wertheim, H. Goldberg, A. Roelvink, R. van Vloten, J. Cramerius, all well known figures from the financial business world at that time. L. Wertheim, for instance, was a member of the Society of Stock Traders, supporters in 1870 for the foundation of the Society for the Stock Exchange, which eventually took place in 1876.

A. Roelvink was a stockbroker and a member of the Board of Directors of the Society from 1901 to 1915. At the outbreak of the First World War in 1914, he took the initiative for the founding of a syndicate for support of the members of the Exchange who were threatened with financial difficulties by the closure of the Exchange.

R. van Vloten, also a well known stockbroker, was a board member of the Society from 1912 to 1927. Cramerius was one of the founders of the stockbrokers office Cramerius E Vorstius Gleichmann E van Heemstra. All this leads to the conclusion that Gans had very good personal connections among the well known stockbrokers of those days.

Gans had his office at Keizersgracht 631. No information has been kept about the nature of stock in which he traded or about his client base, no more than about his turnover. By oral tradition, we know that Gans was a modest man who was not fond of the limelight, and who did not wish to expand his company too much. Stability and trustworthiness in business were his most outstanding characteristics. He was married, but there were no children to carry on the business.

He had a couple of employees, two of which were L. Wertheim and I. W. Doms in 1883. Nothing is known of the relationship between these three; we only know that Wertheim and Doms resigned their membership in the Society on August 24th of that year. This is clear from a letter from Gans to the Board of Directors in which he asked for their resignation. It is not improbable that Gans had, by then, employed his later partner, I. Mendes. The two of them had an excellent relationship. Their partnership ran smoothly until the death of Gans in 1928.

III Stockbrokerage office of Mendes Gans

In 1889, Mendes was made a partner by Gans. In a letter dated May 23rd of that year, he was nominated by ten members of the Society and shortly thereafter, the company name changed to Mendes Gans and Company.

Both partners had, or so we can assume, their own client portfolios but traded for common account. Their personal relationship was one of two good friends. Isaak Mendes was of Portuguese Jewish descent. He was small of stature and just as modest as his partner. In contrast to Gans, however, Mendes was strongly involved in the profession of stock trading and conducted business with an expertise which commanded respect. By word of mouth, we also know that he had a great interest in administrative affairs. Most initiatives came from him.

Illustrative of the business conducted at that time, is a letter dated February 22, 1899 from the Incassobank in Amsterdam to Julius Gans. It reads as follows:

'Herewith we have the honour to confirm that we will pay to you one sixth part of the net profit we made from the placement, through your mediation, of the following mortgage bonds of the undermentioned mortgage banks, to wit:

$4^1/_2\%$ mortgage bonds from the Innerstädtische Sparkasse AG of Budapest;

$4^1/_2\%$ mortgage bonds from the Mitteldeutsche Baden Kredit Anstalt of Greiz;

$3^1/_2$ and 4% mortgage bonds from the Orange Nassau Mortgage Bank in the Hague;

as such net profit is indicated in our books.

This with the remark, that the agreements for issues as made between us and the aforementioned mortgage banks have been made by way of your mediation. We will pay as well, from the aforementioned agreement, a sixth part of the profits we will make from all subsequent business with the first two mentioned institutions.'

The same payment as decribed here was also promised to I. A. Mendes and, in case of his early demise, Mendes' part would go to Gans. The letter of the Incasso Bank ends as follows:

'With this agreement, all earlier agreements made between you and us under the earlier company Goedewagen and Co. have been superseded.'

No further sources or documents have been kept about the further history of the firm Mendes Gans & Co until 1911. One may assume that business was not unsuccessful and that Mendes was the driving force behind the company. Furthermore, circumstances favoured him. The first 14 years of this century, the stock market in Amsterdam was booming, but this was ended by the First World War. The Amsterdam Stock Exchange still traded mainly in foreign funds, and international money traffic had more freedom than it would ever again obtain. Mendes had extensive relations with Jewish companies from Germany and the Austrian-Hungarian empire. His partner, Gans, devoted his time, in addition to business, to charity. So did his partner, who founded the 'Clara Mendes foundation', a children's home named after his mother.

IV From Stockbrokerage Office to Bank

In 1911, the stockbrokerage office was converted into a bank. We are not sure of the motives for this step, but the initiative will have undoubtedly come from Mendes. Gans had a lot of faith in his partner because of his business talents and, therefore, gave his approval for the founding of a bank. They were of the opinion that in that way they would be able to give more services directly (and not via other banks) which could not be provided by a stockbrokerage office. Moreover, the strong rise of the financial world in the Netherlands and the upward industrial movement could have been of influence. The issue activities, especially of industrial shares, increased considerably, and the banks in particular, profited from this. This caused more rivalry between bankers and stockbrokers in the Society for the Stock Exchange, and at the Amsterdam Exchange. The banks were the ones who won ground from the brokers and traders, and this treatening loss for the stockbrokers could have been the ground for the conversion of the stockbrokerage office into a bank. In any event, as per a letter dated December 16, 1911, the founding of the 'Banking House Mendes Gans & Co' was officially announced and, at the same time, membership in the Society was requested for the Bank and its Board of Directors. This Banking house would continue the business of Mendes Gans & Co., according to the brochure in which the foundation was announced. From this announcement it is clear that it fundamentally concerns a securities bank.

Neither founder became managing director, but had themselves appointed as Board members, together with Walter Hethey, referred to in the founding deed as 'merchant, living in Amsterdam.' The latter did not play an important role in the Bank, as far as we know. Some years later, his name is no longer mentioned in papers at all.

The purpose of the company was, according to the statutes, 'the practice of banking in its broadest sense, including money and funds trade, for ourselves as well as for third parties, the carrying out of administration, and everything connected therewith.'

The capital of the company was DFL. 2 million divided into 2,000 shares of DFL. 1,000 each. The capital was issued in series of 100,000 guilders of which five series were placed at the time of founding. 'The remaining series will have to be placed before November 1, 1921, except when this term is extended by a decision of the shareholders meeting. '(art. 4 of the statutes of the founding papers).

The shares were registered and the placed shares were paid in full at the time of founding. At the issue of further stock, the shareholders had first option on the new shares, in proportion to their owned stock. Transfer of shares needed the approval of the Board of Directors.

The company was run by two managing directors under the supervision of at least three and a maximum of five members of the Board. Each managing director and Board member had to own at least ten shares, which had to remain in his possession for the duration of his position. The first Board of Directors consisted of the following people: I. A. Mendes,

J. L. Gans and Walter Hethey; the first managing directors H. Salomonson Mauritszoon and M. L. Heybroek.

'The books of the company will be closed annually on the 31st of December (for the first time in 1912), and a balance sheet and profit and loss account will be made, which will be presented at the shareholders meeting for approval by a majority vote, after investigation by the Board of Directors.' (art. 18)

In the statutes of the founding papers, nothing is mentioned about investigation or endorsement by a chartered accountant. In those days, this was not legally required, and only a few companies did it voluntarily; the accounting profession was still in its infancy. At most companies, supervision was exercised by the Board of Directors.

According to the statutes, a part of the profits, determined by the managing directors and the Board of Directors, was destined annually for personnel and the management accountant. Ten percent of the annual profit had to be added to the reserve.

I. Mendes was appointed by the founders to request royal approval. Moreover, he was empowered to make changes in the statutes, if demanded by the Minister of Justice. One can conclude from this that Mendes was, indeed, the most important influence in the founding of the Bank. The royal approval was given on November 23, 1911. The first management accountants were Messrs. M. J. Meerburg and T. Holkema.

After founding the Bank, Mendes and Gans both resigned their membership in the Society. The Bank itself, and the managing director, M. J. Heybroek, became members of the Society in their place. The Bank remained in the same location where the stockbrokers office had been, i.e. Keizersgracht 631. Although we do not have any authentic documents from this period, we can assume that the activities in these first years were directed mainly towards trade in securities and deposits, and in coupons and drafts. So the activities of the stockbrokerage office were more or less continued with this difference that before, one had to go through an external bank relation whereas now, bank servicing could be provided in house.

Around 1911, historians note the rather radical changes in Dutch finance, which consisted of the big banks aiming for issuance of more loans to Dutch industry. Before, this was done by The Netherlands Bank. But The Netherlands Bank gradually transferred credit issuing to the commercial banks in the period between 1889 and 1914. Then, as well, the first consolidations in the banking world took place. At the beginning of March, 1911, there was a merger between the Rotterdam Bank and the Deposit and Administration Bank in Rotterdam, under the name of the Rotterdam Bank Society.

The former was, by then, specialised in extending loans to the business world, and the latter in stock trade. A couple of weeks after the merger, the Rotterdam Bank Society was able to acquire an interest in the Amsterdam stockbrokers company of Determeijer Wesling and Son, and through this, gained admittance to the Amsterdam Stock Exchange. For according to the rules then in practice, one had to trade stock in Amsterdam to become a member in the Society for the Stock Exchange; and only through this membership was one admitted to the Stock Exchange.

When Mendes Gans started as a bank, there was tumult in the Dutch financial world. The larger banks for the first time started establishing branches throughout the country. Three banks gained a clearly superior position by this. These were the aforementioned Rotterdam Bank Society, the Amsterdam Bank, and the Twentsche Bank Society.

Nothing has shown us that the Bank Mendes Gans also worked in the field of credit financing to industry in this starting period. At the Stock Exchange, there was a rather hostile attitude towards the big banks, and this is probably the reason for the aloof attitude of Mendes towards industrial financing. In addition to this, Mendes himself and both managing directors came from the stock market. That was the field of their expertise. In the days that they gained this expertise, the Amsterdam Stock Exchange rarely traded in Dutch industrial shares.

The clutch that the Amsterdam banks and stockbrokers had on the rest of Holland was obvious. Thanks to the aforementioned restriction (that the Exchange only gave admission to stock brokers and banks situated in Amsterdam) the provincial banks and stockbrokers had to work the Exchange through their Amsterdam colleagues. For securities and exchange business, one depended on Amsterdam stockmarket agents. The privately wealthy also had their stock business taken care of by offices situated in Amsterdam. Mendes Gans will have already profited from this as a stockbrokerage-office, and the Bank Mendes Gans will have continued their tradition in this field. Undoubtedly, this is the origin of the activities which, later on, were practised so succesfully by the Bank, i.e. the management of private wealth, mainly stock portfolios in which foreign shares dominated.

At the Stock Exchange, with the rivalry between banks on the one side, and stockbrokers and commission agents on the other, Mendes had foreseen the dominating position of the banks. As already stated, this could have been a stimulans for him to convert the stock brokerage office into a bank. Mendes Gans was a small bank, among many other small banks. They did not differ from the others in any way, but they profited from the fact that they were situated in Amsterdam. The Amsterdam stock market was known then for its international character, and its attraction for investors from the provinces.

V The Years of the First World War

Only three years after the foundation of the Bank Mendes Gans, the First World War broke out. In spite of the neutrality of the Netherlands in the conflict (which was anxiously maintained by the government), the war economy was deeply felt. War overtook Western Europe in a period of high economic growth. The Amsterdam banking and exchange world was gradually cut off from foreign countries.

One of the first results of the war was the growing interference of the government in the economy in general, and in the stock market and finance in particular. The gradual and quiet growth of the economy came to an end.

On June 28, 1914, the Austrian crown prince was assassinated by a Serbian nationalist in Sarajewo. The already existing tensions suddenly became explosive. On July 23rd followed the Austrian ultimatum to Serbia and this led to an extensive offer of funds on all markets. The ultimatum led to a true panic. The international money exchange traffic became completely chaotic and the dealers could no longer cover their positions. The big money lenders were calling in their loans from every source, the public masses started to hoard food, and there was a run on the banks to exchange banknotes for coins, mainly to silver. In the Netherlands, the panic concentrated itself on The Netherlands Bank. The Vienna Exchange was closed at the end of July, followed by the Exchanges in London, Brussels, Frankfurt and New York. After lengthy discussions, and not without strong internal opposition, the Board of Directors for the Society for the Stock Exchange decided to close the Stock Exchange, on July 29, 1914. The push for closure came especially from about 50 representatives of companies, who feared that by the further fall of price quotations 'undoubtedly a number of firms would no longer be able to supply sufficient cover, while moreover, the aloofness of the creditors, and the tendency to calling in their loans by them, would make it impossible for a lot of companies to rollover the margin transactions.' (quoted from the minutes of the Board meeting of July 29th).

That same day, about 30 stock brokers and bankers, all member of the Society, gathered for a meeting to decide on emergency measures which would make it possible to re-open the Exchange as soon as possible.

The decision was made to found a syndicate for the financing of the exchange business. The idea was to have a great deal of credit available to place margin transactions again, with the aid of The Netherlands Bank and under guarantee of a number of bankers and stockbrokers. The Netherlands Bank was expected to contribute an amount of DFL. 50 million, and those present at the meeting were prepared to add to that an amount of DFL. 10 million. Later, it became apparent that The Netherlands Bank only wanted to provide half of the amount requested, and that is why the

Herengracht looking towards the Amstel, from a water-colour by Hubert Pieter Schouten (1747-1822)

other members of the Society halved their contribution as well.

The following day, renewed heavy discussions took place about the re-opening of the Exchange. Everything revolved around the margin transaction market, which controlled a large part of the Exchange. Through the closure of the Exchange, executions were prevented: debtors received an extension. From the 70's of the last century, the Dutch stock market was based mainly on margin transactions, i.e. one bought stock for a certain amount. These stocks remained with the strockbrokers, who advanced 90% of the purchase sum with the stock as collateral, thus called a margin transaction.

The Society could not come to an agreement about the re-opening. The interest of the creditors and those of the debtors were diametrically opposed. During these discussions, the initiative was taken from the Society by the intervention of the Minister of Agriculture, Industry and Commerce on the grounds of a hastily accepted Exchange Law of 1914. On February 29, 1915, the Exchange was openend again.

The closure had probably prevented a financial disaster. The syndicate founded in haste for the support of the exchange trade became superfluous, but a new syndicate was formed to which The Netherlands Bank made available an amount of DFL. 200 million to which the three largest banks added another DFL. 32 million.

The Exchange Law of 1914 empowered the Minister of Finance (who then had the responsibility over the Exchange instead of the Minister of Agriculture, Industry and Commerce) to determine the opening and closure of the Exchange and to set down regulations for notations of price quotations and the way in which business was conducted at the Exchange. Furthermore, liquidation of the margin transactions, advances on current accounts and other loans, which were from before July 29, 1914, and for which funds were given as collateral, were also under the responsibility of the Minister. Under certain conditions, the current margin transactions could be frozen to give the borrowers time to gradually meet their liabilities. It was a protectionist measure for the thousands of small investors, who would lose from executions at uncontrolled rates after the opening of the Exchange.

In the fierce discussions about re-opening, only about 30 bankers and stockbrokers took part. And among them were not the representatives of the Banking House Mendes Gans & Co. This is a clear sign of this bank's modest place in the Amsterdam stock market and in the Society.

The Board of the Society, together with that of the Society for Stock Trade in Rotterdam, and the Board of the Union for Money and Stock Trade in the Provinces (both were started shortly before the war) informed the Minister, in 1914, that in their opinion, practice had shown that under normal circumstances, there was no need for government intervention in the stock market.

In the last article of the Exchange Law of 1914, for that matter, it was already determined, that the law would be replaced as soon as the extraordinary circumstances came to an end.

The Exchange Law of 1914, however, was not replaced or withdrawn after the war, so that the stock market remains under the force of this law to this day, with only a short interruption during the Second World War. The undecisiveness of the Board of the Society at the beginning of the First World War thus caused government intervention which became permanent.

Gradually, however, on the basis of this law, a practice of consultation grew between the Society and her sister organisations in Rotterdam and the provinces on the one side, and the government on the other; although private organisations kept hammering at the fact that their own internal regulations made direct government intervention unnecessary. In this way they succeeded in preventing a threatened intervention, shortly after the war, which would forbid trade in foreign funds. The Bank Mendes Gans probably escaped disaster in view of its extensive foreign business.

VI The Bank Between Two World Wars

The first important event for the Bank Mendes Gans, after the First World War, was the purchase of the stately building at Herengracht 619, where it is established to this day. By a notorial act, of October 10 of that year, the building was purchased from the then owner, Notary Hendrik Wertheim, by Messrs J. Heybroek and Karel Lansberg, on behalf of the Banking House Mendes Gans and Co. for the amount of DFL. 180,000, free of mortgage. Notary Wertheim had bought it at a public auction in 1881.

The 17th century Amsterdam mayor Jan Six had it built for living quarters in 1667, by the well known architect Adriaen Dortsman, a friend of Six. This can be seen from a 'Liber Amoricum' (called The Little Pandora) in which architectural drawings are shown next to drawings of Rembrandt, handwritten poems by Joost van den Vondel and other manuscripts of 17th century artists.

In the beginning of the 18th century, the house was probably radically altered, but since then it had remained intact, at least as far as the facade and interior was concerned. The majority of the interior had to be drastically adapted however, for a new purpose by the bank.

Shortly after the move to the Herengracht, two small stock brokers offices were taken over, i.e. the firms Edersheim and Heymans. From this and from other sources it is clear that the Bank was doing well in the 20's, even though there are no annual reports which can prove this in figures.

For instance, the Bank in those years participated in syndicates and gave credit, although modestly, to industrial undertakings.

Not much is known, either, of the practices of the Bank in the years of the crises between 1930 and 1940. From indirect sources we know that the Bank, which had a lot of German and Austrian Jewish business relations, experienced drawbacks from the many suspension of payments of banks caused by the great stockmarket 'crash' of 1929 in New York. Extra business was taken on, however, by the bank acting as trustee for capital of German and Austrian Jews who fled to the United States. In general, however, we could also say for this period, that the bank was mainly concerned with the trade of stock and the control of private wealth.

It was also in the 20's that Mendes Gans opened a branch in The Hague. This office originated from the takeover of the stockbrokerage office of André Heymans and Eli Edersheim in The Hague, which took place in 1923.

The Banking House Mendes Gans knew how to hold their own as an independent enterprise in the crises years, contrary to many other small banks, which went under through bankruptcy or were taken over by larger banks. This was caused partly by the wild growth of the Dutch banking world during the 20's, and partly by the crises of the 30's, and the difficulties emanating from this for the international stock trade. Added to that were the problems of international payment traffic and international currency trade which were particularly dependent on the weakening position of the Pound Sterling. The Rotterdam Bank, Marx & Co., fell victim to the depression in 1929. The Rotterdam Banking Society and the Bank Mees & Co. gave a credit guarantee to the creditors under a counter guarantee from The Netherlands Bank. The latter lost an amount of DFL. 28 million on that arrangement. The Bank Association in Amsterdam was re-organised because of solvency problems in 1922. In 1937, however, it again had difficulties. Then, the viable departments were taken over by the Incasso Bank. Even the Rotterdam Bank Society encountered a crises in 1924 with a loss of DFL. 24 million. A bankruptcy could only be staved off by a loan from The Netherlands Bank, in turn supported by government guarantee.

If the banks were too optimistic in their extension of credit to industry in the 20's – most difficulties originated from this – in the 30's they seemed to have learned from bitter experience and were very reticent. Maintaining broad solvency was concentrated upon. The Banking House Mendes Gans was engaged with extending loans to industry on a very limited scale. We know of only two instances. These related to a leather goods factory in Oosterwijk and a factory of office machines, the name of which we can no longer trace.

By then, however, the bank had control over a limited number of important private fortunes. The majority of the activities involved currency exchange deals and, because of the chaotic currency relations, these were very difficult and risky. The Bank, however, managed to survive, which was a big achievement for a small bank during the depression.

VII The Perils of a Banker Under Nazi Occupation

The most trying ordeals from the history of the Bank Mendes Gans occurred during the Second World War and the occupation of the Netherlands by the Germans. If this period was difficult for all banks, it was even more so for Jewish banks. The shareholders of the Bank then were I. Mendes and the families Menko, Heymans and Edersheim. Samuel Edersheim resided in the United States at the outbreak of war in 1940. The son-in-law of Menko was there as well, as a client of Mendes Gans, as well as a member of the Board of Directors – he left because of rumours in 1939 that 'the Germans were coming', to take shares of the Bijenkorf and Menko together safely in one portfolio.

Mauk Edersheim, son of S. Edersheim, already resided by then in the United States so that he could apprentice for a New York brokerage firm. Later, he became a naturalised citizen. After the war, his father returned to the Netherlands.

We know very little about what became of I. Mendes. It is only known that, before the German occupation, he fled to the south of France during the sad 'May Days' of 1940. There, before the end of the war, he died in abject poverty. He was about seventy years old and left no children, as did his partner and co-founder of the Bank, Julius Gans, who had died in 1928, at the age of 65.

C. Lansberg resigned as managing director at the beginning of the oc-cupation. He resigned as a member of the Board as well as a member of the Society voluntarily before the German occupiers forced the Society for the Stock Exchange to expel its Jewish members, and forbid them entrance to the Stock Exchange. He obviously felt the coming malevolance and so made it easy for his colleagues on the Board. They did not have to remove him in the autumm of 1940, when the first anti-Jewish measures for the Society were enforced. C. Lansberg was the only managing director of Mendes Gans who had ever been active on the Board of the Society.

Meanwhile, it did not end with the exclusion of the Jews from the stock market. 'Arianization' of all companies was demanded. As a consequence, the Jews could no longer function in any position in business, therefore, not in the banking and the stock market. The next step was that Jews were robbed of practically all their possessions.

In August 8, 1941, an order was issued that money, cheques, shares of stock, goods and bank deposits belonging to Jews, had to be handed in to Bank Lippmann, Rosenthal & Co. on the Sarphatistraat in Amsterdam. Before, this was a branch of the bank of the same name which had its headquarters on the Nieuwe Spiegelstraat. When the head office appointed a 'Verwalter' (attorney) in the person of A. Flesche, he separated the branche office from the head office and placed it under the management of the German Dr. von Karger. He was given responsibility for all Jewish wealth and possessions.

The Bank and its managing director, von Karger, applied for membership in the Society and, against juridical advice proving the possibility of refusing membership, the Society decided to accept both. For the then chairman, Mr. A.J. d'Ailly, the treatment of the Jews was cause to resign as Chairman and member. His position was filled by the Vice Chairman C. Overhoff.

The German occupiers, by 1940, had the entire Dutch business world placed under government authority, conforming to the German example. The companies were divided into Industry Groups. For the stock market, this meant that the Society was appointed as 'Industry Group', which had a regulating authority over the entire trade, and therefore, over the Stock Exchange as well. This caused the Society to be a direct organ of the German occupation authorities. It could do nothing but follow German orders. It ceased to exist as a private organisation. Based on the change of the Society to Industry Group, the Society had to execute and practice the decisions of the occupational power to exclude Jews from the stock trade, and eventually to hand over Jewish possessions to Lippmann, Rosenthal and Co.

However, not all elements of Jewish wealth were surrendered. According to L. de Jong, the Dutch historian of the Second World War, stocks worth a total value of DFL. 213 million were surrendered, but as we do not know at which rate this sum was calculated, this does not say much about the extent of the surrendered stock.

Dr. H. Fischböck, the German Commissioner General for Finance, who instituted the anti-Jewish regulations in this field, inititally had the intention of transferring the stock from Jewish possession to Berlin, to have them sold there by German banks. Under the influence of the German 'Beauftragte' (agent) for The Netherlands Bank, Dr. A. Bühler, he decided to sell the Jewish shares in the Netherlands. The sale was commissioned to the management of Lippmann, Rosenthal & Co, and took place via the Amsterdam Stock Exchange and with the approval of the Society which could not refuse to comply with this German order. The Jewish shares were, indeed, often sold for rock bottom prices on the Amsterdam Stock Exchange.

The Bank Mendes Gans was not left undisturbed by the German occupiers. When the demise of Mendes became known through the Red Cross, his shares had to be deposited with the Handelstrust West (Commerce Trust West) in Amsterdam. The brother of S. Edersheim (residing in the U.S.) Mr. K. Edersheim, resigned on behalf of his brother as managing director of Mendes Gans. K. Edersheim managed to save his life by going underground.

A cousin of both, W. H. Edersheim, resigned in November 1940 as managing director of the branch office of Mendes Gans in The Hague.

Messrs. M. J. Heybroek and T. van Holkema were the new managers of the bank. They recruited H. Mulder as delegated Board Member. The management contrived to escape a 'Verwalter' by taking of the deposited shares by 80% of the value. Also, all other shares in Jewish possession were purchased by the Bank, so that they could prove to the German authorities that the 'Arianization' had taken place according to the rules concerning composition of the personnel as wel as Jewish possession.

The name was adapted to the situation and the name 'NV Banking House formerly Mendes Gans' was adopted. Only in 1963 was the old name 'Banking House Mendes Gans N.V.' restored in honour, to be changed in 1969 to 'Bank Mendes Gans N.V.'

Both directors, M. J. Heybroek and T. van Holkema, kept business going throughout the war and after the 'Arianization' as best they could. The last year of the war, business came to a standstill almost entirely. Personnel was reduced by half, either by being exiled to Germany for forced labor, or by being forced to the underground to avoid this banishment. This applied to all men under 40. The rest needed all their available time to search for food and fuel, especially during the 'starvation winter'. Traffic was barely possible during the last eight months of the occupation. The railway strike of September 1944, had paralysed all train traffic. Buses and trams for public transport had come to a stop as well, and bicycles became rare or were confiscated by the Germans. As a result of one thing and another, the managers, who lived in the Gooi (a distant suburb of Amsterdam), were barely able to reach the office. Only the senior members of personnel, who lived in Amsterdam, still showed up for work at the office, but only during certain hours of the day since during the last winter of war, the supply of gas and electricity was halted. On May 5, 1945, the misery of war came to an end by the surrender of the German army. With that closed one of the darkest periods in Dutch and European history and undoubtedly the most sombre phase of the history of Mendes Gans.

VIII Restoration of Law and Flagging Existence

The post-war restoration of property rights was set in motion with great difficulty, and took considerably longer than was expected. Principly, all Jewish owners had to regain possession of their property. In most cases, it was their heirs. The majority of the Jewish Dutch did not survive the war. They belong to the six million European Jews who fell victim to the horrible Nazi extermination process. The personal property of the Jews was scattered everywhere and all sorts of juridical procedures made the restoration of law more complicated and more difficult. It was not until 1955, that the restoration of stock commerce was completed.

The end of the war very slowly set into motion the trade of stocks at the Amsterdam Exchange. The occupiers had, as mentioned, made the Society into a semi-governmental institution, which was ruled by National Socialism leadership principals. This meant, among other things, that the chairman of the Society had the only right to decision making, and the board was only an advisory body. The chairman was also the only one responsible to the German authorities. The Society acted as industry group for the stock market in the scheme of the enacted business re-organisation.

Immediately after the liberation on May 7, 1945, the Dutch government forbade all trade and transfer of stocks. It was not until January 7, 1946, that the Stock Exchange was open on a limited basis. There was trade allowed only in domestic stocks and bonds and payment could only be made with frozen money. By the currency purge of October 1945, huge sums were deposited in frozen accounts, which gradually, after investigation by the revenue office (within the scope of the capital gains tax and the capital levy) were released.

The normal functioning of the stock market was delayed primarily due to the stock registration instituted by the government in association with the restoration of lay regulations. Moreover, currency circulation was monitored very closely by the government while international money traffic was subject to a licensing system, in such a way that foreign stock and currency commerce was virtually impossible. Only gradually was this liberalised.

It took until May 10, 1946 before the trade in bank and industrial shares was re-opened. Upon sale, half of the revenue had to be paid in frozen capital, and the other half in free money.

In October 10, 1946, the Exchange went on strike for one day in protest at the continued absence of a license to trade in certificates of American shares. This was permitted again in February 1947, but only in one direction, and under the restricting conditions that at the Amsterdam Exchange, shares could only be sold to members who committed themselves to selling the documents in America.

In April 1947, stock commerce was completely returned to the free money sector, at least as far as 'non-contaminated' stock was concerned.

It was not until 1953, that the end of the restoration of law drama came into view by way of change of law which cleared up a period of juridical procedures and confusing findings of courts. What made the year more important for the stock market was that the industrial organisation from the German period was abolished, and the Society could function again according to the pre-war statutes, albeit that it was restricted in its activities by new government measures and it had to be prepared to declare, as a private organisation, to operate under certain government regulations.

Very important for the stock market was in that same year as well, the abolishment of dividend restrictions and tax on speculation profit. Only the prohibition of the purchase of shares other than with one's own money – which was the prohibition of margin transaction credit – was maintained.

All this revived the stock market. The turnover of stocks increased from 318 million guilders in 1952 to 474 million guilders in 1953. The general quotation average according to ANP-CBS was 136.78 on December 30, 1952, and at the end of December 1953 was 167.88.

Other favourable conditions that year were the increasing demand from abroad, the growing interest of institutional investors in stocks, the tax relief for the business world which raised expectations for higher dividend payments and the tremendous drop in interest on bonds. 1954 showed a continued growth in the stock market, with a turnover in shares of 855 million guilders, and a rate of exchange index at the end of that year of 227.06.

The Dutch economy found itself in a long growing phase, and this benefitted the stock market, especially in shares.

Furthermore, there was a recovery of the interweaving of the Dutch economy with international trade. This was made most clear in the growing tendency towards greater inter-European cooperation, which led in 1952 to the foundation of the Common Market for coal and steel under the name of the European Community for Coal and Steel. This was made possible by the increasing inter-European money traffic, on the basis of the European Payment Union, one of the by-products of the Marshall Plan which put an end to the 'dollar gap' by making European currency convertible.

This was followed by attempts at military and political integration between the six member states of the ECCS. These attempts failed when in 1955, France turned down the plan for a European defense community because it included re-armament of Germany.

The mutual initiative of the Dutch and Belgium governments to found a common market for free traffic of goods, people and services, made it possible to open negotiations, which in 1957 resulted in the signing of the treaties of Rome and Paris for the foundation of the European Economic Community, and the European Community for Atomic Energy, both of which started on January 1, 1958. They would have a profound influence on the explosive growth of the inter-European trade and the internationalisation of business, the Netherlands as well. This was coupled with among other things, the process of up-scaling companies and investments by American companies in European countries. It was especially the latter which had, as we shall see, a determining influence on the new blossoming of the Bank Mendes Gans, which started at the end of the 50's. It was exactly the gradual founding of the Common Market which encouraged

American investments and created new opportunities for the Bank.

But in 1953, it was not yet so far. The Bank had to first go through a period of struggle, and attacks on its independence, to survive. Under the management of G. van Lanschot – owner of a small stockbrokerage office in Amsterdam which had to close its doors shortly after the war – the Bank resumed its ties with pre-war traditions broken in 1940. It recommenced being a bank trading mainly in shares.

Van Lanschot, from 1953 to 1958, was a member of the board of the Society for the Stock Exchange. His management of the Bank was characterised by lack of initiative and dynamism so that there was hardly any expansion in spite of the fact that the economic climate for banking business was favorable.

In 1956, J.E.M. Kramers, owner of a small stockbrokers office in Amsterdam, made an offer for the shares of Mendes Gans at the loftly rate of 140%. He made this offer on behalf of a group of friends, the identity of which was unknown. The offered bid (which was considered especially high considering the profit of the preceding financial year had decreased by 20%) gave him possession of the majority of shares. On this basis, he was appointed a delegated board member. Disagreements soon arose between the managing director, Van Lanschot, and the delegated board member. Kramers received governing authority and Van Lanschot left in 1957. Kramers then became substitute director as well. In that same year, the present managing director M. Ligtenstein was employed as assistant managing director.

IX Modernization and Reformation

The year 1957 was, in spite of a brief drop in the market trend, a year of change, and a turning point in the post-war history of the Bank. There was a considerable increase in profit, and a dividend of 8% was paid out. That year's annual review states that 'in the frame work of the Euromarket, it seemed sensible to participate with a majority share in a branch in Brussels, under the name of Mendes Gans & Co., Belgique S.A.'

In 1960 this branch was closed after having led a flagging existence. The branche in The Hague had already been liquidated in 1954. As of 1957, all the Bank's activities were concentrated at its seat in Amsterdam.

1957 was also a noteworthy year because the internal modernisation of the administration, which had been left untouched since after the war, was systematically undertaken. Until that time, the administration had been done manually. Cashbook, coupon book, purchase and selling ledgers for shares of stock, daily log, auxiliary book, post-giro columns, etc. were all kept with pen en ink, and the demarcation for each separate client was done by hand as well. The current account for each client was closed after three months. The balance was then sent to the client and after it had been signed as correct, would by written down in the books.

Ligtenstein, then still assistant managing director, introduced S. Swaab, an expert in the field of machinised and later automated administration, and former managing director of IBM Netherlands, as advisor. He designed, for those days, modern administration and introduced a punch card system, among other things. It was on his advice, that Ligtenstein later on introduced the computer.

In 1960, Kramers was relieved of his governing position; his interest in the Bank was put in a holding. He was not involved with the management of the business any more. Ligtenstein was appointed managing director. The following year, Kramers also resigned as delegated board member. Under his control, the net result of the Bank had remained the same for three consecutive years.

In the first annual report that was signed by the new managing director, the report concerning 1961, the fact was commemorated that Mr. Julius L. Gans in 1883 obtained the membership of the Society for the Stock Exchange in Amsterdam.'

The celebration of this anniversary was restricted to the employees of the Bank. To business relations was offered 'a special edition of our monthly bulletin.' In it Prof. Dr. J. E. Andriessen wrote a dissertation about the economic growth of the Netherlands. The management wrote an introduction in which 'the place of a banking institution like ours, and the nature of our service' was described. Moreover, a change in statutes was announced, which cancelled the change of name made during the Occupation, which meant that the word 'formerly' disappeared so that the official name was again 'Banking House Mendes Gans & Co.' In 1969 'Banking House' was replaced by 'Bank.'

In the same annual report, it was carefully announced that the business of the Bank would undergo a 'gradual expansion.' Also, there was the first indication 'of the international orientation' of the Bank. Gradually the Bank would choose its final position in the Dutch banking world. This choice was determined, mainly by two external factors, as can be seen from the following: The first was the abovementioned European integration process and therewith was connected the second factor, the up-scaling and internationalisation of the Dutch business world, and of Dutch banks in particular.

In the industrialisation brief of 1958, the Minister of Economic Affairs, Dr. J. Zijlstra, indicated a merger as the best means to strengthen and maintain the international competitive position of Dutch business affairs. The reduction of cost prices, improvement of quality by research, application of 'in depth investments,' export promotion, market control and so forth, according to the minister, could 'be obtained more successfully by mergers than by business agreements.'

According to historians, in the 60's the Netherlands experienced two merger-waves, the first one in 1961 and 1962, and the second one between 1965 and 1970. These consolidations led to a greater demand for capital. This caused a merger movement in the banking world. The most important mergers were those between the Nederlandse Handelmaatschappij and the Twentse Bank, resulting in the Algemene Bank Nederland (ABN) and the one between the Amsterdam and Rotterdam Bank to Amsterdam-Rotterdam Bank (AMRO Bank). In 1970 followed the amalgamation of the Cooperatieve Centrale Boerenleenbank with the Cooperatieve Centrale Raiffeisenbank to RABO Bank. This was followed by the takeover of the Mees and Hope group by the ABN and the amalgamation of the Bank Pierson, Heldring and Pierson with the AMRO Bank.

Those consolidation activities in the banking world raised the question of the possibility of remaining independent for, amongst others, the Bank Mendes Gans N.V.

There was no doubt among the management of the desirability and possibility of remaining independent as a bank. The annual report of 1966 expresses this for the first time. 'Over the past few years, we have gradually reached the opinion that we have other functions to fulfil than the operation of mass routine transactions and the supply of credit on a large scale. The well established larger banks' close net of branches in our country already provide for the needs of carrying out general banking business, derived from numerous clients. Therefore, we have intentionally striven to aim our service at a limited number of business relations. We were able to accomplish this by training our employees te become an expert team of specialists, who are always at the disposal of our clients. As a result, a tight band developed between our current client base and our institution.'

Amidst the consolidation activities in the banking world, the management decided to remain independent. To make this possible, it was decided to forego activities like retail banking and provision of general credit. This market was left to the larger banks in order to be able to look for its strenght in those activities that the big banks had to abandon, especially because of their large scale. They decided to forego broad expansion and looked for in-depth expansion.

The search for this 'alternative market', together with the abovementioned international orientation of the bank, practically coincided with the great interest that was aroused by the American business world for Western Europe as a result of the success of the Euromarket. The sensational book by the Frenchman, J.J. Servan Schreiber: 'Le défi Americain' pointed out almost dramatically to the mass public in Europe the obvious fact, in the opinion of the author, that American companies had spotted that the opportunities offered by the Euromarket became especially a 'défi' (challenge) for the American business world.

The American penetration of the Euromarket started in the beginning of the 60's with direct export, strongly promoted by the U.S. Export Trade Act of 1962, which offered tax relief facilities and was motivated by the deficit of the American balance of payments. One of the many companies which was directing its exports to Western Europe was the Dow Chemical Company, Midland, Michigan, U.S.A. The management was looking for a bank for its European operations for the collection of its debit monies, as was usual in the U.S. In Europe, however, one had to take into account the different currencies, their rate of exchange and the deviating currency procedures. This led to the conclusion that a European bank would have much more experience in this specific field than an American.

The management of Mendes Gans was already then in contact with Dow Chemical. They had reached the conclusion that the Bank had a triple choice as above mentioned. Either one could be taken over by a big bank, or one could form a cooperation with a number of smaller banks, preferably in the Netherlands, but possibly also smaller foreign banks, or one could offer services to the American industrial companies which were invading the Euromarket. This last possibility was intentionally chosen and exactly at that time the possibility arose to meet Dow Chemical needs for European banking services. The contacts with Dow Chemical led this American giant to decide to join with Mendes Gans, but they also wanted a participating contract in the capital investment of Mendes Gans. The negotiations were succesful and its results were announced in the annual report of 1963 as follows: 'On August 15, 1963, we privately placed DFL. 800,000 nominal shares of our company with the Dow Chemical Company, situated in Midland, Michigan, resulting in this American enterprise now owning 40% of our placed capital shares. The signature of our company will not change as a result of this. We hope to be able to expand our activities further as a result of this relation with Dow Chemical.'

The capital of the Bank reached two million guilders once more. At the same time, in the same year, the prime shares were purchased. 'Fifty prime certificates of our company, which have been outstanding since 1911 were purchased as well, and will now be withdrawn.' This required an amount of DFL. 100,000. The statues had to undergo a small change in connection with these transactions.

The relation with Dow Chemical openend completely new opportunities but, at the same time, the operation of the Bank had to be adapted. The first phase was the development of a so-called 'lock-box-system', which consisted of collecting debit monies for Dow Chemical and putting them into a Mendes Gans account with a central bank, chosen by Dow in every country.

In the next phase, American companies, amongst which Dow Chemical was one, moved from direct export to the establishment of production units in the countries of the Euromarket. The need for a clearing system became acute because of the tangle of currencies within the Euromarket with which the American companies had to work, and because of having to supply their European branches, as well as collecting from their clients in many countries. Mendes Gans succeeded in bringing order to the flow of payments with which Dow Chemical was working.

The successful service given to Dow Chemical appeared to have a recruiting quality which enabled Mendes Gans to expand its services to multinationals. This lead to specialisation of knowledge and experience. Moreover, it was a strong stimulus to machinise, later automate, the service with the most modern available technology. In this field, the Bank was using the expert advice of S. Swaab, who gained much experience at IBM.

In the annual report of 1967, this technical modernisation was described and motivated as follows: 'In the past year, we had to spend considerable sums for the modernisation of our equipment from which we now benefit. We are of the opinion, although the modernisation program is not yet finished and a great deal of money will have to be invested in the years to come, that we can increase the payment to our shareholders by raising the dividend to 9%.'

In the same annual report, the 'basic philosophy' of the Bank was repeated and elaborated upon. The chances of remaining independent were considered very high by the management. The cooperation with Dow Chemical was succesful. 'We have' – according to the report of 1967 – 'specialised our services – in view of our position in the financiel world in the Netherlands – in those activities for which special expertise is necessary and demands are being made for accuracy and speed of information. We expect that the on-going consolidations within the banking world in our country will cause the need, also in the future, for services which an institution like ours can supply.'

A second aspect of the Bank's activities received special attention as well: The stock market. Since its foundation in 1911 – and before when Mendes Gans was still a stockbrokerage office from 1883 – the Bank had concentrated on this. But to stay 'withit' in this field needed a lot of re-orientation. That was at least the conclusion the management had come to. We find this reflected in the same annual report. 'For the stock market business, which is so important for our Bank, holds that to manage wealth, so many aspects have to be taken into account that the wealthy can hardly do this on their own. The dynamic developments in the fields of finance and economics, and the great diversity of publications in the field of investment policy, make it almost impossible for the private person to exercise good management adapted to the most current problems. This has become the work of specialists who have a great deal of experience. Our experts in this field give our clients the advice they need and by frequent personal contact, they are able to consider the individual circumstances. Furthermore, necessary information such as, for instance, periodical portfolio surveys and annual wealth and income statements, are being provided.'

Both activities – the clearing for multinationals and the stock market, particularly concerning the control of private wealth – need the most modern information and communication systems. That is why it said in the same annual report: 'in order to be able to fulfil the high demands which our management makes of the administrative organisation of our company, we are striving for the application of the most modern tools in our administration. A short time ago we installed a computer so that we will be able to extend our service even more.'

With that, in an early stage for the Netherlands, the era of automation was heralded in.

In 1968, the first computer was put into use. 'Thanks to extensive pre-studies, the conversion of our administration took place without much difficulty,' according to the annual report in 1968. 'This equipment has had a good influence on the speed and accuracy of our entire organisation.' All company sectors achieved better results than the previous year, and the dividend was increased from 9% to 10%. From the achieved results, the management concluded that 'also in the future, the need will continue for the services of a bank institution like ours.' The Bank Mendes Gans had found its own route. Amidst the mergers in the Dutch banking world, it chose the route of independence and identified a clearly designated market.

The annual report of 1968 further announced that a plan had been made for further automation, for which 'a second computer – of the same type as currently in use – will be necessary. This plan provides for the means to meet the demands of the future gradual expansion of our company and contains information about the expansion of the service to our relations with the use of the greater processing and memory capacity of the equipment then available.'

The management put special emphasis on 'further training for our employees in order to be able to follow the rapid evolution in the field of administrative organisation and the dynamic developments of the currency and stock markets.'

In 1969, the second computer was put into use. 'We are more than ever convinced,' as quoted from the annual report from 1969 'of the desirability of having our computers process routine accounting work. This elevates the work of our employees to a higher level.' This last very sober remark of the management hides a social policy which is aimed at the continual training of personnel. From this one can conclude, at least for Mendes Gans, that automation does not eliminate jobs, but implies a qualitative growth of education and training. 'We place great value on the education of bank experts as well as computer experts to whom we can entrust a great deal of independence and responsibility.'

In spite of a considerable rise in costs as a result of a general wage increase in the banking business, the increase of social premiums connected with this, and the introduction of the Value Added Tax, a higher profit was made in 1969, and, as in previous years, a dividend of 10% could be paid.

In view of the continuous rise in costs, also caused by the high inflation rate in the Netherlands, it was decided in 1970 to hold an extensive investigation into the cost price of different services and operations performed by the Bank. In the annual report of 1970, this is mentioned. 'Our system of costing and composition of development surveys is based on modern principles of cost division and cost imputation as applied in industrial enterprises. The in-depth insight into our company operation will contribute much to the planning of our future activities.'

From the same annual report, it can again be seen which activities the Bank considers its speciality. Thinking about its industrial relations, it was said that the Bank 'helped some of them with the coordination of multi-lateral money traffic between the daughter companies of one concern: for this purpose we have developed a number of systems.'

In 1971, in order to promote efficiency, and based on the abovementioned costing investigation, an order was placed 'for the most modern systems of disc memories which will, after an initial period, lead to further cost savings and increased accuracy.'

It was further announced, that 'the systems designed by us for coordination of multi-lateral money traffic of internationally operating concerns have proven their value. We will continue to strive to attract new clients.'

A new activity was announced in the annual report of 1971. 'Our profit on interest was favorably influenced by our making a start with the application of techniques called 'Operations Research'.'

Besides that, and as a result of the important memory capacity of the computer, it became possible to enter the complete administration and all transactions of the Bank. All this information became immediately available and therefore an important improvement of the insight into and the information about company operations was achieved.

Furthermore, the conventional procedures, which included sending client bills as well as daily accounts as separate documents, could be replaced by a new, more efficient system, whereby on the bills themselves, the old and the new balances were mentioned, as well as the new account per fund, in case of stock transactions.

These reformations had favourable results as was shown in the 1973 annual report. They led to a more effective 'asset management' which resulted in higher profits on interest in markets, which showed great fluctuations in 1973.

Among the most important external events of that year was, besides the unfavourable situation of the stock market, the entry of Great Britain into the Common Market, resulting in a increased interest in the Dutch stock market. This influenced the income from stock arbitration of the Bank favourably.

In the annual report of 1973, another new activity was announced. 'As is known, we give services to multinational industrial concerns which are generally termed as 'cash management.' The systems designed by us for coordination of money traffic for big internationally operating companies, have been used by us for some years successfully. In this financial year, we have made a start with a special service to institutional investors. We will further develop systems which can aid with asset management of financial institutions and industrial companies. Again, new computer systems were put into use, and new projects were being prepared whereby in-put of basic information – 'data entry' – was further automated by using interactive display terminals. All this meant an acceleration and improvement of management information.

The oil crisis, which set in at the end of 1973, had little direct influence on the business of Mendes Gans. This was not coincidental, but contributable to purposeful management. In 1974's annual report, management wrote that 'the problems of the banking business caused by these developments (meant here are the problems of coinciding inflation and recession) have increased. This is shown from reports in the past months about a number of collapses in foreign countries, especially caused by the extending of long term loans, financed by short term raised money (referred to as oil dollars), and by the risky trading on the currency market in combination with insufficient internal control.' 'We are,' declared the management, 'not involved in any of these infamous affairs, and our Bank has not suffered any losses in these matters.'

At the beginning of this, for the banking world, so dangerous period of massive offer of so-called surplus dollars by OPEC countries and the extensive granting of loans to, for instance, governments of developing countries to cover their balance of payments shortage, the management formulates the policy of Mendes Gans quite clearly: 'The considerable restrictions which we have put upon ourselves concerning the supply of credit (as was pointed out again and again in the previous years), is maintained undiminished. As well as in the past, our Bank will not keep currency positions for its own account; the third party in our transactions is always a first class relation of long standing.

We always evaluate, very carefully, business contacts with new national and international relations. Internal control is always given our most careful attention.' The policy was aimed as well, at maintaining a very strong liquidity position and a high solvency, which were much higher than the norms enforced by The Netherlands Bank.

The same premises, Herengracht 619, the registered office of Bank Mendes Gans since 1919

In 1975, Messrs. A. J. Ch. van der Noordaa, Esq., responsible for 'General Business and Organization' and J. H. N. Zijlstra, M. A., responsible for 'Stock Operations and Economic Research,' were accepted in the excutive management after having worked at the Bank for a number of years as assistant managers.

X Stable in Economic Recession and Crises

As early as in 1975's annual report, the management of Mendes Gans clearly indicated the coming economic recession. In this report they point out: 'Now we can expect the first big post-war recession with an unprecedented high unemployment unknown in the Netherlands since the 30's.'

The situation was characterised by a 'rapid succession of events, shift in the main problems and increasing international influence. In a short period of time, the emphasis of the problems were successively on the position of the dollar and the gold, the international fight against inflation, the oil crisis, and the adaptation to the changed monetary relations.' These quick shifts of emphasis caused the business world and the institutional and private investors to make swift changes in policy. 'Our Bank has,' according to the management, 'a duty to its clients to assist them with their policy decisions by way of expert advice, if need be, by its own initiative, if the economic situation so requires. For internationally operating companies and investors, this advisory function in the field of financing, money and capital market, currency business and investments, has become permanent. The speed of information for clients is helped by the short communication lines with our specialists. Furthermore, there is a large measure of continuity because there is very little turnover in the expert staff of our team, which stimulates awareness of the specific problems of every client.'

In the meantime, the Bank continued giving its attention to technical improvements which offered new and better possibilities in handling its client relations. At the end of 1974, a new computer from the IBM Series 370 was put into use meaning larger memory capacity and higher processing speed. 'In this new system, the data has continuous 'on-line' availability for which VDU terminals are being used in every department.' In the course of 1976, an interactive data-entry and approval system was introduced so that every transaction could be entered, checked and approved by the department responsible.

At the same time, the Bank participated in the international banking project known as 'SWIFT' (Society for Worldwide Interbank Financial Telecommunication), with which a modest start had been made in 1977, and which turned out to be very successful. Automation had reached a new phase with this. Terminals with alphabetical and numerical keyboards and screens were introduced. These VDU terminals, installed in the operational departments of the Bank, were connected with the computer at the computer center. 'Apart from the production of client statements from the daily transactions, and the Bank's own administration, the terminals made it possible for the specialists of the departments to retrieve and display on the screen information about the status of an account, the composition of stock portfolios, etc. In general one can say: 'the Bank specialist can ask the computer a question via his terminal and receive an answer displayed immediately so that the advice to the client is based on complete up-to-date information.'

XI Expansion and Redistribution of Capital

The year 1977 was very important for the Bank due to agreements with three relations. In October of that year, the Philips Finance Company N.V. – a 100% subsidiary of the Philips Light Factories – obtained an interest of 32% of capital stock in Mendes Gans N.V. As a result of this, the long standing relationship with Philips was confirmed.

Furthermore, with the approval and cooperation of Dow Chemical, which then owned 40% of the capital stock of the Bank, an agreement was reached with the Manufacturers Hanover Trust Company, under which this bank obtained an interest of 16% in the Bank Mendes Gans N.V. This bank, with a total balance of 35 billion dollars, the fourth largest bank in the U.S. and with worldwide operations, did not have its own branch or representative in the Netherlands. The relationship of this bank with Mendes Gans had by then existed for many years. Eight percent of the Dow Chemical shares were transferred to the Manufacturers Hanover Trust, and another 8% was obtained from Dutch holding.

> The distribution of the capital stock –
> two million guilders – was as follows:

Dow Chemical Company, Midland	32%
Philips Finance Company, Eindhoven	32%
Manufacturers Hanover Trust Company, N.Y.	16%
Other holdings noted at the Amsterdam Stock Exchange	20%

An option was extended to Manufacturers Hanover for another 4% to be exercised between November 1978 and November 1979. This option was, indeed, taken up in 1979 so that Manufacturers Hanover Trust obtained 20%. At the same time, 1,200 shares of Mendes Gans N.V. were placed with the AGO insurance Co. in Amsterdam. In view of both transactions, on December 20, 1979, 2,200 new shares for DFL. 100,00 were issued as a result of a commitment made in the annual report of 1977, which stated that the interest of both American companies in Mendes Gans N.V. would remain below 50%. As a result of these transactions, the capital stock reached DFL. 2,220,000.00, distributed as follows:

Dow Chemical	28.83%
Philips Finance Company	28.83%
Manufacturers Hanover Trust	20.00%
AGO Life Insurance Co.	5.40%
Holding via Amsterdam Stock Exchange	16.94%

XII A New Way of Reporting

As of 1979, Mendes Gans' annual report was published in a totally new layout, contributing to the clarity and cognizance of the results. Used for this were the well known block diagrams as used for organisation charts. This has also proven invaluable in computer programming. In a number of diagrams the policy objectives were successively shown, the tools to achieve them, the financial structure, the external circumstances influencing activities and results, the most important activities and results of the department, the expectations for the coming year with regard to external circumstances, and the forecast for the current financial year.

Notable is the very clear description of the policy objectives. Foremost is – and that determines the special position and place of this small bank in contrast to the big banking concerns – the 'supply of services of high quality, *keyed to the individual and specific needs of each client.'* This distinguished the Bank from other banks. It is its 'Trade Mark,' as it were. The other objectives are additional and are the logical consequence of the main objective. These include the maintenance of a compact and clear organisation by which means decision making is made along short and direct lines. Employees are easily involved with management in this manner, they carry a large responsibility, and are therefore able to develop themselves. A further objective is the productiveness of all departments of the company. Connected with this is the striving for the further increase of profit per share, which guarantees the liberty and independence of the Bank.

What is noteworthy as a tool to achieve the objectives is the 'frequent personal contact between employees and clients,' the 'study, development, and application of innovative methods and systems' for clients, as well as for internal use. 'Intensive, anticipatory and restrained internal controls' allow the management to stay in contact, rapidly and completely, with operations and to take immediate action when necessary. The Bank aims at investing the entrusted money as selectively and as safely as possible.

The annual review does not elaborate on the general economic situation in the Netherlands and the world. The management limits itself to summarising the external circumstances which influenced the activities of the Bank directly and clearly. The same holds for the declared expectations concerning future external circumstances. The Bank's policy over the last 15 years can be characterised as being purposeful and consistent. The management has clearly seen and identified the place of the Bank and the market available for its activities. It has penetratingly cultivated this market. The results show the aptness and the viability of the concept. Mendes Gans' total balance, which amounted to 5 million guilders at the end of the 50's, increased in 1981 to about 800 million guilders. The price of shares in guilders rose, in that period, more than five times in value.

Managing director M. Ligtenstein declared to a journalist for the magazine 'Euromoney' in 1979: 'We have seen an average annual compound growth rate of 15% in our earnings since 1963.'

The future of the Bank lies in further development of the cash management for internationally operating companies and in control of private wealth. Undoubtedly, there are many other banks, especially small ones, which are looking for work in this field, but Mendes Gans has the advantage of an early start, and therefore leads in experience.

Julius Gans started his modest stockbrokers office a century ago. His friend, and later partner, I. Mendes, knew how to manage this successfully by building up a network of primarily international relations. For the sake of more complete services, it was decided to convert the office into a bank, whereby it was favoured by the blossoming of the Amsterdam stock market in the period after the First World War. In the difficult period during the crises of the 30's, the Bank managed to stay alive. It stuck to its speciality, the stock market. The Bank survived the darkest period in its existence, that of the Second World War and the German occupation. It led a flagging existence during the restoration period of the Dutch post-war economy. The then management of the Bank did not know how to take advantage of the general recovery of the 50's. Not until the beginning of the 60's did it see its position and its possibilities. Amidst the merger activities in the Dutch banking world, the management kept a cool head and chose for maintaining its independence. This needed a clearly defined market, different from the one cultivated by the large banks. 'To compete with the big banks, Mendes Gans concentrated on being different. We need to do things differently from the American banks and our style is not dissimilar to the London Merchant Banks.' (M. Ligtenstein in the abovementioned interview with 'Euromoney'.)

This history of Mendes Gans proves that the motto 'small is beautiful' is not without a grain of truth. In any event, it is its deliberate management, its solid team of employees, its selective choice of relations as well as investments, and its high level of automation, which give the Bank Mendes Gans a strong basis to defy the storms of the somber prospectives for the world economy in this centennial year.

August 1983
drs. L. Metzemaekers

Table of contents

List of illustrations

Monetary uncertainty: the fear of future inflation, which will melt away the purchasing power of long-term government paper, keeps real interest rates high

chapter 1

Analysing interest rates

"Many financial executives say that although they are interested in hearing others' interest-rate forecasts, they don't have much faith in them. 'Over a one- to two-year period, the record of very intelligent people is so bad that you have to come to the conclusion that it isn't the fault of the people but that it's essentially an unpredictable situation', Felix Rohatyn concluded."

The Wall Street Journal, January 4, 1982.

"A long tradition of misleading statements, a sequence of broken promises to pursue anti-inflationary policies, the many contradictions observed between statements made by Fed officials since October 6, 1979, a more or less veiled opposition of important Fed officials to a policy of effective monetary control, and lastly, the variability of monetary growth after the promise offered in October 1979 to tighten control and improve performance, all contributed to a diffuse and pervasive uncertainty about the trend in monetary policymaking. The array of experiences imposed on financial markets lowered the credibility of the Fed's monetary strategy. The resulting uncertainty imposed a substantial risk premium of several percentage points on the gross real rate of interest."

Karl Brunner, 'The voices of "failure" and the failure of monetary policy-making', in: Shadow Open Market Committee, Policy Statement and Position Papers, Graduate School of Management, University of Rochester, September 12-13, 1982, pp. 8-9

1.1 The importance of uncertainty

The greatness of John Maynard Keynes derived from his joint proficiency in financial economics and in macroeconomics. He understood both the psychological factors that affect the moods of the market-place and the abstract aggregates – national income, personal consumption, aggregate investment – studied by the theoretical economists. His suggestions for economic policy were based on careful consideration of their likely impact on investors' expectations, and he stressed the necessity of a stable investment climate for a lasting reduction of unemployment.

The Keynesian revolution changed all that. A stylized version of the Keynesian 'model' became the centerpiece of modern textbooks on economics. Later, this so-called 'IS-LM framework' served as a basis for economic computer models of national economies pioneered by Jan Tinbergen in the Netherlands and Lawrence R. Klein in the U.S. The Keynesian model became more and more elaborate, both in the classroom version with its short-term and long-run dynamic 'multipliers' for indicating the effects of increases in government expenditure, and more especially in statistical computer implementations which expanded into interconnected systems of hundreds of equations.

To an extent, availability of statistical data has had an influence on the increasing sophistication of macroeconomics. It is much easier to measure production, shipments and sales than to estimate rates of return on plant and machinery, let alone to gauge representative expectations about future profits and inflation or about required risk premia. The multiplier-accelerator mechanism provided a means of connecting the different components of national income and produced interesting oscillations in laboratory experiments with computer models of national economies. As the analysis became more intricate, the self-confidence of the corps of economic engineers grew and their advice to policy makers took the form of precise recipes for 'fine-tuning' the economy. Politicians were to select goals for important variables such as unemployment, the trade balance or inflation, and hypothetical experiments with a large-scale computer model were used to show the appropriate values for the instruments of monetary and fiscal policy.

At the same time, financial economists were testing hypotheses about price-setting in the financial markets which were derived from two basic laws of the market-place:

- riskier assets will offer a higher expected return over the long term.;
- future short-term changes in interest rates and share prices are unpredictable to the extent that no sure opportunities exist for realizing excessive rates of return.

Statistical investigations of changes in security prices contributed to deeper insights into the relationship between risk and return and the concept of efficient markets, but most financial research took as given changes in an aggregate stock market index or a representative interest rate on default-free government debt, and concentrated on comparing price changes for different (groups of) securities to movements in the market index.

The late 1960's and the first part of the 1970's witnessed the maximum gap between the two fields. On the one hand, macroeconomists began to connect their national econometric models, so that hypothetical experiments with the world economy became feasible. In spite of all the statistical sophistication, however, considerations of risk and uncertainty were virtually absent from the models and there was no guarantee that the interplay of interest rates and exchange rates satisfied the postulates of efficient financial markets. By contrast, the financial specialists pushed the so-called 'Capital Asset Pricing Model' (CAPM) to its limits. Their local findings for the financial sector, however, could not be transplanted easily into a model for the macroeconomic fundamentals of market prices.

One group of macroeconomists attempted to integrate considerations of risk and market efficiency into macroeconomics: the monetarist school. Monetarists viewed economic policy as different from setting dials in some imaginary macroeconomic control room, but rather as the design of *institutions* and *rules* which could lower uncertainty and variability for society as a whole. From Milton Friedman's 'A monetary and fiscal framework for economic stability' (1948) to Allan Meltzer's 'On Keynes's general theory' (1981), monetarists have been closer to Keynes in this respect than many 'Keynesians':

> 'Keynes's main concern in the General Theory and after is to reduce the instability of the economy by eliminating fluctuations in the most volatile elements, not to substitute one source of variability for another. Keynes, the probabilist, appreciated that variable policies affect expectations and can increase uncertainty.'
>
> Allan H. Meltzer, 'On Keynes's General Theory',
> Journal of Economic Literature, 19 no. 1, March
> 1981, p. 62.

To a financial economist, who sees returns as being related to risk, such statements are obvious; many macroeconomists and econometricians, however, relegate uncertainty to the uninteresting residual errors in their multi-equation models or assume something called 'certainty-equivalence', implying complete certainty about the structure of the economic system and perfect foresight regarding the future. However convenient such artificial assumptions are for theoretical analyses, the principle of certainty-equivalence impoverishes the analysis of economic policies, because the social costs of volatile, erratic, and unpredictable policies have been defined away.

Macroeconomics and financial economics have grown far apart indeed: even when dealing with the same economic magnitude, the two disciplines offer their respective predictions without much attempt at integration. For example, consider what a macroeconomist and a financial economist might contribute to a discussion about the prospects for the airline industry. The macroeconomist would exploit the likelihood that business and pleasure travel are related to the health of the economy. Once the relevant elasticities are known, the macroeconomist could concentrate on his real job, to predict the economy's path over the near term.

A financial economist would apply the technical toolbox of his trade in a quite different area. Since airline revenues vary with the strength of the economy, whereas many cost items are fixed, profits in the industry exhibit greater-than-average sensitivity to the business cycle. Airline stocks move up and down with the stock market as a whole, but rather more so than most other industry groups. Their 'beta' is larger than one, implying a somewhat higher long-term rate of return, because of the cyclical risk of such investments. If investors were particularly uncertain about the cyclical outlook, the risk premium in the average rate of return on airlines would have to increase, and their stock would suffer more than share prices in less cyclically sensitive areas.

Whereas the macroeconomist specializes in future scenarios, his colleague in finance lectures about diversification of risk and estimates the required compensation for uncertainty. On a practical level the two approaches have long been integrated. The microeconomics of uncertainty shows that 'certainty equivalence' does not at all apply to the pricing of hotel rooms, the length of individual spells of unemployment or the assessment of an investment project. On the national or supra-national level, however, the only concession most macroeconomists are prepared to make is to offer multiple scenarios instead of a single forecast. But, according to the current philosophy of the standard macroeconometric models, it makes no difference to the economy's prospects whether businessmen's uncertainty about future inflation is average, extreme, or minimal. If their clients have diffuse beliefs about the future, the macroeconomic consulting firms will offer many different scenarios, but the degree of uncertainty itself has no place in each separate scenario.

Fortunately, attention given to the impact of uncertainty has grown in some areas of macroeconomics during the past ten years. Lucas (1972, 1975) offered a theoretical analysis of the business cycle based on persistent but unavoidable difficulties facing businessmen and consumers in interpreting the current state of aggregate demand. Later, Brunner, Cukierman and

Meltzer (1981) showed how confusion between transitory and permanent changes in the economic environment could help explain many features of economic behaviour, and in some sub-fields of macroeconomics much research has been done on specific effects of increased uncertainty. The academic debate on the economic costs of inflation, for example, focussed on the relationship between uncertainty about the future path of the average price level and uncertainty about the relative prices of individual goods and services. Indices for both types of uncertainty were postulated to have effects on the economy (see Cukierman, 1983, for an authoritative survey).

In spite of these examples showing a greater role for uncertainty in macroeconomic analysis – which, I am sure, will be the trend in other areas also – standard analyses of national economies and of the Western world as a whole continue to simply take note of uncertainty when the research is finished. Such concern is used as a rationale for low coefficients of determination in an econometric model over some historical period, or to excuse poor forecasting performance. Instead, uncertainty should be important right at the outset, when equations are specified to capture the economic regularities of supply and demand. There is little or no room for indices of uncertainty in the macroeconomic equations; an unpredictable economic environment shows up in the residual errors, but regrettably does not affect the coefficients in the equations.

The aim of my co-authors and myself in this book has been to measure the impact on long-term rates of interest of one particular type of macroeconomic uncertainty, viz. uncertainty about the future course of inflation. To this end, we compute historical indices of both inflationary uncertainty and monetary uncertainty, hypothesizing that uncertainty about the future rate of growth of the money supply is the prime reason for uncertainty about future inflation rates, and test whether changes in these indices have something to contribute to an explanation of the surprisingly high real rates of interest during the early 1980's. All the statistical analysis is in agreement with a few basic notions on the role of risk factors in the determination of long-term rates of interest, which were developed originally by financial economists and are now starting to be used in macroeconomic research. To provide the reader with a quick feeling for the way in which the subsequent analysis differs from the traditional macroeconomic treatment of interest rates, I offer some illustrated worked-out examples in the next section of this chapter. The aim has been to bring out basic instances where considerations of risk must be important for determining interest rates and to indicate how much macroeconomic analysis neglects such arguments. Section 1.3 terminates this introductory chapter with an overview of the subject-matter of the remaining chapters.

1.2 Uncertainty and interest rates

The vignettes in this section are meant to convey how important uncertainty can be for the determination of interest rates. A more formal analysis in chapter 3 attempts to integrate some effects of uncertainty into a system of equations describing a national economy, but the busy reader will get an adequate impression from the three brief sketches in the present section.

The two panels of figure 1.1 depict the rate of inflation in two hypothetical countries. Inflation reached a peak in both countries approximately three periods (years) ago and has declined to a current level of five per cent per annum. I assume that not only the current inflation rates are identical, but that the two hypothetical economies are presently indistinguishable in all other relevant aspects but one: businessmen and consumers in country B are even more uncertain about the future outlook for inflation than residents of country A. Although inhabitants of both countries expect on average that inflation will stay at its current level of 5% per annum, expectations in country B are considerably more diffuse, with 30 per cent of the respondents to surveys of public opinion expecting a rebound in inflation and an equal number counting on a significant further decline to an almost zero rate of price change. By contrast, in country A small minorities only hold views on future inflation that diverge from the consensus opinion that inflation will remain approximately at current levels.

Country B thus suffers from greater inflationary uncertainty defined here as greater variability in individual forecasts of future inflation at a given moment. Some evidence has accumulated that greater inflationary uncertainty in this sense has harmful effects on economic growth and employment (see Mullineaux, 1980, Levi and Makin, 1980). Long-standing surveys of inflationary expectations together with an estimate of their variability across respondents are available for the U.S. (the so-called Livingston series, see chapter 4), but not for many other countries. Therefore, we shall perform our statistical analysis with a computed measure of the amount of inflationary uncertainty in the different sense of large average forecast errors in predicting inflation. Cukierman and Wachtel (1979) have shown that, at least in the U.S., the variability of inflation on this definition goes up and down with the amount of disagreement regarding inflationary expectations as measured by the Livingston survey.

Despite this evidence, most discussions of interest rates neglect the potential effect of inflationary uncertainty on real rates of interest. The flow-of-funds technique of forecasting interest rates, probably less influential than 10 years ago in academic circles, but highly popular in Wall Street, bases its projections on numerical estimates of the supply and demand for funds in the capital market, but considerations of uncertainty are hard to incorporate into this approach.

Figure 1.1   Inflationary risk and the real rate of interest

Long-term bonds will be less popular if inflationary expectations are more diffuse

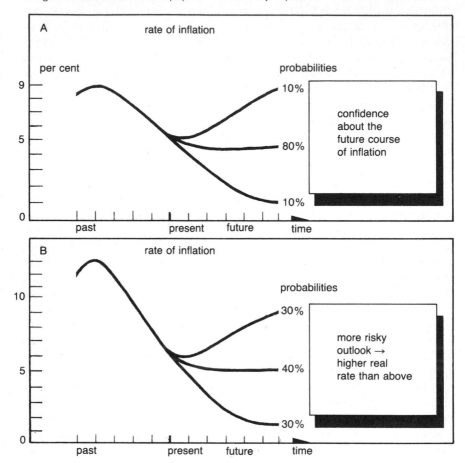

Other forecasting organisations based their analysis of interest rates on large scale-econometric models. To my knowledge, the current generation of big computer models for national economies regards uncertainty as something showing up in the error terms, not as a factor which should be given due attention when specifying the individual equations of the model. Both major approaches can offer multiple scenarios with varying assumptions about government deficits, for example, but fail to draw the logical inference that the demand for many scenarios implies special uncertainty about the future. If the corporate clients require not only a "base line" projection, but also several alternative forecasts, then each set of predictions should reflect the effects of such manifest uncertainty on investment intentions, for example, but changes in the degree of inflationary uncertainty do not seem to affect the way in which the base line forecast and its alternatives are put together.Thus, both major approaches to analysing and forecasting interest rates have great difficulty in coping with the effects of increased uncertainty about future rates of inflation.

However, the degree of uncertainty regarding future rates of inflation does have important consequences for the evaluation of financial portfolios. Although nobody in countries A and B expects truly dramatic increases in inflation over the next five years – the rate of inflation stays in single digits even in the view of the most pessimistic forecasters – a moderate increase in inflationary uncertainty does affect immediately the likely error made when forecasting the future purchasing power of fixed-interest investments. Since only 10 per cent of the respondents in country A expect inflation to increase from its current level of 5% to 9% over the next five years, as against 30% in country B, the downward risk is perceived to be considerably smaller in country A. The same applies to the possibility that the purchasing power of fixed-investments will increase beyond expectations through a lower-than-expected future rate of inflation. For simplicity, assume that a nominal rate of 5 per cent can be obtained presently in the capital markets for a five-year investment. In that case the purchasing power in today's constant dollars of a $ 1000 investment ranges between $ 1101 and $ 910 in both countries, with exact conservation of purchasing power the most likely outcome.

The standard error in an estimate of the purchasing power five years hence is very sensitive, however, to the probabilities on the different forecasts of future inflation. In country B, where the expectations are more diffuse, the standard error in our hypothetical example would be $ 74, as against a smaller error of $ 42 in country A.

Some important conclusions for investment strategy follow from this difference between the two economies:

- Investors in country B will appreciate more those investments that are

Figure 1.2   Real rates of interest and the business cycle
Real interest rates may be less pro-cyclical if risk factors become more important

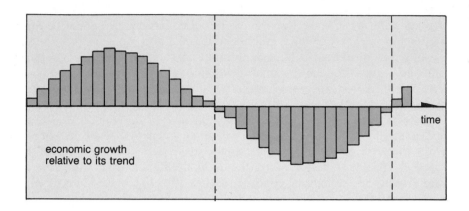

economic growth
relative to its trend

time

I supply/demand factors

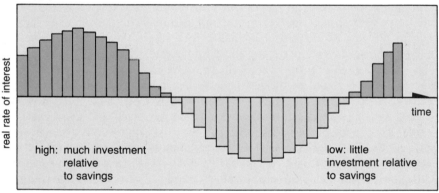

real rate of interest

high: much investment
relative
to savings

low: little
investment relative
to savings

time

II risk factors

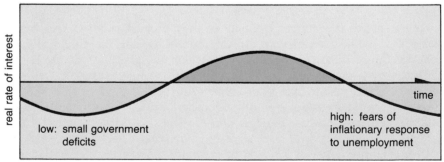

real rate of interest

low: small government
deficits

high: fears of
inflationary response
to unemployment

time

inflation-proof, or even better, move positively with inflation. Prices of real estate for example will be somewhat higher than in country A, ceteris paribus.

- Prices of equity shares may be a little higher in country B for given projections of future dividends since investors will be prepared to accept a slightly lower expected real rate of return if equity shares are viewed as less vulnerable to unanticipated inflation than long-term investments at a fixed rate of interest. In other words, the yield gap between bonds and equity shares will become smaller in country B. The differences between countries A and B become even more pronounced if a return to higher inflation would imply a general loss of investors' confidence and a slump in fixed investment. In that case, large losses of purchasing power on fixed-interest investments would come together with a special need for liquidity because of weaker-than-expected personal income and losses on equity shares. Conversely, fixed-interest investments might do better than expected (the low-inflation scenario), when capital gains on their stock market investments made investors happy anyway. Under such circumstances, the riskiness of fixed-interest investments over the longer term would be especially high, and investors would surely require an additional risk premium in the interest rate to compensate for inflationary uncertainty.

Figure 1.2 illustrates two views on the determination of long-term real rates of interest. The top panel of the figure shows an idealized business cycle, during which the rate of economic growth accelerates from through to peak and subsequently declines to its long-term average value in the centre of the diagram. This corresponds to the point where the actual rate of output would reach its maximum over the cycle. After the relative peak, the rate of output declines below its long-term average, and the negative phase of the business cycle ensues.Output reaches its cycle low at the right-hand side of the diagram, at which time the rate of growth of output begins again to accelerate above its long-term average.

The two remaining panels of figure 1.2 correspond to complementary theories about the determination of long-term real rates of interest. Before proceeding to these theories, we require a hypothesis about what causes the business cycle. Convenient for present purposes is the assumption that (unexplained) variations in the expected rate of return on real capital cause corresponding swings in investment which in turn require a changed real rate in order to equate the flow of savings to the demand for investment funds. If this mechanism is important indeed, there should be pro-cyclical influences on real rates of interest, as indicated in the centre panel of figure 1.2. In the drawing the real rate slightly leads the cycle, but a strong positive covariance between the real rate and the rate of growth of real output would remain even if peaks and troughs did not coincide exactly.

A different view on real rates of interest is illustrated in the bottom part of figure 1.2. Once again, I assume that unexplained variations in the expected rate of profit on business investment underly cyclical fluctuations in the rate of output. This time, however, we focus on a different aspect of the supply side of the market for investment funds. Investors will only be prepared to hold financial claims issued by firms or governments if they are compensated for the risks attached to holding these securities. During the positive phase of the business cycle, various risk factors will be below average. Few firms will go bankrupt and unemployment will be decreasing together with the probability that the government will succumb to the pressure for more expansionary policies.

With an adverse change in the economic climate, however, many risk factors will increase. There is bound to be more uncertainty regarding government policies, as increasing unemployment may lead to pressure on the authorities to inflate the economy. Revenues from taxation will drop in a recession, and government programs to assist the unemployed will require more funds, so that the measured budget deficit goes up, which in turn may increase inflationary uncertainty.

If changing perceptions of risk were the major factor determining long-term rates of interest, the movement of real rates over the business cycle could be as in the bottom panel of figure 1.2. Instead of exhibiting procyclical movements, real rates might drop when the economy improves and rise when the economic outlook becomes more clouded. The counter-cyclical risk factors would then have become more important empirically than the pro-cyclical changes in the 'risk-free' real rate.

Figures 1.3 and 1.4 attempt to illustrate in yet another way the impact of uncertainty on analysis of interest rates. I assume that a protracted period of high money growth has recently been terminated, with investors pondering the consequences for nominal interest rates. The figures show how greater emphasis on monetary uncertainty would alter the terms in which they discuss their dilemma. Previously, the main question could have been whether prices were going to be sufficiently flexible to prevent a sharp fall in real money balances with its major contractionary effects on the economy. By contrast, if the real worry is not so much whether prices are flexible but whether the recent deceleration in the money supply is temporary or permanent, the outlook for interest rates would be discussed in the terms of figure 1.4. Emphasis has shifted from concern about the 'real' sector of the economy to a problem of distinguishing between permanent or transitory changes in monetary policy, and monetary uncertainty plays a much more important role than in the past. In chapter 5 I shall present evidence suggesting that the dilemma in figure 1.4 captures the most important single reason why U.S. interest rates were high in the early 1980's.

1.3 Remainder of the book

As exercises in economic logic, the illustrative arguments of the previous section may be persuasive enough; what remains to be seen is whether a greater emphasis on uncertainty – likely to be achieved at the expense of reduced attention for some competing other factors – is relevant empirically. Does it pay to construct indices for uncertainty regarding inflation, money growth and other macroeconomic factors or are the gains in understanding and predictive power trivial?

Our evaluation of the evidence is in chapter 5, which documents a very significant impact of monetary uncertainty on long-term rates of interest in the U.S. Since U.S. rates have an influence on interest rates in Western Europe, either directly or via their effects on German long-term rates, uncertainty regarding future money growth in the U.S. is relevant for long-term rates in Europe also. In addition, we obtain some rather weaker evidence regarding other effects of economic uncertainty on European long-term rates.

Three chapters precede this pivotal chapter and three others follow it. Chapters 2–4 prepare the ground both theoretically and statistically. Chapter 2 addresses the issue why so much more speculation takes place regarding the money supply in the United States economy than about monetary trends in other developed nations. The higher quality of the monetary statistics together with their speedy and frequent release provides a partial explanation; I shall argue that there are additional economic factors, related to the importance of exchange rates as goals of monetary policy, which explain why monetary statistics in Europe contain more 'noise' and carry less information about future inflation rates. In chapter 2, I propose a method for correcting the European data on the money supply (M1) which takes out some temporary contaminating effects. This results in a corrected series for the money supply which relates more closely both to short-term changes in economic growth and to variations in inflation.

Having established that money matters, I continue in chapter 3 with a theoretical analysis of the risk premia which are incorporated in rates of return on financial assets. Three abstract models of increasing complexity attempt to weave financial insights into a macroeconomic framework. No complex mathematics are required, but simplicity is achieved at the cost of some incompleteness: I continue to use standard macroeconomic assumptions about the relations between consumption, income, and wealth, even though the traditional 'consumption equation' should be derived afresh on the basis of the new research in financial economics.

Most of the discussion in chapter 3 is related to how increased monetary uncertainty – defined as erratic rates of growth for the domestic money supply – affects interest rates, but I consider also the effects on required rates

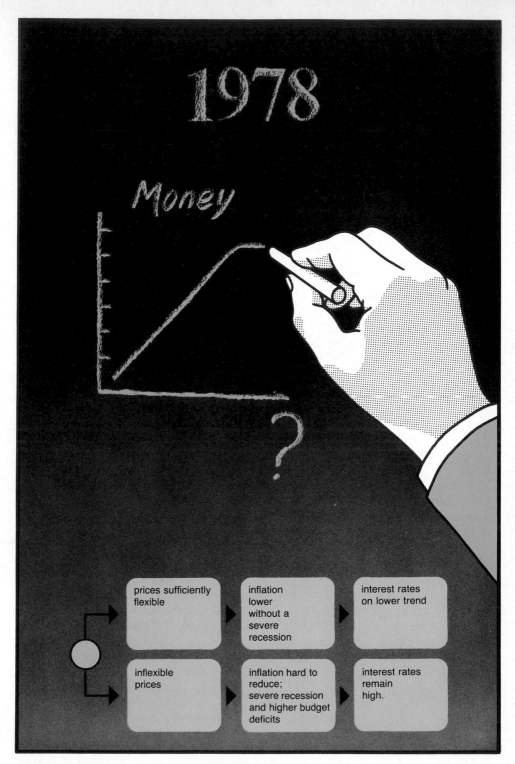

Figure 1.3   Pondering unexpected monetary restraint, 1978

Money growth has halted: are wages sufficiently flexible to prevent a severe recession?

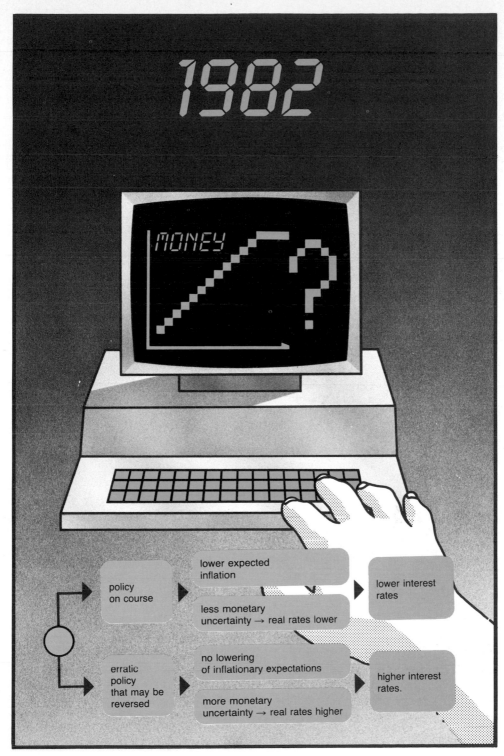

Figure 1.4   Pondering unexpected monetary restraint, 1982
Money growth has halted: is there a method in this monetary policy?

of return of great uncertainty about future economic growth in a small system of mathematical equations. I believe that the admittedly sketchy treatment of uncertainty in a small macroeconomic model does serve already to suggest answers to some puzzling questions about the economic record of the past few years:

- Why were the negative economic effects of monetary contraction larger than many expected on the basis of earlier evidence regarding the temporary positive effects of monetary expansion?
- How could prices and wages in the U.S. be so much more flexible than expected, whereas at the same time the sharp decline in actual inflation was less helpful for long-term interest rates than many economists had thought?
- What caused the sharp decline in the income velocity of money in the U.S. during 1982?

The theoretical analysis of chapter 3 suggests some answers to these and similar questions; the next two chapters investigate whether the postulated effects can be traced in the historical statistics for the U.S. and other countries.

In chapter 4 Clemens J.M.Kool and I expand our earlier published research on the connections between the money supply and the aggregate price level. We contrast two ways of forming forecasts of future inflation rates: on the one hand extrapolative forecasts that are based on nothing but previously realized rates of price change, and on the other hand monetarist forecasts which exploit a version of the quantity theory of money to compute predictions of the underlying rate of inflation. Since our statistical analysis uses quarterly data and concentrates on the short-term, it stands to reason that the extrapolative forecasts do better than the quantity-theoretic predictions. For, the aggregate rate of inflation should be regarded as a weighted average of the rates of increase of innumerable individual goods and services, many of which are not priced in the auction markets so popular with theoretical economists. This explains the typical inertia seen in movements of the aggregate price level: the current quarterly rate of change is nearly always a fair benchmark for forecasts regarding the rate of change for the next quarter. Extrapolative forecasts of inflation are bound therefore to perform relatively well over the very short term.

The quantity theory of money, on the other hand, points towards the necessary and sufficient cause of secular inflation, namely sustained growth in the money supply in excess of the rate of increase in the demand for real money balances. But, fluctuations in the demand for money reduce its value as a short-term forecasting tool. Our statistical analysis for the period 1971–1982 confirms that the extrapolative forecast does better than the monetarist forecast of inflation, but that forecasters act unwisely if they over-look the monetary signals. We propose a combined forecast of near-term inflation incorporating both extrapolative and monetarist elements.

Chapter 5 provides the proof of the pudding in the form of a statistical investigation of long-term interest rates on government bonds in seven countries for the period 1971–1982. Paul T.W.M.Veugelers and I conclude that the extreme variability of the U.S. money supply (M1) since 1980 contributed some 2 percentage points to the high interest rates of the recent period. High interest rates in the U.S. get translated into high interest rates elsewhere, so that the rest of the world has suffered also from monetary uncertainty in the U.S. In addition, we find that an uncertain outlook with respect to domestic inflation also may have an upward effect on some European interest rates. These findings suggest that monetary policy affects interest rates not only through a short-term liquidity effect and a more important permanent effect on inflationary expectations, but also through increasing or decreasing perceived monetary uncertainty. The more uncertain businessmen and consumers are about the future purchasing power of their nominal assets, the higher the risk premium which they will want to see incorporated into interest rates on such risky paper investments.

Large-scale econometric models pretend also to be useful in analysing interest rates, perhaps even to the extent of being able to forecast future rates. In chapter 6, I try to explain why the big computer models of national economies may suffer a fate similar to that of the ancient dinosaurs: slow-footed because of their giant size, they exhibit curious trembling movements that hamper their capacities for survival. A non-technical discussion of the oscillating dynamic characteristics so typical of the current generation of large-scale models serves to show why the quest for ever-increasing complexity has not served economic understanding well. I also provide some informal evidence about professional forecasts of interest rates in the United States. Predicting future changes in interest rates appears to have been very difficult indeed; the neutral forecast that interest rates will remain at current levels performs equally well according to two surveys discussed in chapter 6. I conclude that the current generation of large-scale econometric models is not sufficiently reliable to be of help in solving disputes about what moves interest rates. Specialized research on a smaller scale is still more likely to foster our understanding of interest-rate patterns over time.

After monetary uncertainty has become high, it may take considerable time before businessmen and consumers are prepared to believe once more in anti-inflation rhetoric. After all, the direct costs of printing paper money are practically zero, and a surge in the money supply always has some positive short-term effects on economic growth and employment. Policies have turned expansionary before, and how are we to trust that we are not condemned to repeat the past? Chapter 7 makes a plea for one way in which government can show its anti-inflation resolve, namely indexation of long-term debt. Monetary specialists have long advocated indexation of private mortgages and long-term government debt, both for reasons of economic efficiency and a better matching of assets and liabilities, and because index-ation of the national debt implies that the taxpayers instead of rentiers gain when the authorities deliver on their anti-inflationary pronouncements. In chapter 7 I summarize the arguments in favour of indexation, now that a substantial risk premium for inflationary uncertainty in nominal long-term interest rates has made it even more imperative to search for better debt policies.

A brief concluding chapter comments on the main results about monetary uncertainty and interest rates, and indicates some limitations of this re-search. Technical materials on the statistical techniques used to compute the extrapolative and monetarist forecasts of inflation are contained in two technical Appendices after which a source listing of statistical data used terminates the book.

chapter 2

Watching the money supply

"Forecasters typically underpredict changes in inflation rates. Most often, formal econometric models rely heavily on past inflation rates to predict future inflation... As a result, even when monetary policy changes as dramatically as it did in 1981 (when shift-adjusted M1 grew by 2.3 percent, down sharply from 6.6 percent growth in 1980) many forecasters will predict little change in near-term inflation rates."

Roy H. Webb, "Forecasts 1983",
Economic Review, Federal Reserve Bank of
Richmond, January/February, 1983, p. 5.

"A powerful advantage of monetarism, therefore, is that it does not concentrate on a single segment of the total stream of expenditures. Moreover, the effects of money-supply changes can be expected to be more pervasive than changes in the cost of credit, or in the volume of autonomous expenditures, both of which directly affect a relatively small part of the public. Money, after all, is held by everyone in the economy."

A. James Meigs, "Money Matters", Harper &
Row, New York, 1972, p. 51.

2.1 U.S. citizens only?

Fed-watching is much more prominent in the United States than in Western Europe. The American financial press contains extensive discussions of the weekly M1 numbers: did they come out surprisingly high, or were the latest figures lower than expected? Questions such as these are not put often in Europe, where the degree of attention is in no way comparable to the keen excitement generated by the latest data on the U.S. money stock M1. In this chapter we shall look at some potential explanations for the more modest interest in the money numbers in Europe.

One obvious factor that helps explain the lower visibility of the monetary statistics in Europe does not require much discussion: the basic data tend to be published with substantially greater delays by the respective central banks, which reduces their usefulness for gauging short-term trends in the financial markets. It is unlikely, for example, that the most recent available data on the Dutch money supply are of much help to market participants in forecasting short-term interest rates, since the numbers become available with a lag of approximately three months. It remains true that trends in such an important measure of aggregate nominal demand as the narrow money stock may continue to be influential in shaping inflationary expectations, even if published with substantial delay. Also, the lag in publication does not totally destroy their incremental usefulness in forecasting short-term movements in the business cycle, but the immediate interest in the M1 numbers will obviously be much reduced if they are published after three months instead of after two weeks as in the U.S. The longer the publication lag, the more market participants will look at other, more readily available economic indicators.

But, more needs to be said about other reasons why the data on the growth in the national money supply attract so much less attention in Europe than in the U.S. According to monetary theory, changes in the money supply should be important both for short-term movements in real output and for longer-term inflationary trends. Even if delays in publication, institutional differences between the small open economies of Western Europe and the United States, or less developed financial markets reduce the value of the European M1 numbers for assessing short-term interest rate trends, the well-established connections between money and both the price and volume components of national income should continue to be of interest. Unexpected accelerations or decelerations in the money supply should have significant effects on the business cycle, whereas longer-term trends in the growth rate of the money supply should be a major factor in determining the rate of inflation.

How useful the data on the money supply really are for understanding changes in real economic activity and the general price level depends on

how well-behaved the income velocity of money tends to be. In the equation
of exchange

M.V = p.y

> *Symbols*
> M = nominal supply of money
> V = income velocity of money
> p = aggregate price level
> y = index for real national income

velocity, V, is the crucial factor in determining whether the identity serves
only as a definition of V or whether we can reliably make assumptions about
the average behaviour of velocity, so that the identity becomes theoretically
and practically useful and may be called the 'quantity theory of money'.

The evidence in this chapter will show that the published data on the
money supply are less useful for explaining prices and output in Europe
than in the United States: the income velocity of money is much less well-
behaved. Fortunately, there is something we can do about this, since the
raw data are contaminated by temporary movements in the money supplies
that are largely irrelevant for nominal national income, but may be removed
with little difficulty. Correction for these temporary disturbances leaves us
with new time series of the European money supplies that are of more help
in understanding the patterns in the price level and in real activity. I shall
present one method for purging the data on the European money supplies
and compare statistically and graphically the relevance of the corrected and
the original series for contributing to an explanation of the business cycle.

The links between unexpected movements in the money supply and short-
run movements in real economic activity never become as tight as in the
U.S., but the attempt to correct the money stock data does help in most of
the six European countries to reduce the gap. Fed-watching will remain
more popular in the United States, but paying attention to the money stock
can be worthwhile in Europe as well.

2.2 The official numbers

Numbers on the supply of money are available in national sources and
reprinted in the 'International Financial Statistics', published by the International Monetary Fund, together with the I.M.F.'s estimate of the
seasonally adjusted series. The I.M.F. publication also contains a comparative table that shows growth rates over a 12-month period for the money
supply in different countries. Such growth rates over a 12-month period are
reported also in the 'Economist'. The British weekly gives growth rates over

a 3-month period as well, but these are based on data that have not been adjusted for seasonal variation in all countries.

For certain types of statistical investigations into the efficiency of financial markets it is preferable to work with point-in-time data that have not been corrected for seasonal patterns. Questions whether two economic time series are related through a causal mechanism that leads from one series to the other or whether feed-back channels exist are best studied with such point-in-time data, that are gathered once during each period. A quarterly analysis, for example, would use financial data observed during a single week, or if feasible, a single day in the course of each three-month period even though many more statistics would be available.

In this study, however, we shall work exclusively with quarterly averages of seasonally adjusted monthly data. It is true that many common procedures for seasonal adjustment apply two-sided filters to the raw data, which introduces some amount of future information into the definitive published data on the seasonally adjusted series. Also, the averaging procedure whereby end-of-month numbers are aggregated into quarterly averages automatically induces first-order serial correlation of the moving-average type into the resulting series (Working, 1960). But, one has to weigh these drawbacks against the advantages of seasonal adjustment and temporal aggregation. It is not likely that the seasonal pattern in the money supply is useful in explaining changes in aggregate prices and real output. Nominal national income has its own seasonal shape that presumably depends more on the weather and on patterns in holidays and schoolyears than on seasonal factors in the financial sector. Differences in seasonality are likely to be more important than similarities. The inference problem is much more complicated, therefore, if one decides to work with data that are not seasonally adjusted since seasonal patterns and causal connections have to be estimated jointly.

If the raw figures contain a lot of transient noise – purely temporary disturbances that contaminate the data and are void of useful information – then temporal aggregation, for example replacing end-of-month numbers by quarterly averages, will improve the quality of the data. Furthermore, our interest here is in the connections between movements in money growth and subsequent changes in the price level and in real economic activity, and the availability of data on these variables also points towards working with quarterly averages rather than with monthly data. Real gdp or gnp is not estimated with greater frequency than on a quarterly basis and the available monthly indices of changes in consumption prices are less suitable for macroeconomic analysis than the quarterly values for the gdp or gnp deflator, both because of their more restricted coverage and because the particular way in which the monthly indices are constructed seems likely to differ more from country to country than the techniques for computing the deflators in the national accounts. In some countries, for example, the component of the monthly index that measures housing cost is based on infrequent observations of rents for (quasi-) public housing. Such an index may be useful for wage adjustments, but most researchers would prefer a deflator from the national income accounts for macroeconomic analysis.

We shall use quarterly averages of end-of-month numbers for all analyses in this book for the six European countries. The Federal Reserve System in the United States publishes also monthly averages of daily figures that are a preferred alternative to the end-of-month numbers for the type of macroeconomic analysis that we are undertaking here, since the averaging process reduces the amount of irrelevant 'noise' in the end-of-month numbers. Superior quality of the U.S. data is one reason why the month-to-month and quarter-to-quarter variability is less there than in the average European country.

Apart from this purely statistical factor, there are also economic reasons why the variability is larger in the six European countries than in the U.S. In the next section I shall document the higher variability in Europe and provide an explanation for some of the violent short-term swings in the growth rates of the European money supplies. We shall see that many of the short-term accelerations and decelerations can be explained by corresponding short-term movements in domestic or international interest rates that alter the opportunity costs of holding money instead of interest-bearing money substitutes. To the extent that these frequent shifts between non-interest-bearing money and interest-bearing substitutes for M1 are clearly temporary, the reported M1 numbers will give a distorted image of the underlying growth rate of the money stock. Removal of the estimated effects of the temporary shifts in and out of M1 will then result in higher-quality data on the economically relevant money supply.

The advantages of correcting the rough money stock data are greatest for some of the smaller countries in the D-mark block. In Holland and Switzerland approximately one third of the variation in the money supply disappears if one takes short-term transfers in and out of interest-bearing substitutes for money into account. Less urgent is the need to correct the data for Germany and the other smaller countries, but with one exception for Austria our method removes at least some short-term variability that is mostly irrelevant for macroeconomic analysis. Comparative tables with results for all six European countries and graphs of the money stocks after correction are supplied at the end of the chapter.

2.3 Temporary distortions in the monetary data

A handy source for quarterly averages of the narrow money supply (M1) in different countries is 'International Economic Conditions', a publication of the Research Department of the Federal Reserve Bank of St. Louis, Missouri, U.S.A. Figure 2.1 has been reproduced from the issue that was released in late January of 1983 and relates to the Netherlands, which I shall use as an example in this section. The corrections that will be made to the money supplies are of more than average importance in Holland, but our method applies as well to almost all the other European countries under review.

The staff of the Federal Reserve Bank of St. Louis splits the complete period in different parts, each with its own trend rate of growth. Note, for example, the very strong acceleration in the money supply between the third quarter of 1974 and the first quarter of 1976, and the subsequent absolute decline in M1 during the first three quarters of 1976. Another remarkable change in the growth rate is located in the second half of 1977, when the average rate of growth decelerates from 21.5% to little over 3%.

Several analysts have argued on the basis of these data that the Dutch monetary authorities executed a monetary policy that was far too permissive during certain periods, but very restrictive at other times. Michael Parkin of the University of Western Ontario has claimed that the deceleration during 1973 and part of 1974 was extremely severe and very costly for the Dutch economy (Parkin, 1981). For, according to standard monetary analysis, unexpected declines in the rate of growth of the money stock that persist over more than a few months have temporary contractionary effects on real output. Similarly, unanticipated accelerations in the money supply will lead to a temporary boom in the economy. Economists still argue about the precise theoretical basis for these effects, but there is little doubt that unexpected changes in the growth rate of the money supply have such temporary effects on the rate of economic growth. The time delay between unanticipated changes in money growth and their consequences for economic growth varies between countries and periods, but 3-9 months seems to be a reasonable estimate.

One should expect, therefore, that the major accelerations and decelerations in the figure are followed after little time by corresponding temporary accelerations and decelerations in the rate of economic growth in the Netherlands. The relevance of swings in the growth rate of the money supply for economic growth in the Netherlands can be investigated by comparing the pattern in figure 2.1 to that of real gross national product (gnp) presented below in figure 2.7.

The verdict is clear: the money stock numbers in figure 2.1 are not helpful in predicting future movements in economic growth. Not only are the major

Figure 2.1   Money growth in Holland-original numbers
The uncorrected data are hard to interpret

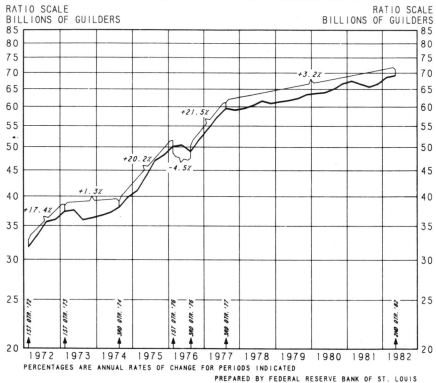

MONEY SUPPLY – NETHERLANDS

RATIO SCALE
BILLIONS OF GUILDERS

RATIO SCALE
BILLIONS OF GUILDERS

PERCENTAGES ARE ANNUAL RATES OF CHANGE FOR PERIODS INDICATED
PREPARED BY FEDERAL RESERVE BANK OF ST. LOUIS

Quarterly averages of monthly figures

upswings and downswings in the period 1972-1977 of limited relevance for the subsequent behaviour of the real sector, the dramatic and persistent decline in industrial production that started during 1980 is not at all preceded by any clear decline in the growth rate of the money supply. Part of the loss of industrial production must be blamed on the second OPEC oil price hike, but it remains implausible that production could collapse as badly as during the first oil crisis without once again an adverse monetary shock super-imposed on the energy crisis.

Some standard monetary theory is required by way of introduction to our proposal to change (and improve) the raw data on the money stock. The actual amount of money in circulation is determined by the banks and the public together with the central bank which is responsible for the growth over time of the so-called monetary base, roughly defined as the sum of cash balances outside the banking system and bank reserves. The central bank is capable of regulating this monetary base, as the base is nothing more but the sum of two major items on the liabilities side of its own balance sheet. The so-called 'money multiplier' connects the monetary base to the money stock. Control of the money stock would be a simple matter if there were a fixed proportion between the size of the monetary base and the outstanding money stock. But, this is not the case: the factor of proportion, the money multiplier, varies over time and is determined in part by the behaviour of the banking system and the public. A strong increase in the public's preference for cash balances over demand deposits, for example, implies that the money multiplier decreases, so that the money stock has to contract. This is what happens during a banking panic. The public's behaviour may also have strong effects on the size of the outstanding stock of money that are of a visibly temporary nature. A bout of speculation against the currency, for example, will usually be countered in countries that have commitments to defending fixed exchange rates by a sharp rise in short-term money market rates, and this induces many firms to change some demand deposits into higher-yielding time deposits or money market instruments. As a result the money stock declines temporarily, until more orderly conditions resume.

Obviously, money market rates will be sensitive also to changes in inflationary expectations or to more lasting changes in real rates of interest. If such causes are operative we would expect agents to consider the resulting changes in interest rates as permanent (until further notice) rather than temporary. There is a simple way to distinguish between changes in the money stock that are caused by temporary actions on the part of the banks and the public – which we may wish to disregard for macroeconomic analysis – and changes in the money supply that cannot be classified straightaway as temporary and should therefore not be erased out of the published data. We can make use of the likelihood that interest rates such as those on savings deposits, where the costs of changing the interest rates are high for the financial institutions, will be adjusted approximately in step with rates that are determined continuously by the market-place if market rates are deemed to have changed permanently, whereas the financial institutions will tend to hold back if in their judgement market rates respond to temporary factors that will be reversed shortly.

For our empirical analysis we have used the differential between a market-determined rate on three-month time deposits (i_T) and a rate on three-month savings deposits (i_S) that is more of an administered interest rate. We assume that the normal value for the interest differential is constant and that changes in it are predominantly due to temporary factors. If i_T rose far above i_S temporary increases in time deposits would occur at the expense of savings and demand deposits, so that the narrowly defined money stock would decrease. If the rise in the interest differential were indeed temporary, then it would be wrong to assign the same importance to the resulting decrease in money as one would to a drop in the money supply that was considered as a signal of persistent tighness. Therefore, we shall remove the effects of changes in the interest differential on the money stocks before relating changes in money to economic growth and inflation. The correction hinges on the assumption that the normal value for the interest differential is constant. Such an assumption would be implausible if the terms to maturity of the two respective assets where not identical, but we work throughout with rates on 3-month deposits. The constraint that the terms to maturity had to be identical forced us to opt for 3-month interest rates instead of even shorter-term rates, although movements in call money rates may even more obviously have temporary causes than changes in 3-month rates on time deposits. Unfortunately, we could not find comparable data for seven countries on administered rates for periods under 3 months.

In our attempt to purge the raw data on the money stocks from temporary disturbances we use the interest differential together with one other explanatory variable. Holland, Belgium and Denmark attempted throughout the sample period to maintain a fixed rate of exchange with respect to the German mark. Austria did not join the 'snake' or the E.M.S., but was quite successful in unilaterally pegging the exchange rate of the schilling to the mark. In all four economies one could claim therefore that the normal value for the forward premium (signed to become positive if the domestic currency is expected to depreciate with respect to the D-mark) should be approximately zero. If the forward premium suddenly became significantly different from zero, then rational agents might well consider this to be a temporary phenomenon, to be resolved either by a currency realignment or by a victory for the central banks in their counter-attack on the speculators.

Under quasi-fixed exchange rates a forward premium that deviated from zero for protracted periods would imply systematic profits from open interest arbitrage in the foreign currency markets (however, see Krasker, 1980, for a qualification to this statement). Here we assume that large changes in the forward premium vis-à-vis the D-mark were temporary and thus caused temporary and reversible changes in the money stocks. Our research does not distinguish between deliberate central bank actions as the proximate cause for large changes in the forward premia and endogenous changes in the money multiplier for a given path of the monetary base. We simply hypothesize that if increases in the forward premium with respect to the D-mark in any of the countries that tried to maintain a fixed exchange rate with that currency were associated with declines in the measured stock of money, agents would not immediately adjust their inflationary expectations, but would rather consider such changes in the money stocks to be not permanent.

For our empirical work we first computed a quarterly series for the underlying level of nominal national income. The Multi-State Kalman Filter technique with which these underlying levels were computed is explained in Appendix 1 at the back of the book. In chapter 4 we shall compute multivariate expectations of the aggregate price level and the rate of real output, but since these indices are based in part on the corrected series for the money supplies, they obviously were not available for the regressions in this chapter.

The underlying values for expected nominal income, Y^e, are divided into the nominal money supplies, which results in a quarterly time series for the inverse of the income velocity of money. The first difference of this variable, $\Delta(M/Y^e)$, is the left-hand side variable in the statistical analysis of this section. We regress it on the interest differential and – in the case of Holland, Belgium, Austria and Denmark – on the forward premium with respect to the D-mark. Both explanatory variables are also employed in first-difference form. Either current values for the explanatory variables were entered, or their one-quarter lagged values, but no lags beyond one quarter were allowed.

Table 2.1 provides information about the trend and variability of the inverted income velocity of money both for the complete period of analysis and for three sub-periods, corresponding roughly to the final years of fixed exchange rates between the dollar and the European countries in our sample (1965III-1970IV), the transitional years of high uncertainty about the future monetary order (1971I-1973IV) and the most recent years during which the D-mark floated against the U.S. dollar (1974I-1982II). It is clear from the table that trends in velocity shifted considerably over time in several of the European countries, especially in Switzerland and Belgium. One cannot say, however, that the variability of velocity, measured simply as the standard deviation of the residuals, increased all-round over time; only in the case of

Switzerland do we see a significant increase in the short-run variability of velocity. Our procedure for removing temporary distortions from the money supply will reduce this jump in the variability of Swiss velocity, although the standard deviation of the changes in velocity over the 1974-1982 period remains twice as high in Switzerland as in Denmark and Belgium, three times as high as in Austria and the Netherlands, and over five times higher than in West-Germany. Table 2.2 provides information on the explanatory power of our two measures of temporary disturbances in removing some short-term variation from the data. The regressions are clearly significant for Germany, the Netherlands, Switzerland, and Denmark, marginally so in the case of Belgium ($F_{65}^2 = 3.04$ with the 0.05 significance level at 3.14) and insignificant for Austria. Note that the regressions remove a considerable amount of positive serial correlation from the dependent variable in Germany, Holland and Switzerland.

In the Netherlands, the explanatory power of the regressions is reduced, but the correct (negative) signs are obtained if we replace the interest differential by the forward premium. This finding suggests that the interest differential is also in the first place a gauge of changes in the degree of pressure on the national currency. Tests of this issue are less telling for Belgium, Austria and Denmark where no specification is capable of explaining much of the variation in velocity. The analysis would have to be different in Germany, where it would be much harder to construct appropriate time series for the forward premium. On the basis of the evidence we assume that both explanatory variables measure in the first place the same type of phenomenon: short-term changes in the foreign exchange markets together with the reactions of the monetary authorities. Thus, it would be inappropriate to attempt a similar analysis for the U.S., where we shall work with the standard data on the narrow money stock.

Our explanation for some of the temporary disturbances to the money supply helps to make the evolution of the income velocity of money smoother and more predictable. A separate analysis for the three sub-periods shows that changes in the interest spread or changes in the forward premium with respect to the D-mark contribute to an explanation of changes in velocity during the transition period to floating exchange rates (1971-73) and afterwards. The separate regressions for the 1960's show that virtually all the coefficients have their correct signs, as in table 2.2, but are insignificant. The coefficients of determination (R^2) reach 0.4 or above in the regressions for the sub-period 1971-73 in Germany, Holland and Switzerland. Currency substitution was of particular importance during these years when many market participants agreed about a fundamental overvaluation of the US dollar and placed their one-way bets accordingly.

The coefficients of determination (R^2), are lower in these three

Table 2.1. Shifting Trends in Velocity

	1965III - 1982II	1965III - 1970IV	1971I - 1973IV	1974I - 1982II
D : Δ (M/Y^e) =	$-.008$ (.033) σ_u = .27 DW = 1.2	$-.066$ (.058) σ_u = .27 DW = 1.7	$-.027$ (.098) σ_u = .34 DW = 1.2	.037 (.042) σ_u = .25 DW = .9
NL : Δ (M/Y^e) =	$-.060$ (.060) σ_u = .49 DW = 1.4	$-.118$ (.084) σ_u = .39 DW = 2.4	$-.039$ (.18) σ_u = .63 DW = 1.2	$-.029$ (.087) σ_u = .51 DW = 1.0
CH : Δ (M/Y^e) =	$-.099$ (.14) σ_u = 1.19 DW = 1.5	$-.146$ (.13) σ_u = .61 DW = 1.1	$-.270$ (.35) σ_u = 1.21 DW = 1.1	$-.009$ (.25) σ_u = 1.46 DW = 1.5
B : Δ (M/Y^e) =	$-.220$ (.070) σ_u = .58 DW = 1.3	$-.422$ (.12) σ_u = .58 DW = 1.1	.038 (.10) σ_u = .36 DW = .9	$-.179$ (.11) σ_u = .61 DW = 1.6
A : Δ (M/Y^e) =	$-.069$ (.050) σ_u = .41 DW = 2.2	$-.128$ (.092) σ_u = .43 DW = 2.0	$-.014$ (.12) σ_u = .41 DW = 2.5	$-.049$ (.069) σ_u = .39 DW = 2.1
DK : Δ (M/Y^e) =	$-.059$ (.077) σ_u = .64 DW = 1.8	$-.075$ (.12) σ_u = .57 DW = 1.5	$-.122$ (.18) σ_u = .64 DW = 3.0	$-.026$ (.12) σ_u = .69 DW = 1.6

- 1979I and II have been discarded in the case of Austria (see Data Appendix).
- The dependent variable has been multiplied by 100.
- σ_u standard error of estimate.
- DW Durbin-Watson coefficient for first-order serial correlation.
- Standard errors have been printed below the coefficients.

Table 2.2 Correcting the raw data on the Money Supply.

$$D \; : \Delta (M/Y^e) = \begin{matrix} .008 \\ (.030) \end{matrix} \quad \begin{matrix} -.052 \; \Delta \; (i_T - i_S) \\ (.040) \end{matrix} \quad \begin{matrix} -.131 \; \Delta \; (i_T - i_S)_{-1} \\ (.041) \end{matrix}$$

$$R^2 = .19 \quad \sigma_u = .25 \quad DW = 1.6$$

$$NL : \Delta (M/Y^e) = \begin{matrix} -.052 \\ (.049) \end{matrix} \quad \begin{matrix} -.146 \; \Delta \; (i_T - i_S) \\ (.031) \end{matrix} \quad \begin{matrix} -.091 \; \Delta \; (i_T - i_S)_{-1} \\ (.031) \end{matrix}$$

$$R^2 = .33 \quad \sigma_u = .40 \quad DW = 2.0$$

$$CH : \Delta (M/Y^e) = \begin{matrix} -.072 \\ (.12) \end{matrix} \quad \begin{matrix} -.437 \; \Delta \; (i_T - i_S) \\ (.14) \end{matrix} \quad \begin{matrix} -.525 \; \Delta \; (i_T - i_S)_{-1} \\ (.16) \end{matrix}$$

$$R^2 = .33 \quad \sigma_u = .97 \quad DW = 2.1$$

$$B \; : \Delta (M/Y^e) = \begin{matrix} -.199 \\ (.069) \end{matrix} \quad \begin{matrix} -.098 \; \Delta \; (i_T - i_S) \\ (.068) \end{matrix} \quad \begin{matrix} -.123 \; \Delta \; (i_T - i_S)_{-1} \\ (.068) \end{matrix}$$

$$R^2 = .06 \quad \sigma_u = .56 \quad DW = 1.4$$

$$A \; : \Delta (M/Y^e) = \begin{matrix} -.68 \\ (.050) \end{matrix} \quad \begin{matrix} -.028 \; \Delta FP_{DM} \\ (.030) \end{matrix}$$

$$R^2 = -.00 \quad \sigma_u = .41 \quad DW = 2.1$$

$$DK : \Delta (M/Y^e) = \begin{matrix} -.050 \\ (.073) \end{matrix} \quad \begin{matrix} -.084 \; \Delta FP_{DM} \\ (.034) \end{matrix} \quad \begin{matrix} -.075 \; \Delta FP_{DM-1} \\ (.035) \end{matrix}$$

$$R^2 = .10 \quad \sigma_u = .60 \quad DW = 2.1$$

Period of analysis : 1965III – 1982II.
- 1979I and II have been discarded in the case of Austria (see Data Appendix).
- Due to data limitations ΔFP_{DM} has been set to zero in 1965III – 1967III for Austria and in 1965III – 1973I for Denmark.
- The dependent variable has been multiplied by 100. All interest rates are percentages (e.g. 5, not 0.05).
- R^2 coefficient of determination, after correction for degrees of freedom.
- σ_u standard error of estimate.
- DW Durbin-Watson coefficient for first-order serial correlation.
- Estimated standard errors are printed below each coefficient.

countries for the 1974-1982 period, but the coefficients on the interest rate differential remain significant at the .05 level in Germany, Holland and Switzerland. Changes in the forward premium with respect to the D-mark are helpful in explaining changes in velocity in Denmark over this period as well ($R^2 = 0.2$, t-values greater than 2). Limited availability of Danish data precluded separate investigation of the two earlier sub-periods.

Combining the information in table 2.2 with the additional insights from the regressions for the three-sub-periods, I conclude that analysis and prediction of velocity in Germany, Holland, Switzerland and Denmark is made easier by accounting for changes in the spread between market-determined and administered 3-months interest rates or by correcting for the effects of changes in the forward premium with respect to the D-mark. Neither method produces great results in the case of Austria where the t-value on the change in the forward premium is approximately 1.7 for the 1974-82 sub-period, but the coefficient has the wrong – positive – sign in 1971-73. In Belgium the explanatory variable makes a modest contribution with t-values between 1.0 and 1.5 for both the 1971-73 and 1974-82 sub-periods.

Multiplying both sides of all the equations in table 2.2 by the expected level of nominal GDP gives us equations that partially explain the quarterly changes in the money stock. Most changes in the European money supplies are, of course, relevant for the business cycle and for the trend in inflation ; our transformed regression equations tell us about changes in the money stocks that are induced by temporary phenomena in the financial markets. Earlier research (Bomhoff, 1980) indicated that removing the temporary disturbances from the published data on the money supplies leaves us with corrected time series that are of greater use in explaining the business cycle and the rate of inflation. The older analysis utilized annual data for a longer period of time, which makes it easier to investigate the medium-term connections between money growth and inflation. In this study we use quarterly data over a shorter span, and therefore I shall focus attention on whether the corrected money supplies are better in explaining short-term movements in real output. A positive finding for the corrected data on M1 will make us prefer the corrected data for all the analysis in the subsequent chapters.

Using the estimated coefficients in table 2.2, together with the computed series for Y^e, nominal gdp, we thus calculate the size of the quarterly adjustments to the money stock in all European countries, except for Austria where the measured effects are alltogether insignificant. Figures 2.2, 2.3, and 2.4 show the original and the corrected series for Germany, the Netherlands and Switzerland, the three countries where the corrections are most substantial. Note how

Figure 2.2   Money stock in Germany – before and after correction
Correction removes some of the extreme movements in the uncorrected monetary statistics

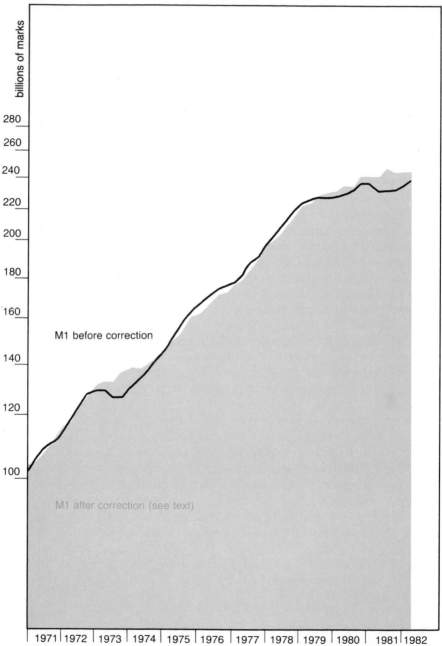

Quarterly averages of monthly figures

Figure 2.3　Money stock in Holland – before and after correction

The corrected monetary data show how restrictive monetary policy became in 1980

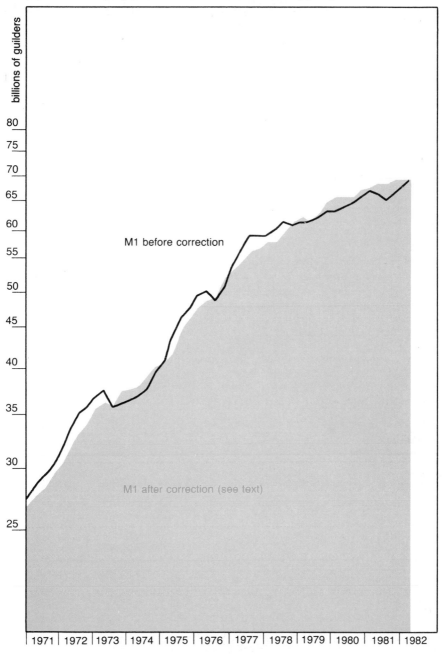

Quarterly averages of monthly figures

Figure 2.4   Money stock in Switzerland – before and after correction
The corrected data on Swiss M1 show better the restrictive monetary policy in 1974-1975

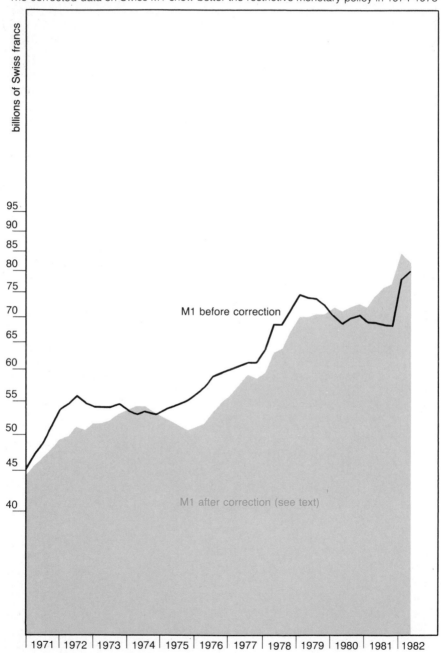

Quarterly averages of monthly figures

much smoother over time the series become. In many instances, sharp decelerations in the measured money supplies coincided with a rapid rise in the difference $i_T - i_S$ between the 3-month time deposit rate and a 3-month administered rate on savings deposits. Correction for such temporary increases in this interest rate spread generally leaves us with less erratic patterns over time.

Some of the distinct features of the uncorrected series have disappeared : consider, for example, the declines in the Dutch money supply in 1973III and 1976III, or the deceleration in the original data on the Swiss money supply between 1976 and 1977. The Swiss money supply in particular looks much less erratic after corrections ; we shall investigate whether the corrected series is not only easier on the eye but also more useful in understanding Swiss output and inflation.

2.4 Monetary influences on real output.

Money matters and corrected money matters even more. That is the message of table 2.3 which shows to what extent a looser or a tighter monetary policy can temporarily influence the pace of economic growth and at the same time conveys information about the relative usefulness of the raw versus corrected data on the money stock in predicting the business cycle.

One can compute an indicator of monetary looseness and monetary restraint in different ways. One oft-used method consists of taking the change in the growth rate of the nominal money stock as the measure of monetary stimulus. The results tend to be even better if one replaces the observed changes in the growth rate by the unexpected accelerations (see, for example, many of the papers in Brunner and Meltzer, 1978, and the seminal paper by Barro, 1977 ; see Bomhoff, 1980,for a critique of Barro's preference for a stationary long-term growth rate).

An alternative approach to measuring the contribution of monetary policy to the business cycle consists of taking (unexpected) changes in real balances as indicating whether money is loose or tight. This has been our choice for the regressions in table 2.3, where the aim has not been to achieve the richest possible specification for each country, but to provide some simple evidence regarding the potency of monetary actions to influence the real sector. To this end, we have run identical regressions for all six European countries in our sample plus the U.S. : the quarter-to-quarter growth rate of real gross domestic product is regressed on a constant term, a linear time trend, the previous quarter's rate of economic growth and the amount with which real balances increase or decrease. If the nominal money supply goes up faster than the aggregate price level, so that real money balances become more plentiful, agents

Table 2.3 Monetary effects on real activity.

US   : $\hat{y}$ =   3.19   − .011 T   + .591 $(\hat{M/P})^e$ − .014 $\hat{y}_{-1}$
                        (1.2)   (.026)   (.13)   (.13)

                                                   R^2 = .30 σ_u = 3.65   h = 0.25

D   : $\hat{y}$ =   4.85   − .063 T   + .288 $(\hat{M/P})^e$ − .080 $\hat{y}_{-1}$
                        (1.5)   (.031)   (.077)   (.11)

                                                   R^2 = .24 (.11) σ_u = 4.26   h = − 0.66

NL   : $\hat{y}$ =   9.71   − .153 T   + .294 $(\hat{M/P})^e$ − .432 $\hat{y}_{-1}$
                        (2.5)   (.056)   (.12)   (.11)

                                                   R^2 = .26 (.19) σ_u = 7.41   h = − 1.16

CH   : $\hat{y}$ =   2.65   − .035 T   + .164 $(\hat{M/P})^e$ + .272 $\hat{y}_{-1}$
                        (1.4)   (.031)   (.067)   (.12)

                                                   R^2 = .22 (.15) σ_u = 4.23   h = − 0.86

B   : $\hat{y}$ =   5.91   − .073 T   + .103 $(\hat{M/P})^e$ + .095 $\hat{y}_{-1}$
                        (1.7)   (.034)   (.076)   (.13)

                                                   R^2 = .11 (.09) σ_u = 4.49   —

A   : $\hat{y}$ =   8.94   − .111 T   + .018 $(\hat{M/P})^e$ − .357 $\hat{y}_{-1}$
                        (1.8)   (.038)   (.077)   (.12)

                                                   R^2 = .16 σ_u = 4.83   h = 0.56

DK   : $\hat{y}$ =   6.05   − .070 T   + .288 $(\hat{M/P})^e$ − .353 $\hat{y}_{-1}$
                        (2.0)   (.044)   (.080)   (.12)

                                                   R^2 = .20 (.21) σ_u = 6.05   h = − 1.07

− Period of analysis : 1967I − 1982II.
− 1979II - 1980I have been discarded in the case of Austria (see Data Appendix)
− T signifies a linear time trend that increases by 1 each quarter.
− R^2 coefficient of determination after correction for degrees of freedom
− σ_u standard error of estimate.
− h Durbin's h-statistic for first-order serial correlation in the presence of the lagged dependent variable.
− Estimated standard errors are printed below each coefficient.

will start bidding up the prices of financial and real assets, and this – combined with more direct effects of higher wealth on spending – will boost production. Conversely, if the rate of growth of the money supply falls below the rate of inflation, actual money balances drop below the desired level, and consumers as well as business firms will want to cut back on their planned expenditures.

The relevance of such elementary textbook scenarios stands or falls with the behaviour of the income velocity of money. If changes in the growth rate of nominal or real money balances are compensated by opposite short-run changes in velocity, then Fed-watching remains vital for assessing inflationary trends – the income velocity of money can hardly go to zero or infinity – but chances of predicting a business cycle from monetary data are slim.

All regressions in table 2.3 have been executed twice: once with the original quarterly averages of the national money supplies and again with the corrected data for the nominal money stocks. In both cases we used the Multi-State-Kalman filters of Statistical Appendix 1 to discover the 'underlying' or 'basic' levels of the series for the logarithms of money and prices. A linearly decreasing lag structure has been used, with the greatest weight on the current estimate of the underlying levels of M and p, and a zero weight on the end-point at lag (-3) (First-order Almon lag with coefficient at $t-3$ constrained to 0). The coefficients shown in table 2.3 refer to the first difference of this weighted average of current and lagged underlying levels of log (M) minus log (p).

Shown are the regressions based on the corrected money stocks ; the numbers in brackets directly after the coefficients of determination for these regressions show the R^2's for the identical specification when run with the uncorrected money data. There is no alternative measure of R^2 for the United States where we did not want to correct the money supply or for Austria where our attempts at correction were unsuccessful. In four out of the five remaining countries the corrected money numbers produce a higher value for the coefficient of determination and a more significant value for the coefficient of the change in real balances.

The regressions aim for simplicity and a uniform specification across countries and the many potential explanatory variables that have been omitted surely influence the size and statistical significance of the few determinants of economic growth that have been included. What the regressions do serve to show is that no desperate data-mining is required to show that money matters. The simplest possible specification for testing whether changes in real balances can help predict real growth, having taken into account the information hidden in past rates of growth, shows that money matters significantly (0.05 level) in five out of seven countries, and has the correct sign everywhere. Separate regressions (not shown here) for the two sub-periods 1967I – 1973I and 1973IV – 1982II work better for the second sub-period where the coefficient of the change in real balances is positive and significant at the 0.05 level in all countries apart from Switzerland and Austria. The first period produces a positive coefficient in all countries apart from Belgium, but the coefficients are smaller in size and less significant. For both sub-periods the highest coefficient on the change in real balances is obtained for the U.S. as is the case in table 2.3 for the complete period.

Figures 2.5 – 2.11 provide informal visual support for the monetarist contention that short-run (unexpected) changes in money have consequences for short-term economic growth. For each country we show the path of the nominal money stock – after the corrections described in section 2.3 – together with the level of economic activity. I want to use the graphs for a closer look at Holland and Switzerland, the two small countries where correcting the money supply makes the greatest difference.

A comparison of figure 2.7 for Holland and figure 2.1 where the raw data on Dutch M1 are displayed, shows the following differences :

- the growth rate of the corrected money supply accelerates somewhat in the second half of 1974. The recovery in industrial production starts during the second half of 1975, and is slightly more vigorous than in West-Germany, but not significantly so. If the trend rate of growth of the Dutch money supply had indeed been perceived to accelerate from 1.3% to 20.2% – as in figure 2.1 – then the difference in the growth of industrial production between Holland an Germany should have been larger. Also, inflationary expectations would have gone up sharply in Holland and the guilder would have lost more ground vis-à-vis the D-mark.

- Dutch monetary policy turned more restrictive during the Winter of 1976-77 in order to reduce the inflation differential with West-Germany and to protect the value of the guilder. This change in monetary policy is not at all visible in figure 2.1, where the trend changes in 1977III only. The figures on industrial production confirm that monetary policy became more tight in early 1977 : between 1977I and 1978IV industrial production rose by 1.4% in Holland, but by 3.8% in West-Germany.

- The corrected data on Dutch M1 show that the effects of the second oil price crisis in 1979-80 have been reinforced by a simultaneous change to a more restrictive monetary policy.

Figure 2.5   Money and output in the U.S.

Changes in the growth rate of M1 explain much of the U.S. business cycle

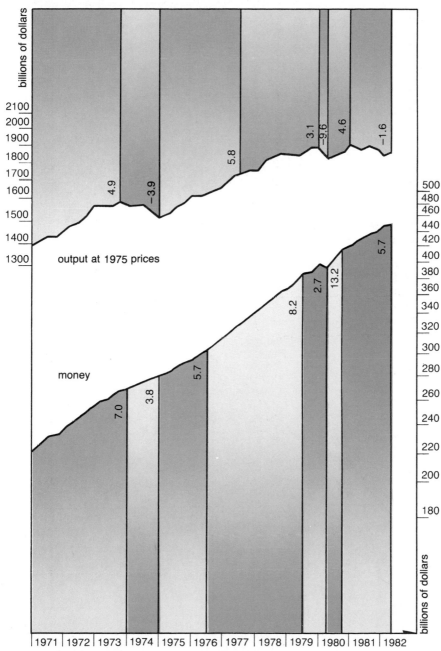

money: quarterly averages of monthly data
gnp: quarterly values at annual rates in 1975 prices
Percentages are annual rates of change between the indicated quarters

Figure 2.6   Money and output in Germany

Highly variable monetary policies aggravated the negative effects of the two oil crises

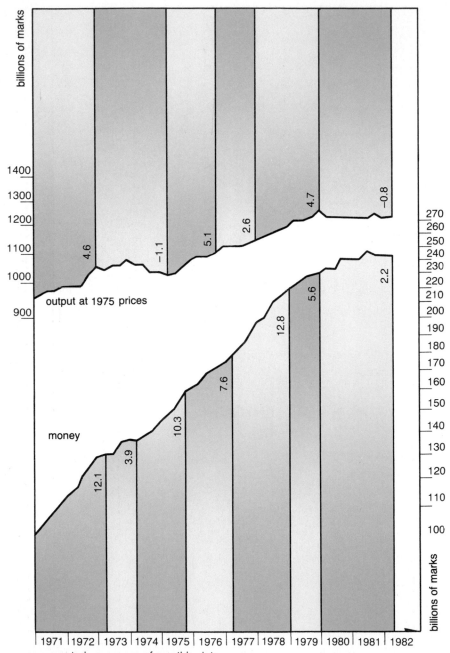

money: quarterly averages of monthly data
gnp: quarterly values at annual rates in 1977 prices
Percentages are annual rates of change between the indicated quarters

Figure 2.7   Money and output in Holland
Very restrictive monetary policies in 1980-1981 contributed to negative economic growth

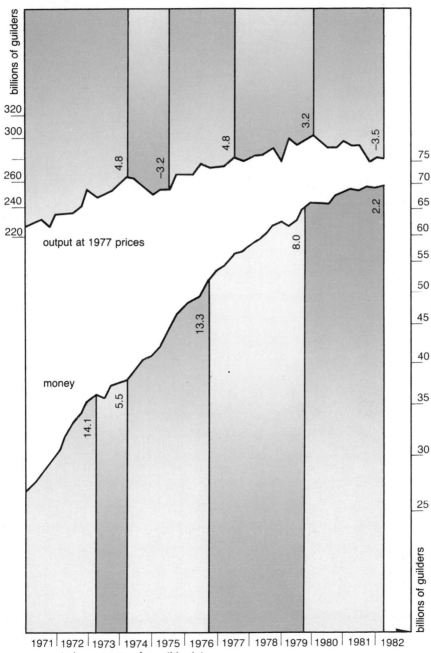

money: quarterly averages of monthly data
gnp: quarterly values at annual rates in 1975 prices
Percentages are annual rates of change between the indicated quarters

Figure 2.8   Money and output in Switzerland

A severe monetary policy in 1974-1975 caused a particularly sharp fall in real output

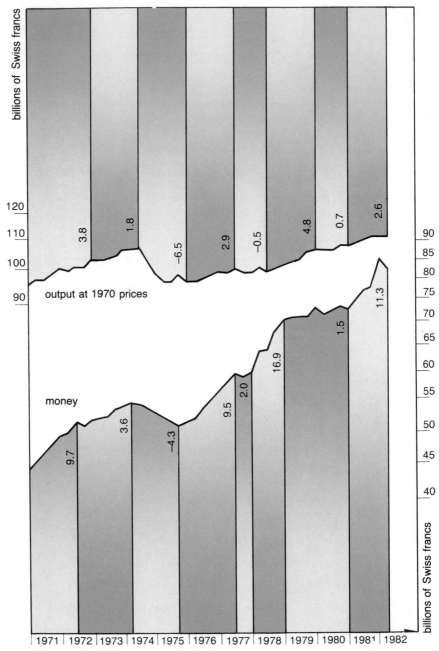

money: quarterly averages of monthly data
gnp: quarterly values at annual rates in 1970 prices
Percentages are annual rates of change between the indicated quarters

Figure 2.9   Money and output in Belgium

As in Germany and Holland, monetary policy made the 1974-1975 and 1980-1981 recessions more severe

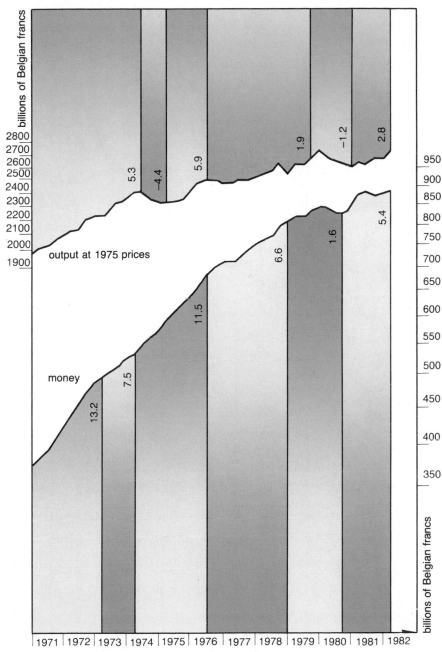

money: quarterly averages of monthly data
gnp: quarterly values at annual rates in 1975 prices
Percentages are annual rates of change between the indicated quarters

Figure 2.10   Money and output in Austria
No clear effects of changes in monetary policy on the pattern of real output

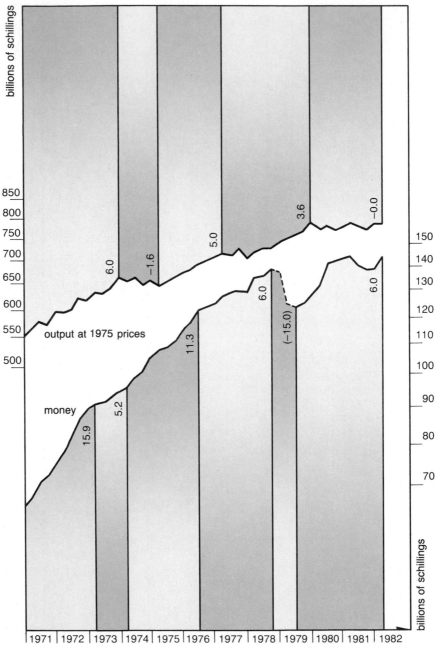

money: quarterly averages of monthly data
gnp: quarterly values at annual rates in 1975 prices
Percentages are annual rates of change between the indicated quarters

Figure 2.11 Money and output in Denmark

Continued high money growth after 1979 reduced the drop in the growth rate of real output after the second oil crisis, but at a cost of persistent high inflation

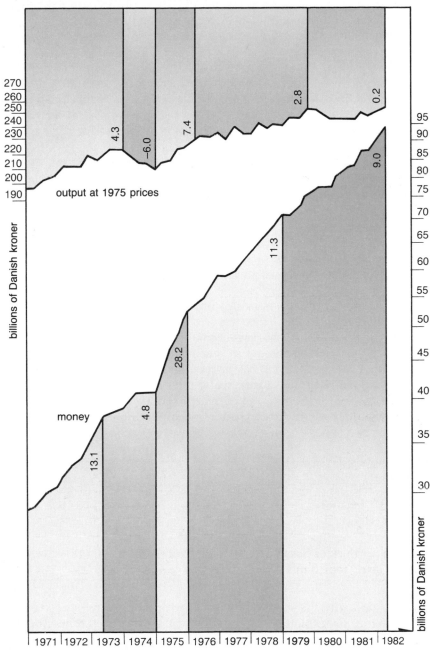

money: quarterly averages of monthly data
gnp: quarterly values at annual rates in 1975 prices
Percentages are annual rates of change between the indicated quarters

The corrected data are more in line also with the broad movement in the Dutch inflation rates :

• The spurt in money growth during 1975III – 1976IV corresponds to the observation that consumer prices in Holland went up by 7.6% (on an annual basis) in 1976 – 1977 as against an increase of 4.1% in Germany.

• The sharp decline in the trend of Dutch money growth after 1976 is translated into a corresponding decline of the rate of inflation in 1978-79. Over these two years prices went up by 4.2% (at an annual rate) in Holland, versus 3.4% in Germany.

For Switzerland I should like to focus on the behaviour of the money supply in 1977 – 1978 which continues to be debated for its implications regarding monetary policy (see Büttler and Schiltknecht, 1983). The Swiss monetary authorities allowed the monetary base and the money supply to accelerate sharply in 1978, although monetary policy in the mid-Seventies had been carried out in accordance with a strong dislike of the (imported) inflation during the terminal years of the fixed-exchange rate period. The Nationalbank's purpose was to avoid a further strengthening of the Swiss Franc in the foreign exchange markets at a time of increasing disenchantment with the U.S. dollar. To achieve this, they decided to make the Franc less scarce, but their actions created two puzzles for observers of the Swiss economy : (1) how could the growth in the money supply accelerate so much without great consequences for the inflation rate ? (2) if real balances became much more plentiful, why did Switzerland not achieve spectacular rates of growth in 1978-79 ?

A comparison of the raw and corrected figures on the growth rates of the Swiss money supply throws some light on both questions. Figure 2.4 shows the two series ; annual rates of growth are as follows :

	1975	1976	1977	1978	1979
raw data	3.8	8.2	2.5	16.5	0.6
corrected data	−4.9	7.2	7.2	14.5	4.5

Note : growth rates have been computed between the quarterly averages of the fourth quarters of each year.

The question why the money supply in Switzerland could accelerate in 1978 without a concomitant acceleration in the price level remains open for now (see chapter 4 for further comments), but at least the size of the question mark can be halved if we go from the raw to the corrected data. The corrected data show an increase of seven percentage points as against an acceleration of fourteen percentage points for the raw published data.

A more detailed look at the numbers shows that the first two quarters of 1978 witnessed a 22 percent increase in the official series (annual rate) as against an 17 percent in the corrected numbers. Not only was the increase during the first half of 1978 much less after correction, the growth rate during the preceding year also looks more reasonable if we correct the numbers by taking into account that temporarily high values for the interest rate differential led to a decline in the demand for money that was not expected to persist. I could claim that the corrected numbers make more sense also for 1977 in view of the pattern of real output in Switzerland during the same period :

	1975	1976	1977	1978	1979	1980
growth rate of real gnp (estimated)	−4.4	−0.1	1.7	1.0	4.1	2.2

Note : growth rates have been computed between the quarterly averages of the fourth quarters of each year.

The raw data on the growth rates of the money supply show a sharp decline in 1977 followed by the spectacular advance in 1978 and an equally spectacular deceleration in 1979. Since these changes in the growth rate must have been unexpected to a large extent, one would expect a corresponding short-run pattern in the growth rate of real gnp. But, the numbers show that real output did not behave that way. The fluctuations in economic growth correspond rather better to the pattern of the corrected data on the growth of the money stock, namely recovery in 1977, a normal year in 1978, acceleration in 1979 and a return to a normal level for the growth rate in 1980.

The informal analysis confirms the statistical message in table 2.3 : correction for temporary disturbances makes the resulting numbers on the European money supplies easier to interpret for business-cycle analysis. We shall continue to work exclusively with the corrected data in the remaining chapters of this book.

2.5. Conclusions.

Paying attention to the money supply is worthwhile – in Europa as well as in the United States. This chapter has provided some additional support for the standard monetarist contentions that money matters for short-term fluctuations in economic growth and for longer-term trends in inflation.

Simple analytical techniques confirm the informal message of figures 3.5 – 3.11 that economic growth quickens significantly when money becomes more plentiful and stalls temporarily if money becomes more scarce. Monetary uncertainty thus implies additional uncertainty about the short-term prospects for economic growth, employment and profits. As we have seen in chapter 1 that uncertainty about the real economy can effect long-term real interest rates, we have a potential channel from monetary uncertainty to long-term rates of interest.

To analyse on a quarterly basis what changes in money growth mean for future inflation is more difficult than to assess the real effects of monetary policies, since inflation is better measured in terms of year-over-year changes in a general price index, or perhaps even as an average rate of increase over a complete business cycle. Only if the rate of inflation becomes very high do contracts in the product and labour markets become short and flexible enough for inflation to become undeniably sensitive to quite short-term changes in the rate of money growth. Inflation never went up that far in the countries of our sample, so that more refined statistical techniques are required for an investigation of the short-run connections between money and prices. Our study of the issue in chapter 4 will be made a little easier by the corrections to the raw data on the money stocks that have been made in this chapter.

Before turning to an analysis of inflationary expectations I first return to the general analysis of interest rates that was introduced in chapter 1. Investigation of its short-term effects on real output has shown that monetary uncertainty is no trivial matter ; before tackling the technically harder question how monetary uncertainty effects the formation of inflationary expectations, we shall try to formalize a framework for analysis in which both phenomena can find a place.

chapter 3

Risk premia for uncertainty

"Proposed capital expenditure projects typically have cash flows that are more significantly related to aggregate consumption, than to the market portfolio. This may make the distinction of projects with different risk levels more precise and more intuitive, thereby facilitating the use of asset pricing theory in capital budgeting."

Douglas T. Breeden,
"An intertemporal asset pricing model with stochastic consumption and investment opportunities", Journal of Financial Economics, vol. 7, nr. 3, 1979, p. 292.

3.1 Risk and return

This chapter on risk premia and uncertainty will be much more abstract than other parts of the book. After trying to convey informally the thrust of the analysis for the reader who is not interested in algebraic manipulations, I shall attempt a detailed treatment of the required rates of return on financial assets under different assumptions about the sources of uncertainty in the economy.

The most common framework for analysis of rates of return on financial assets and the risk premia incorporated in these instruments remains the 'mean-variance' model of Sharpe (1964) and Lintner (1965). The essence of the approach is that investors rate the riskiness of the securities in their portfolio according to whether these securities move with the market as a whole. If the returns on a security tend to exhibit a high degree of correlation with an index for the market as a whole, then the expected average return on such a stock will have to be somewhat higher than the return on a security that tends to be less sensitive to market movements. A security that tends to appreciate when the market as a whole declines and vice versa is particularly attractive from the point of view of risk diversification, and therefore will be priced with a lower prospective yield.

One problem with this 'Capital Asset Pricing Model' (CAPM) has been the construction of an appropriate index for the return on the aggregate capital market. Most research has concentrated on assessing the riskiness of (portfolios of) equity shares as measured by the degree of covariation between the return on such securities and the return on a value-weighted index for the complete stock market. 'Betas' have been computed to gauge this riskiness. Extensions to include the bond market have been undertaken, and some researchers also have tried to extend the CAPM-framework beyond the capital markets. Mayers (1972) shows how variation in labour income should, in principle, be taken into account when computing the required returns on marketable financial assets such as shares and bonds, but an influential study by Fama and Schwert (1977) concluded that as a statistical matter the variation in personal income did not alter significantly the required returns on financial assets in the United States. The issue remains open, however, since Fama and Schwert made restrictive assumptions about the stationarity of (expected) returns.

The basic approach towards riskiness which underlies the Capital Asset Pricing Model has been retained in recent research: what matters is not how uncertain the return on a financial asset may be, but whether adding one unit of this asset to one's portfolio will increase or decrease the overall degree of risk about future returns on the complete portfolio. Whereas empirical applications of the CAPM take the unexpected element in the total return on a market portfolio of financial assets as the indicator of aggregate risk, a different measure of risk is used in a number of recent studies on the relationship between risk and return (see Breeden, 1979, Shiller, 1982, Hansen and Singleton, 1983 and the references therein). No longer is the unpleasantness of a lower-than-expected return on a financial asset measured according to whether total financial wealth has also come out lower than could have been expected, but the inconvenience of a meager return on a share or bond is assessed by investigating whether such surprises tend to occur when our need for the investment income is above average. This 'intertemporal consumption CAPM' as set forth by, for example, Breeden, rates financial assets according to whether they produce unexpected gains (or losses) when we find it most convenient to increase (decrease) spending or whether the opposite is more true on average.

The economic literature uses the marginal utility of consumption to indicate how attractive it would be to dispose of one additional unit of spending power, on the assumption that the marginal utility of consumption equals the marginal utility of business investment and the marginal utility of wealth. We frequently shall use these identities in the analysis. If the marginal utility of consumption increases by more than was expected between the previous period and the present, for instance because economic growth and consumption have been disappointing, then financial assets that yield greater-than-expected returns under such conditions have attractive hedging qualities that will lower the average return on such assets as required by the financial markets. Financial assets that turn sour in step with the economy as a whole and inconvenience their owners by yielding less when they need it most, will have to promise a higher average return in order to compensate for this unfavourable covariation.

On certain occasions changes in financial wealth will indicate quite well what we should assume about the unobservable marginal utility of consumption, but – as pointed out by Breeden – this is not always the case. For example, the marginal utility of consumption which equals the marginal utility of business investment in equilibrium may be exceptionally high due to a sunny investment climate; at the same time financial wealth may increase more than expected because of the accompanying stock market boom. Alternatively, the marginal utility of consumption may be increasing because a prolonged recession forces people to cut back on earlier consumption plans. Real income has decreased below earlier forecasts and so has financial wealth, with the result that people would really value more spending-power. Therefore, to speak about the covariance between the unexpected part of the return on the financial asset and the unanticipated future change in the marginal utility of consumption, is not the same thing as to analyse asset returns in terms of covariation with unexpected changes in total financial wealth.

In this chapter I attempt to use the central ideas of the intertemporal consumption CAPM to analyse how different kinds of macroeconomic uncertainty affect the returns on financial assets, in particular for money and long-term bonds. Earlier writers have paid attention to the effects of inflationary uncertainty on the required rates of return on nominal assets (see, for example, Klein, 1977, Blejer, 1978, who estimated demand for money functions, Friedman, 1979, who included an index for inflationary uncertainty in loan demand equations and more recent work by Mascaro and Meltzer, to be discussed in detail in chapter 5). Whether increased economic uncertainty increases or decreases the demand for financial assets is no trivial matter. Blejer notices that inflationary uncertainty, for example, can affect the demand for money in opposing directions: 'on the one hand it will increase the precautionary demand and on the other by increasing the risk of holding assets whose value is not constant in real terms, it will induce changes in portfolio composition which tend to reduce the demand for money. The net effect of increased variability of the rate of inflation remains, therefore, open to empirical determination' (1978, p. 545).

A formal framework of analysis can thus be of help in understanding these different effects and in interpreting the empirical results of the following chapters. I begin in the next section with a simple exposition of the determination of the real rate of interest as the compensation for postponing consumption from the current to the next period. The remaining sections of this chapter build on this by introducing various assumptions about uncertainty in the economy. Section 3.6 contains a more elaborate model that combines different aspects of the simpler structures in sections 3.3-3.5. Sections 3.7 and 3.8 show that monetary uncertainty (forecast errors with respect to money growth) and real uncertainty (difficulty in predicting economic growth) have different effects on long-term interest rates and the spread between the yields on bonds and on equity shares.

The formal analysis employs the fiction of a discrete-time model in which economic agents experience unexpected news about money growth, world trade, and other macroeconomic variables at the beginning of each period and subsequently act to adjust without delay the current values for variables such as interest rates, the aggregate price level and real output, and also update their expectations regarding the future developments in all these variables. The assumption that any news occurs exclusively during the mornings of January 1st, April 1st, July 1st and October 1st and that all financial and real 'markets' reach the appropriate equilibrium values before lunch on these four days after which nothing unexpected occurs until the start of the next quarter makes it possible to develop the argument without the need of using advanced mathematical techniques.

There have been few empirical applications of the intertemporal consumption CAPM, so that it is not yet clear whether our choice of working with quarterly average data is justified, or whether a different unit of time or perhaps an approximation of a continuous-time model would be a more appropriate vehicle. Macroeconomics – where use of models with discrete intervals of time is common – and the theory of finance – an area in which many researchers work in continuous time – are bound to converge (see Lucas, 1982), but it is unclear, at least to me, how that will influence the existing practices in applied macroeconomics. In this book I try to use the insights from the financial literature within the traditional macroeconomic framework of a discrete-time model.

As movements in interest rates will depend on actual and anticipated changes in the marginal utility of consumption, all theoretical constructions in this chapter require clarity about the dynamics of these unobservable variables. Several pathbreaking studies (Merton, 1973, Lucas, 1981, for example) have succeeded in deriving the pattern over time of the marginal utility of consumption through solving a formal intertemporal optimization problem. The price for this approach is that quite simple assumptions have to be made regarding the amount of uncertainty in the economic system. In this chapter I consider different assumptions about monetary and real uncertainty and in the empirical analysis of chapter 5 we shall test for the effects of uncertainty about inflation, the world business cycle, government deficits and energy prices. With so much emphasis on different sources of economic uncertainty, I have been unable to construct the theoretical models in such a way that the characteristics of the marginal utility of consumption could be derived from more basic assumptions. I shall simply postulate how the marginal utility of consumption depends on changes in income and wealth and concentrate on the effects of uncertainty on the economy.

3.2 Consuming nów or later

The rate of return on a financial asset depends on the answer to the following question: how much is needed to induce the holder not to dispose of the asset nów and obtain one additional unit of spending power, but to keep the asset until at least the following period for sale at some future time. If agents find it costly not to liquidate their assets now – in terms of temporary consumption or investment opportunities foregone – then a high expected rate of return is required to induce them to nevertheless continue holding these financial assets in their portfolio. The marginal utility of consumption during the current period, $u'(c)$, will be our measure of the utility that can be derived from selling the financial asset without delay and consuming (or investing) the proceeds.

Conversely, if agents are not very keen to liquidate their portfolios during the current period, but plan to sell financial assets during the next period because of their future consumption or real investment needs, they will accept a low real rate of return as compensation for something they feel inclined to do anyway, namely to keep the financial asset in their portfolio until at least the following period.

We measure the usefulness at the margin of being able to dispose of one unit of spending power during the next period by the marginal utility of consumption at that future time:

$$u'(c)_{+1}$$

On combining the two assumptions that we have just made, it follows that expected real rates of return will be related to

$$_tE \frac{u'(c)}{u'(c)_{+1}}$$

The higher this quotient, the higher the expected rate of return that is needed to induce holders of financial assets not to sell parts of their portfolios.

When people compare the benefits of more consumption now to more consumption later, they nearly always display a general preference for the present over the future: time has a positive price of its own. Although there are rare situations in which the pure 'rate of time preference' may be negative (see Olson and Bailey, 1981), consumers normally require compensation for postponing some consumption to a future date. Thus, the decision to carry a financial asset until at least the following period depends also on r, the pure rate of time preference. In other words, the more agents feel inclined to discount the future compared to the present, the higher real rates of return will have to be.

If there is no uncertainty regarding actual, ex-post real rates of return, then it is easy to combine the two determining factors, namely (1) the comparison of the utility of current and future consumption and (2) the price exacted for postponing some consumption:

$$u'(c) = \frac{1}{1 + r} u'(c)_{+1} (1 + epR) \tag{3.1}$$

Symbols

$u'(c)$	marginal utility of consumption during the current period
$u'(c)_{+1}$	marginal utility of consumption during the next period
r	pure rate of time preference
epR	ex-post real rate of return on some asset, if held until the beginning of the next period

The equality states that liquidating one unit of the asset presently and consuming (or investing) the proceeds is just as attractive to the owner as keeping this unit for one more period. If kept in the portfolio, the asset will earn a real return equal to epR, so that the owner can spend $1 + epR$ units instead of just 1 unit if he or she is prepared to wait. On the other hand, some discounting of future opportunities is in order, as indicated by the discount factor $1/(1 + r)$. Also, the marginal utility of consumption may change over time and this is represented by the factor $u'(c)_{+1}$ on the right-hand side of eq. (3.1).

Equilibrium in the financial markets requires the above equality to hold, since otherwise people would be better off if they sold or bought some assets in the market. If the existing stock of assets is willingly held, then eq. (3.1) serves to indicate the required certain real return on each type of asset at the margin:

$$(1 + epR) = (1 + r)\frac{u'(c)}{u'(c)_{+1}} \tag{3.2}$$

The formula relates the ex-post realized rate of return to the price of time and to the marginal utilities of consumption now and later. If we make the unrealistic assumption that current disturbances are but temporary ripples on the sea of time, so that $u'(c)_{+1}$ is constant at all times, then we can utilize the formula to investigate how different types of economic news temporarily affect $u'(c)$ and thus the ex-post real rate of return on assets that are held from period t to the beginning of period $t + 1$.

Example 1

An unexpected increase in the money stock at the beginning of period t: M^{ue}. Such a surprise would lessen the liquidity constraint on firms and individuals and reduce the real burden of outstanding nominal debt. Consumption or investment plans that had been constrained due to insufficient liquidity have become more feasible: $u'(c)$ in our formula decreases because agents now decide to increase current consumption (or investment). Those marginal consumption decisions that were not planned originally but have now become worthwhile, bring lower marginal utility than the more essential consumption decisions that would have been carried out even without the additional liquidity. Thus, the ex-post real rate epR decreases.

Example 2

A greater-than-expected foreign demand for domestic goods: m_w^{ue}. If foreign trade temporarily offers exceptional opportunities, business firms will aim at increasing overseas profits which implies that the community will find it advantageous to shift some additional resources into exports and business investment. These alternatives to current consumption have become more attractive so that the marginal utility of the last unit that is nevertheless consumed has to increase. u'(c) goes up, and the ex-post real rate epR is above average.

If we drop the assumption that $u'(c)_{+1}$ is constant, but retain the hypothesis of perfect foresight with respect to the marginal utility of consumption in the next period, we can analyse another simple case:

Example 3
An increase in the rate of economic growth: $\Delta \hat{y}^e_{+1}$.

People now expect to become wealthier at a faster rate and foresee a future in which they can indulge more and more easily in their desires. The age of abundance will approach at a faster rate, so that u'(c), the marginal utility of consumption, will henceforth decline more quickly over time. Eq. (3.2) indicates that 1 + epR, the reward for saving, will have to go up.

3.3 The short-term rate of interest

Our three examples dealt with situations in which there is perfect foresight regarding $u'(c)_{+1}$, but a passing surprise event occurs in the course of the current period that compels firms and individuals to revise their original spending plans. The more realistic assumption that the actual need for liquidity during the next period, as measured by the marginal utility of future consumption, $u'(c)_{+1}$, will be not be known in advance leads to the following relation between the short-term rate of interest, the rate of inflation and the variables that were introduced before:

$$u'(c) = {}_tE\left(\frac{1}{1 + r} u'(c)_{+1} (1 + i_s) \frac{p_t}{p_{t+1}} \right) \tag{3.3}$$

In words: the marginal utility u'(c) of selling a short-term financial asset with a sure nominal rate of return i_s must be equal to the expected usefulness of keeping the asset until the next period, discounted with the rate of time preference r. Holding on to this short-term nominal asset gets rewarded by the nominal interest i_s, but real spending power changes if the general price level moves up or down.

Following Shiller (1982), I move u'(c) within the brackets after the expectations operator. This is permissible, since u'(c) is known when the goods and financial markets reach their equilibrium values for the current period.

Using the notation that was previously introduced (see eq. 3.2), we get:

$$_tE \, (1 + epR)^{-1} \, (1 + epr_s) = 1 \qquad\qquad (3.4)$$

In eq. (3.4), epR stands for the ex-post intertemporal marginal rate of substitution between consumption now and consumption later and epr_s represents the ex-post real rate of return on a one-period financial asset with a sure nominal return i_s.

Now we have a relation for the *expected* value of the product of the ex-post rates of return epR and epr_s; what we need for economic analysis is an explanation for the currently expected real rate of return r_s that is required by the financial markets. Assume that the following relation holds between the ex-post real rate and the currently expected real rate of return on a short-term asset:

$$epr_s = r_s + u_{s,+1}$$

Symbols
epr_s ex-post real rate of return
r_s expected real rate of return
$u_{s,+1}$ expectational error

The differential between the ex-ante real rate r_s and the ex-post realized rate of return epr_s cannot be systematically correlated with any information that is available in the financial markets when they reach equilibrium during period t. Also, there can be no systematic correlation over time among the residuals $u_{s,+1}$. Violations of these two assertions would mean that the expected rate of return r_s is not an optimal predictor of the actual ex-post rate of return epr_s.

In the case of a one-period financial asset, the holders do not have to worry about capital losses: the only reason why epr_s will differ from its expectation r_s is because of a failure to forecast the exact change in the price level between the current and next periods. Thus, the unpredictable error $u_{s,+1}$ represents the forecast error with respect to the rate of change of the price level.

The most convenient assumption about the difference between $(1+epR)^{-1}$ and its ex-ante predictor $(1+R)^{-1}$ is:

$$\frac{1}{1 + epR} = \frac{1}{1 + R} - u_{R,+1}$$

Again, the residual term $u_{R,+1}$ has to be serially uncorrelated and not predictable during period t.

Substitution in eq. (3.4) gives:

$$\frac{1 + epr_s}{1 + epR} = [(1 + r_s) + u_{s,+1}]\left[\frac{1}{1 + R} - u_{R,+1}\right]$$

The expected value of the left-hand side equals one, so that the expected value of the right-hand side has to be 1 also.

Since the expected values of $u_{s,+1}$ and $u_{R,+1}$ are zero, we can expand the brackets to get:

$$_tE\left(\frac{1 + r_s}{1 + R}\right) - {}_tE\left(u_{s,+1} \cdot u_{R,+1}\right) = 1$$

Both r_s and R are ex-ante rates of return that can be observed when the markets have reached equilibrium during period t. Thus, we may neglect the first expectations operator and multiply the whole expression by $1 + R$:

$$(1 + r_s) = (1 + R)(1 + {}_tE(u_{s,+1} \cdot u_{R,+1})) = 1 \tag{3.5}$$

This is conveniently rewritten as:

$$(1 + r_s) = (1 + R)(1 + \text{cov}(r_s, R)). \tag{3.6}$$

Here, $1 + R$ stands for

$$_tE(1 + r)\frac{u'(c)}{u'(c)_{+1}}$$

and $\text{cov}(r_s, R)$ is defined as the expected covariance between the surprises with respect to the short-term real rate and to the intertemporal marginal rate of substitution between current consumption and consumption during period $t+1$. Please note that Shiller and other authors work with the covariance between surprises in r_s and surprises in $1/(1 + R)$. In that case the covariance term in eq. (3.6) has a minus sign attached to it. As long as $1 + R$ is close to 1, the two alternative assumptions about the prediction errors with respect to R do not matter much and we may neglect Jensen's inequality; in empirical work $1 + R$ or its inverse are likely to be measured with considerable measurement errors anyway, so that it will not be easy to determine the stochastic properties of the forecast errors made with respect to this variable.

3.4 A minimal model

In order to see the implications of our formula for the real short-term rate of interest, we require assumptions about some sources of uncertainty in the economy. A very simple context would be:

$$\ln y = \ln y^e + y^{ue} \qquad \text{output of goods} \qquad (3.7)$$

$$\hat{p} = \hat{p}_{-1} + p^{ue} \qquad \text{rate of inflation} \qquad (3.8)$$

$$1 + r_s = (1 + R)(1 + \text{cov}(r_s, R)) \qquad (3.6)$$
$$\text{required real rate of return}$$
$$\text{on one-period nominal assets}$$

$$1 + r_s = (1 + i_s)\, p/p^e_{+1} \qquad \text{implicit definition of } r_s \qquad (3.9)$$

$$1 + epr_s = (1 + i_s)p/p_{+1} \qquad (3.10)$$
$$\text{implicit definition of } epr_s$$

Symbols

y	index for real output
p	index for the price level
y^{ue}	surprise increase in the natural log of output
p^{ue}	surprise increase in the logarithmic rate of growth of the price level
r_s	expected real return on a one-period asset
R	risk-free real rate of return, as measured by the expected marginal rate of substitution between consumption nów and consumption later
i_s	nominal rate of return on a one-period asset
p^e_{+1}	expected value of next period's price level
epr_s	ex-post real return on the one-period asset

In this minimal model the real sector of the economy behaves according to the laws of motion eqs. (3.7) and (3.8). The expected rate of output of goods, y^e, is exogenous to the model, and the actual rate of output, y, fluctuates around this given trend value. In each period an expectational error, y^{ue}, is made. The rate of inflation, $\hat{p}$, behaves as a pure random walk: all future changes in the rate of inflation are unpredictable. People find that the actual rate of inflation changes from period to period by the increment p^{ue}. I assume that both y^{ue} and p^{ue} are serially uncorrelated and mutually independent white noise processes.

The unpredictability of both future output and future inflation define a context of uncertainty in which we can analyse the properties of eq. (3.6). Equations (3.9) and (3.10) are definitional and describe the connection between the nominal rate of interest and the two different measures of the real rate, the *expected* rate of return and the *actually* realized rate of return. The market reaches equilibrium during period t, the current period, at a nominal interest rate i_s, which implies an expected real rate of return r_s (eq. 3.9). This real rate must satisfy the requirements of eq. (3.6). When the actual rate of price change between the current and next period becomes known during period $t+1$, the ex-post real rate of return epr_s may be computed, as indicated by eq. (3.10).

The only financial asset is a one-period nominal instrument; there is no separate role for non-interest bearing money in the model. Uncertainty affects the actual ex-post real rate of return, epr_s. In this minimal model the forecast error with respect to epr_s equals $-p^{ue}_{+1}$. The amount of uncertainty in the system determines also the size of the covariance term on the right-hand side of eq. (3.6). Thus, for the system of equations (3.6)–(3.10) to become operational, we require assumptions about the movement of $(1+R)$ over time, so that we may compute the right-hand side of eq. (3.6).

The required assumptions to close the model are set out in equations (3.11)–(3.15).

$$1 + R = (1 + r) \frac{u'(c)}{{}_t Eu'(c)_{+1}} \tag{3.11}$$

$$epr_s - r_s = -p^{ue} \tag{3.12}$$

$$\ln(W/W^e) = -p^{ue} \tag{3.13}$$

$${}_t Eu'(c)_{+1} = u'(c) \tag{3.14}$$

$$u'(c) = {}_{t-1}Eu'(c) - c_1 y^{ue} - c_2 \ln(W/W^e) \tag{3.15}$$

Symbols

r   pure rate of time preference.
u' (c)   marginal utility of consumption.
W   real wealth.
W^e expected real wealth.
c_1, c_2 positive coefficients.

Eq. (3.11) is the ex-ante version of eq. (3.2): the price at which consumers are prepared to shift some consumption from the current to the next period depends on the pure rate of time preference, r, and on the ratio between the marginal utility of consumption now and the expected marginal utility of consumption during the next period. The expectations operator E has been moved into the denominator in eq. (13.11), although its proper place is in front of the fraction; see section 3.6 for comments about this simplification.

Equation (3.12) shows how the actually achieved real rate of return differs from the expected real rate of return on the nominal asset, r_s. The nominal rate of return is certain since fixed, so the only source of uncertainty is the exact value of next period's price level. Forecasting errors with respect to next period's price level depress the rate of return if they are positive, and increase the realized return above its expectation if they are negative.

Equation (3.13) postulates that real wealth, W, is affected to the same extent by forecasting errors with respect to the price level. Unexpectedly higher prices depress the real purchasing power of the outstanding stock of nominal assets. Equations (3.14) and (3.15) describe the law of motion for the marginal utility of consumption. Here I assume that consumers fix the current volume of consumption at such a level that they can expect to maintain that level during all future periods. As in Hall's (1978) model, the marginal utility of consumption behaves like a random walk over time. Equation (3.15), finally, describes the adjustments in the current volume of consumption that are made when the current surprises y^{ue} and p^{ue} have become known. Favourable news regarding current production y, and current wealth, W, make for somewhat larger consumption and thus for somewhat lower utility of the last unit consumed. Since the surprise in output, y^{ue}, is temporary and has no permanent implications, it may be expected that the coefficient c_1 is smaller than it would be if surprises with respect to output had permanent implications for the future growth of output.

Equations (3.14) and 3.15) are not deduced from an intertemporal optimization problem, but represent more or less plausible assumptions about the relationships between income, wealth and consumption. As argued in section 3.1, a theoretical model that allows for these equations to be derived from a higher-level theory often has to economize so much on the modelling of uncertainty that the price for proving instead of postulating the optimal path for consumption over time becomes very high; I have taken a short-cut with respect to the determination of consumption plans in order to retain the freedom to experiment with different assumption about economic uncertainty in the theoretical structures.

The model is silent about the question how wealth accumulates in the course of time, since only the current expectational error regarding wealth is incorporated into the consumption equation (3.15). In this stationary economy where the expected rate of output is exogenous, I assume that there is no trend in real wealth over time. In the richer model that will be discussed below there will be a changing non-zero growth rate for real output that gets translated into expected changes in the marginal utility of consumption over time. In this minimal model, however, the marginal utility of consumption is a random walk with zero drift.

The covariance term, $\text{cov}(r_s, R)$, equals the expected product of the errors that will be made in predicting this period's epr_s and epR. The outcome depends on what will happen during the next period. The ex-post real return on the nominal asset is vulnerable to price level surprises, p^{ue}_{+1}, the ex-post value of epR will differ from the ex-ante value R, due to both y^{ue}_{+1} and p^{ue}_{+1}. Since I have assumed zero covariance between y^{ue} and p^{ue}, the $\text{cov}(r_s, R)$ depends only on the variance of p^{ue} and is positive. With higher-than-expected prices in the next period, real wealth will be lower, so that the marginal utility of consumption goes up. This decreases $1 + epR$ below $1 + R$, just at a time when the ex-post real return on the nominal asset is lower than was expected:

$$p^{ue}_{+1} > 0 \quad \begin{cases} \mapsto W_{+1} < {}_t EW_{+1} \to u'(c)_{+1} > {}_t Eu'(c)_{+1} \\ \qquad\qquad\qquad\qquad\qquad \to 1 + epR < 1 + R \\ \to epr_s < r_s \end{cases}$$

With a positive value for the covariance between epr_s and epR, the expected real rate of return on the nominal asset has to be higher than the risk-free price for shifting consumption over time, R. The size of the inflationary risk premium in the real rate of interest increases directly with the variance of the forecast errors p^{ue}. The higher the uncertainty about inflation, the higher the risk premium in the real rate of interest.

Within the present model there never is a foreseeable increase or decrease in the marginal utility of consumption:

$$\frac{u'(c)}{{}_t Eu'(c)_{+1}}$$

Thus, the value of $1 + R$ does not change unless the price of time, r, changes. A different situation would arise if we had assumed that some of the decline in current consumption due to lower output or higher-than-expected-prices is temporary only. In that case equation (3.14) would have been more complicated, and the value of $\dfrac{u'(c)}{{}_t Eu'(c)_{+1}}$ could differ from unity.

Assume, for example, that instead of equation (3.14):

$${}_t Eu'(c)_{+1} = u'(c)$$

we had postulated the following relation between the current marginal utility of consumption and the expected marginal utility of consumption in the next period:

$$_tEu'(c)_{+1} = {}_tEu'(c) - \alpha c_1 y^{ue} - \alpha c_2 \ln(W/W^e) \text{ with } 0 < \alpha < 1 (3.14a)$$

Replacing the original equation (3.14) by this more subtle equation means that surprises with respect to income and inflation now have the following effects: current consumption is different from previously expected consumption as indicated by equation (3.15). At the same time, all future consumption plans are adjusted in the same direction, but not to the same extent as before. Technically, the marginal utility of consumption is no longer a random walk, but has become an ARIMA (0,1,1) process. People can now foresee that consumption in the following period will be a little different from current consumption, but they are unable to foresee any changes in consumption beyond the following period.

Let us investigate what happens now to the interest rate if a negative surprise with respect to output occurs during the current period. Equation (3.15) says that people have to cut current consumption somewhat, so that the marginal utility of the last unit consumed increases. They also have to make a slight downward revision in their future consumption plans. As a consequence, the quotient

$$\frac{u'(c)}{_tEu'(c)_{+1}}$$

increases during the current period only, but is expected to return to its normal value of unity afterwards. The result is a purely temporary rise in the expected real rate of interest, r_s.

The analysis of this minimal model shows the two lines of investigation that have to be pursued for describing the behaviour of interest rates over time. In the first place we have to compute the value of the covariance between the ex-post forecast errors in r_s and R. This covariance depends on the types of shocks that may hit the economy during the next period and their effects on epr_s and epR. The higher the covariance, the higher the risk premium in the expected real rate of interest r_s. In the second place we must trace the effects of current shocks on the current rate of interest that equilibrates the markets. For that, we need to work through the consequences of current shocks for the marginal utility of consumption now, $u'(c)$, and for the expected marginal utility of consumption in the immediate future period, $_tEu'(c)_{+1}$. These two aspects of the determination of interest rates will recur in the more complicated models of the next two sections.

3.5 Inflationary uncertainty and the demand for money

The model of the previous section was composed out of two arbitrary laws of motion for real output, y, and the price level, p, together with an exact determination of the real rate of interest on a one-period nominal asset. In this section I want to analyse another miniature model in which the only financial asset is money. I replace the original equation (3.7) for the output of goods by equation (3.16) in which the forecast error with respect to current output now consists of two component parts: the term βp^{ue} indicates that positive price level surprises have a positive influence on output and vice versa whereas the error term ε describes all other influences that make y different from its expected value, y^e.

$$y = y^e + \beta p^{ue} + \varepsilon \tag{3.16}$$

$$1 + r_m = (1 + R)(1 + \text{cov}(r_m, R)) \tag{3.17}$$

$$1 + r_m = p/p^e_{+1} [1 + m_0 + m_1 \ln(yp/M)] \tag{3.18}$$

In this model there is no equation that corresponds to the inflation equation (3.8); the price level is going to be extracted from the demand for money equation, eq. (3.18). Equation (3.18) should be seen in conjunction with the earlier equation (3.9). Equation (3.9),

$$1 + r_s = (1 + i_s)p/p^e_{+1}$$

made clear what the real return on a one-period nominal asset consists of: a fixed nominal return minus the expected rate of inflation during the holding period. Likewise, eq. (3.18) indicates that the real return on money is composed of two parts. One part of the expected real return on money depends on the projected change in the price level between the current and next periods: p/p^e_{+1}. The other part of the real return on money relates to the services rendered by money balances in facilitating economic transactions. I have postulated that the marginal usefulness of a unit of real balances, M/p, is a linear function of the logarithm of yp/M, where the income velocity of money yp/M indicates the relative scarcity of the total stock of real balances M/p with respect to real output, y. The role of y is thus to serve as an index of the number of economic transactions per period. This specification is analogous to, for example, that of Sweeney (1982).
Equations (3.17) – (3.18) correspond to equations (3.6) and (3.9) in the minimal model of the previous section, since equation (3.17) determines the required real rate of return on money as a function of $(1 + R)$ and the covariance between the forecast errors with respect to r_m and R.

As in the case of the earlier model, some additional equations are required to complete the structure. With two changes, we can use again equations (3.11)–(3.15).

$$1 + R = (1 + r) \frac{u'(c)}{{}_tEu'(c)_{+1}}$$ (3.11)

$$epr_m - r_m = -p^{ue}$$ (3.12a)

$$\ln(W/W^e) = -p^{ue} + M^{ue}$$ (3.13a)

$${}_tEu'(c)_{+1} = u'(c)$$ (3.14)

$$u'(c) = {}_{t-1}Eu'(c) - c_1 y^{ue} - c_2 \ln(W/W^e)$$ (3.15)

There is one obvious change in notation: r_s has been replaced by r_m. A non-trivial change had to be made in equation (3.13) which now shows that the unanticipated change in wealth equals the unanticipated change in real balances. If, for example, the nominal money stock increases unexpectedly by five per cent whereas the price level only goes up by three per cent within the same period, then there is an unanticipated increase in real wealth of two per cent. If the price level catches up with the new level of the money stock during the following period, there will be a foreseeable negative adjustment in real wealth during that period, so that the change in the money stock has no permanent effects on real wealth. The coefficient c_2 in eq. (3.15) will reflect the likely absence of long-run money illusion: it should be very small if transitory changes in real balances are the main source of changes in wealth.

It may be recalled that this specification of the auxiliary equations makes $u'(c)$ a random walk, so that the quotient

$$\frac{u'(c)}{{}_tEu'(c)_{+1}}$$

equals 1 at all times. Therefore, if the pure rate of time preference, r, is constant over time, $(1 + R)$ will be constant also. Equation (3.17) shows why this in turn makes the expected real return on money, r_m, constant as long as the value of $cov(r_m, R)$ does not change, which is to say as long as the model continues to hold with no change in the estimated variance of the unpredictable shocks.

Within this model there are two sources of uncertainty: unexplained shocks to real output, ε, and uncertainty regarding the future path of the nominal money supply M. I shall consider two different assumptions about the stochastic behaviour of the money supply over time: a pure random walk for lnM, so that all future changes in the money stock are unpredictable, and a pure random walk for the logarithmic rate of growth of the money supply, $\hat{M}$, so that a monetary surprise has to be equated to a permanent change in the expected future growth rate of the money supply.

In the first instance, then, the economic environment is uncertain because there are serially uncorrelated random shocks ε to output and because there occur random additions or subtractions to the logarithm of the nominal money supply:

$$\ln M = \ln M_{-1} + M^{ue}$$

Consider what this uncertainty implies for the covariance between the forecast errors in epr_m and epR. A positive shock M^{ue}_{+1} will have no effect on the expected real return on money between periods $t+1$ and $t+2$, because the expected marginal utility of consumption in period $t+2$ equals the actual marginal utility of consumption in period $t+1$, according to equation (3.14). Thus, the monetary surprise has to be reflected by changes in other variables on the right-hand side of equation (3.18): an unanticipated increase in next period's money supply, M^{ue}_{+1}, has to be absorbed by a corresponding increase in $\ln(py)_{+1}$. The short-run supply equation

$$\ln y = \ln y^e + \beta p^{ue} + \varepsilon \tag{3.16}$$

then determines the distribution of this unanticipated surge in nominal aggregate demand over equidirectional changes in real output and prices.

Simple algebra shows that the changes in y and p are given by

$$p^{ue}_{+1} = \frac{1}{1+\beta} M^{ue}_{+1}; \quad y^{ue}_{+1} = \frac{\beta}{1+\beta} M^{ue}_{+1}$$

In this way $\ln(yp/M)_{+1}$ remains constant, so that equilibrium in the money market can be maintained. We can now use these results to determine the impact of an unanticipated monetary surprise in the following period on that period's unanticipated change in the marginal utility of consumption. A positive monetary surprise has an effect on real output which will lower the marginal utility of next period's consumption somewhat. Equation (3.13a) shows that there is a positive effect on wealth, which again may diminish the marginal utility of consumption. The denominator of the right-hand side of equation (3.11) will be lower than expected so that $1 + epR$

will be higher than its expectation $1 + R$. At the same time, the unanticipated monetary shock M_{+1}^{ue} will lower the ex-post real rate of return on
money below its expected value r_s, as the price level in period $t + 1$ will
now be higher than anticipated. We see that the covariance term $cov(r_m, R)$
is negative since epR is higher than expected when r_m is lower than anticipated, and vice versa. Eq. (3.17) says that the expected real return on money
balances is lower than the expected risk-free rate of return R. It is worthwhile to deduce this result also for the case of a negative monetary surprise
at the beginning of period $t + 1$. Such a negative shock to aggregate demand
will lower next period's real output and next period's wealth and thus increase the utility of liquid balances during that period. By a happy coinci-
dence, the real value of these balances goes up – because of a lower value
of the price level – at the same time as the need for liquidity increases.
Therefore the required real return on money balances will be lower than in
the absence of monetary uncertainty.

If, on the other hand, surprises with respect to the money supply were
relatively unimportant compared to shifts in productivity, ε, then the covariance would be positive. A positive value for ε_{+1} raises y_{+1} and depresses
p_{+1}, because equilibrium in the money market requires a negative movement in the price level if there is a positive change in output. Thus, a positive
value for ε_{+1} unambiguously lowers the marginal utility of next period's
consumption. Eq. (3.11) shows that $1 + epR$ will be a little higher than
$1 + R$. At the same time, eq. (3.12a) tells us that the ex-post real return on
money has increased, due to the lower-than-expected value for the price
level. The covariance term in equation (3.17) would be positive under these
circumstances. Greater uncertainty about changes in productivity, as modelled by ε_{+1}, would therefore tend to increase the required real return on
money balances in this model, whereas greater uncertainty with respect to
future aggregate demand, as modelled by M_{+1}^{ue}, lowers the required real
return on money.

Assume, then, that the degree of monetary uncertainty, measured by the
variance of M^{ue}, increases significantly, so that the covariance term in equation (3.17) goes down and with it the required real return on money balances. It follows that the right-hand side of equation (3.18)

$$1 + r_m = p/p_{+1}^e[1 + m_0 + m_1 \ln(yp/M)] \tag{3.18}$$

will have to decrease in order to maintain equilibrium in the money market.
An increase in the expected rate of price change would lower the first term
on the right-hand side of eq. (3.18). But, to accommodate a permanent
increase in monetary uncertainty, the rate of inflation would have to go up
permanently, which would have strange and unacceptable consequences for
yp/M, the income velocity of money. Elsewhere, I have tried to argue (1982)

that such an implied path for future inflation and velocity would be at variance with the microeconomic underpinning of the demand for money function. Within the present context, m_0 or m_1 should be affected if the economy started moving along such a path of ever-changing prices with no corresponding increases in M. The thought experiment is 'inadmissible' without a deeper study of the microeconomic foundation of the demand for money (see also Bomhoff, 1980).

If not an increase in the rate of inflation, what else? The specification of eq. (3.18) offers one mechanism for accommodating a decline in the required real return of money: an unanticipated downward shift of the price level, p. The short-run supply curve (3.16) postulates that such an unexpected decline in the price level will come together with a corresponding decline in aggregate output. In the present model an increase in monetary uncertainty lowers the price level permanently, but this has only temporary effects on real output.

Much more burdensome does the price of increased monetary uncertainty become in a context where the necessary decline in the price level has more lasting effects on real output. This would be the case, for example, if m_0 and m_1 in our eq. (3.18) were not constant, so that people were forced to partly rely on the actual rate of price change for their estimates of the expected future rate of inflation. In such a context, an unanticipated decline in the current price level lowers the expected future rate of change of the price level, which has a positive effect on the right-hand side of the demand for money equation (3.18). The current values of p and y will have to decline more to accommodate this increase in the demand for money. The deflationary episode has to proceed even further if the declines in y and p increase the uncertainty surrounding the future marginal utility of consumption. If that happens, the $\text{cov}(r_m, R)$ decreases, so that current y and p have to decline further yet.

The consequences of increased monetary uncertainty will be larger also, if we remove one restrictive feature of the analysis. The assumption that the quotient $u'(c)/Eu'(c)_{+1}$ remains constant even if the degree of uncertainty in the economy increases implies a utility function that is linear in current consumption. For convex utility functions greater uncertainty about future consumption will by itself raise the expected marginal utility $Eu'(c)_{+1}$, keeping the point estimate $E(c)_{+1}$ constant. Thus, $(1+R)$ will decrease and with it $1 + r_m$, with the consequence that p and y have to decline so that real money balances become more plentiful per unit of income. I return to this issue in section 3.6.

The monetary model of eqs. (3.16)–(3.18) can also be used to analyse a country in which the logarithmic rate of growth of the money stock is a pure random walk. We replace the previous equation for the money supply

$$\ln M = \ln M_{-1} + M^{ue}$$

by the dynamic formula:

$$\hat{M}_t = \hat{M}_{t-1} + M^{ue}.$$

Now, the growth rate changes permanently with each perceived error in predicting the money stock. The analysis of the covariance term in the equation for the required real return on money goes through as before, with one exception. An unexpected increase in the money stock still raises current-period income, but the effect on current wealth becomes uncertain. Depending on the slope of the short-run supply curve, β, and on the coefficient m_1 in eq. (3.18) (the inverse of the semi-logarithmic interest elasticity of the demand for money), a one-percent increase in the money stock may increase the current price level by more or less than one per cent. Empirical evidence strongly suggests that even within an annual model the price level goes up by less than the money supply during the initial period. Admitting this to be the case, the price level may nevertheless 'overtake' the money supply during the following periods since the income velocity of money has to rise due to the higher expected rate of inflation. Thus, the unexpected initial increase in the real value of the outstanding money stock will be more than nullified by foreseeable subsequent decreases in the real value of the money supply. Under such circumstances, a temporary increase in real wealth due to an acceleration in the money supply that has not yet worked its way through into the price level, may well make people more pessimistic regarding their future financial wealth which would mean a slight downward adjustment in current consumption plans: the coefficient c_2 in formula (3.15) becomes negative.

Since each jump in the money stock signals a corresponding jump in the future rate of inflation, nominal income, $p \cdot y$, has to increase more than in the previous case where an increase in the money stock had no permanent implications for the rate of price change. It follows from eq. (3.18) that a one per cent increase in the money stock now leads to an increase in nominal income of

$$1 + \frac{1}{m_1} \text{ per cent}$$

The reciprocal of the coefficient m_1 is simply the semi-logarithmic interest elasticity of the demand for money function. The higher this elasticity, the more will nominal income increase following a surge in the money supply. Our model does not allow for any lagged effects of the monetary surprise on real output; therefore, this permanent increase in nominal income will be reflected in a higher path for the price level in all periods after the initial surprise. During the initial period only, part of the increase in nominal income is attributable to higher real income, as the demand curve (3.18) shifts along the short-run supply curve (3.16).

Two conclusions follow from the analysis in this section. The first result is that the required real return on money decreases if there is more monetary uncertainty in the economy. Such a lower required real return on money is achieved in the model by a permanently lower path for the price level. This result is not easily achieved in more common demand-for-money functions that use measured market interest rates as indicators of the opportunity cost of holding money balances. Increased monetary uncertainty will push up such interest rates, as we have seen in the model of the previous section, so that a conventional demand-for-money function would register a *decline* in the demand for real balances. By contrast, the present model shows how viewing the real rate of return on an asset as the price required for postponing the sale of such an asset leads to the opposite conclusion of an *increase* in the demand for money under greater monetary uncertainty.

However, the rise in the demand for money will be modest in the present model because of the way in which uncertainty is introduced into the formal system. The assumption that all markets reach equilibrium during the first day of each quarter is convenient for the (empirical) treatment of expectations, but implies that uncertainty only reigns between periods and not within periods. It follows that there is no room in the theoretical model for variation in the 'quality' of the services rendered by real money balances. In the model money becomes more attractive only because it is a hedge against unforeseen events at the beginning of the following quarter; in reality money can also become more necessary to hold if uncertainty about relative prices, for example, means that we can survive the current period more easily if our real money balances are larger. In other words, changes in the precuationary demand for money might affect the coefficients m_0 or m_1 in the demand for money function, eq. (3.18).

Mascaro and Meltzer (1983) discuss also increases in the demand for money due to greater uncertainty about future periods. They link their analysis of the 1970's and early 1980's to Milton Friedman's investigations of long-term trends in the demand for money in the United States and the United Kingdom, which led Friedman to conclude that the demand for money increases if the economic environment is perceived to become more uncertain. According to these authors long periods of stable growth and low or very moderate inflation lead to a secular decline in the precautionary demand for money, that may be reversed if the economic climate becomes more unpredictable.

Milton Friedman and Anna J. Schwartz write:

> 'Another variable that is likely to be important empirically (for the
> demand for money) is the degree of economic stability expected to
> prevail in the future. Wealth holders are likely to attach considerably
> more value to liquidity when they expect economic conditions to be
> unstable than when they expect them to be highly stable. This variable
> is likely to be difficult to express quantitatively even though the direc-
> tion of change may be clear from qualitative information. For example,
> the outbreak of war clearly produces expectations of instability, which
> is one reason war is often accompanied by a notable increase in real
> balances – that is a notable decline in velocity.'
>
>   Milton Friedman and Anna Schwartz, 'Monetary
>   Trends in the United Kingdom, Their Relation to
>   Income, Prices, and Interest Rates, 1867–1975', The
>   University of Chicago Press, 1982, p. 39.

The covariance term $cov(r_m,R)$ captures some of this effect, but probably
not enough.

The second insight that follows from the money-and-goods model of this
section is that the specification of the demand for money function is sensitive
to the pattern over time of the money supply. The reason is two-fold: first,
the effect of an unanticipated monetary shock on the marginal utility of
consumption depends on whether people view such a monetary surprise to
have lasting or temporary consequences for real income and real wealth.
Changes in income and wealth affect the marginal utility of consumption
and thus the ex-post risk-free rate of return epR. If monetary shocks are
deemed to have important inflationary implications and thus non-trivial
effects on current consumption, then epR will tend to differ significantly
from the ex-ante value R, and this in turn affects the covariance term in the
equation for the short-term rate of interest. As we have seen above, a permanent change in the covariance term in equation (3.17) causes a permanent
shift in the demand for money, eq. (3.18). Thus, if the inflationary implications of a given 'jump' in the money supply become more or less serious
over time, then the parameters of the demand-for-money function will also
change.

The second reason why different perceptions about the supply of money
have an effect on the proper specification of the demand for money is potentially more important, although it has been kept out of the present model
for the sake of expositional convenience. If we allow for the possibility that
$u'(c)$ is not a pure random walk – this was discussed near the end of section
3.4 – then unanticipated changes in the money supply have an effect on the
current rate of interest i_s. Again, the magnitude of this effect depends on the
way in which the monetary news is interpreted: does a positive monetary

surprise have major consequences for inflation or is it just a temporary 'hiccup'? The answer to this question determines to what extent previous consumption (and investment) plans are adjusted, and this in turn determines the current change in the rate of interest.

To sum up: if the 'rule' for the supply of money goes into a higher or lower 'gear', then the consumption equation changes and with it the specification of the demand for money.

3.6 Risk and return in a macroeconomic model

The two models of the previous sections each contained one financial asset: a one-period nominal asset in the model of section 3.4 and money in the model of section 3.5. In both cases, the following five building blocks were combined to get a macroeconomic framework in which to study the effects of macroeconomic uncertainty on rates of return:

1. *Stochastic laws of motion for output* (and for the price level in the minimal model of section 3.4 where the demand for money function was omitted).

2. *Deterministic equations for the required real return on financial assets.* Each return depends on $(1 + R)$, the risk-free measure of the price to be paid for postponing consumption, with adjustments that depend on the covariance between the forecast errors in this risk-free rate and in the real return on a financial asset.

3. *Definitions that show what makes up the real return on a financial asset.* For the one-period nominal asset, the real return consists of a sure nominal return plus an estimated loss in purchasing power; for money the real return consists of transactions services plus loss in purchasing power. For longer-term assets, the expected real return may include the expected capital appreciation during the holding period.

4. *Identities for the ex-post forecast errors with respect to the real rates of return on financial assets.* For one-period nominal assets and for money the forecast error is caused solely by wrong guesses about next period's price level; for longer term financial assets there will be unexpected capital gains or losses during the holding period, because the assets are held until just after the unforeseeable surprises that occur at the beginning of the following period.

5. *Auxiliary equations that are needed to get expressions for the marginal rate of substitution between consumption nów and consumption later.* As a minimum, we need to know how the current shocks affect current con-

Exhibit 3.1   The five building blocks

Expected rates of return on different types of assets incorporate compensation for risk which depends on the relation between the uncertain element in the return and the uncertain element in the economic outlook.

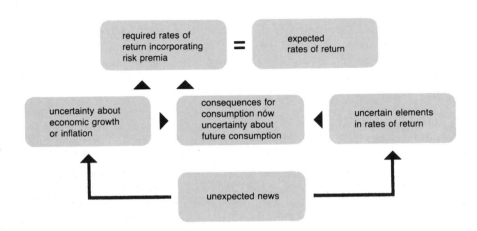

sumption and how the excess returns that will become known at the beginning of the following period will affect period's wealth and next period's consumption.

Exhibit 3.1 shows the main connections between the five blocks. Since our focus here is on systematic analysis of the risk premia in interest rates, I have taken care to include the necessary linkages between blocks 2-5 that jointly determine the appropriate risk premia. Block 1 does provide one of the necessary inputs for risk evaluation, namely the dynamics of economic growth, but there are no feed-back channels as yet in exhibit 3.1 that show reverse influences from changes in real rates of interest and changes in consumption on expected future economic growth. In the empirical work of the following chapters I shall incorporate a feed-back from the financial sector to the trend rate of economic growth, but in this theoretical exposition it is simpler to make such connections on an ad-hoc basis.

A serious analysis of monetary uncertainty requires a model in which people hold both money and longer-term financial assets. The model of this section will be larger, therefore, than the miniature models of sections 3.4 and 3.5. Nonetheless, the five building blocks described above will be used again: they are displayed on the following five pages.

Equations (3.19)-(3.21) deal with the determination of real output. I assume that the trend rate of growth between the current and next period, gr_{+1}, is known during the current period. Equation (3.20) indicates how this underlying growth rate changes as a pure random walk over time. Equation (3.21) has been encountered before; it allows for two sources of discrepancies between expected and actual output: unanticipated shifts in productivity, ε, and output effects of unpredicted changes in the price level. It will be convenient for the dynamics of the model to assume – as in the model of section 3.5 – that these forces have a permanent effect on the level of real output. The opposite assumption of purely temporary changes in the level of real output complicates the dynamics of the price level and thus of the expected rate of inflation.

Equations (3.22)-(3.25) define the required real rates of return. Two new assets are introduced: long-term nominal bonds, on which the required real rate of return equals r_b and claims to equity capital that carry an expected real return of r_q. The definition of $1 + R$ has been discussed in section 3.2 above.

Equations (3.26)-(3.29) explain what exactly the four assets have to offer. Money loses its purchasing power over time due to inflation, but offers transactions services that are captured by the remaining three terms on the right-hand side of eq. (3.26). New is the assumption that the value of these transactions services may depend on the current state of the business cycle,

$$\ln y^e_{+1} = \ln y + gr_{+1} \tag{3.19}$$

$$gr_{+1} = gr + acc \tag{3.20}$$

$$\ln y = \ln y^e + \beta p^{ue} + \varepsilon \tag{3.21}$$

Symbols

y index of real output; y^e expected value of this index
gr logarithmic rate of growth of output
acc change in the growth rate of output
p^{ue} unanticipated change in the price level
ε serially uncorrelated shift in productivity

$$1 + r_m = (1 + R) [1 + \text{cov}(r_m, R)] \qquad (3.22)$$

$$1 + r_s = (1 + R) [1 + \text{cov}(r_s, R)] \qquad (3.23)$$

$$1 + r_b = (1 + R) [1 + \text{cov}(r_b, R)] \qquad (3.24)$$

$$1 + r_q = (1 + R) [1 + \text{cov}(r_q, R)] \qquad (3.25)$$

with $1 + R = (1 + r) \, _tE \dfrac{u'(c)}{u'(c)_{t+1}}$

Symbols

r_m	required real return on money
r_s	required real return on a one-period nominal asset
r_b	required real return (expected capital gain included) on a long-term nominal bond
r_q	required real rate of return (expected capital gain included) on an equity share
r	price of time, rate of time preference
$u'(c)$	marginal utility of current consumption
$_tEu'(c)_{t+1}$	expected marginal utility of consumption during the following period
$\text{cov}(r_m,R)$	covariance between the forecast errors with respect to r_m and R

Other covariance terms are similarly defined.

$$1 + r_m = [m_0 + m_1 \ln(py/M) + m_2 \ln(y/y^e)] \, p/p^e_{+1} \qquad (3.26)$$

$$1 + r_s = (1 + i_s) \, p/p^e_{+1} \qquad (3.27)$$

$$1 + r_b = \left(1 + \frac{I}{B} + \frac{\Delta B^e_{+1}}{B} \right) \frac{p}{p^e_{+1}} \qquad (3.28)$$

$$1 + r_q = \left[q_0 + q_1 \ln(py/Q) + q_2 \ln(y/y^{e)} + \left(1 + \frac{\Delta Q^e_{+1}}{Q} \right) \right] \frac{p}{p^e_{+1}}$$

$$(3.29)$$

Symbols

p   index for the general price level

M   nominal money stock

p^e_{+1} currently expected value of the price index during the following period

I   fixed nominal payment on a long-term bond (a consol)

B   current nominal price of a government bond that promises to pay I units in each period

B^e_{+1} expected price of the bond just after next period's news has come in

Q   current price of an equity claim

Q^e_{+1} expected price of the share just after next period's news has come in

Δ first difference

$$\text{epr}_m - r_m = - p^{ue}_{+1} \tag{3.30}$$

$$\text{epr}_s - r_s = -p^{ue}_{+1} \tag{3.31}$$

$$\text{epr}_b - r_b = -p^{ue}_{+1} + B^{ue}_{+1} \tag{3.32}$$

$$\text{epr}_q - r_q = -p^{ue}_{+1} + Q^{ue}_{+1} \tag{3.33}$$

$$\Delta r_q + \Delta \hat{p}^e_{+1} = -\hat{B} \frac{I}{B} + \Delta \hat{B}^e_{+1} \tag{3.34}$$

$$\Delta r_q + \Delta \hat{p}^e_{+1} = q_1 (\hat{y} + \hat{p}) - q_1 \hat{Q} + q_2 y^{ue} + \Delta \hat{Q}^e_{+1} \tag{3.35}$$

Symbols

epr_m	ex-post real return on money, as measured just after next period's news has come in
epr_s	same for a one-period asset
epr_b	same for a long-term nominal bond
epr_q	same for a claim to equity capital
p^{ue}_{+1}	unanticipated surprise with respect to next period's index of the price level
B^{ue}_{+1}	unexpected capital appreciation on the long-term bond as a result of next period's news
Q^{ue}_{+1}	unexpected change in the share price as a result of next period's news
$\hat{}$	logarithmic growth rate
Δ	first difference

$$W^{ue}_{+1} = -p^{ue}_{+1} + w_b B^{ue}_{+1} + w_q Q^{ue}_{+1} + w_m M^{ue}_{+1} \qquad (3.36)$$

$$_tE\, u'(c)_{+1} = {}_{t-1}Eu'(c) - c_1 W^{ue} - c_2 y^{ue} \pm c_3 gr_{+1} \qquad (3.37)$$

$$u'(c) = {}_{t-1}Eu'(c) - c_4 W^{ue} - c_5 y^{ue} \qquad (3.38)$$

Symbols

W^{ue}_{+1} unanticipated change in next period's real wealth, due to the news at the beginning of that period

w_b weight of long-term government bonds in the total financial portfolio

w_q weight of claims to equity capital in the total financial portfolio

w_m weight of money in the total financial portfolio

as expressed by $\ln(y/y^e)$. The Dutch tradition in monetary economics has stressed the inclusion of such a term in the demand for money function (Den Butter and Fase, 1981).

The short-term nominal asset offers a sure nominal return i_s, but some of its purchasing power over goods will melt away if prices increase between the current and next period.

The equation for the expected real return r_b on a long-term nominal government bond is new. Comparison between equations (3.28) and (3.27) shows that

$$\frac{I}{B}$$

corresponds to i_s. The term

$$\frac{\Delta B^e_{+1}}{B}$$

indicates the expected rate of capital appreciation. There is no corresponding term in eq. (3.27) because the nominal asset of eq. (3.27) reaches maturity just after the shocks of period $t + 1$. For an analysis of longer-term bonds, however, this term plays a vital role, not because holders of bonds normally feel confident about future capital gains or losses, but precisely because capital gains are largely unforeseen. The difference between the actual capital gain ΔB_{+1} and its earlier expectation ΔB^e_{+1} is a source of uncertainty for which a risk premium will be required. This is where monetary uncertainty exacts its pound of economic fat and muscle, and the purpose of the following sections will be to study the size of the risk premium on long-term bonds under different assumptions about the combinations of monetary and real uncertainty in the economy.

Longer-term assets are risky also because of unforeseen changes in the purchasing power of money that will change their real value. But, for both bonds and equity shares, unforeseen changes in the asset's nominal price are generally much more important than unforeseen alterations in its real price or purchasing power. In equation (3.28)

$$\frac{\Delta B^e_{+1}}{B},$$

the rational forecast of

$$\frac{\Delta B_{+1}}{B}$$

refers to the nominal capital gain, whereas p/p^e_{+1} is the current forecast of the actual rate at which money will lose its purchasing power p/p_{+1}.

In equation (3.29) for the required return on equity shares, the expected capital gain is denoted as

$$\frac{\Delta Q^e_{+1}}{Q}.$$

Again, the average expectation in the market will be close to, if not equal to zero. For our analysis of risk factors, however, we need the difference between this unexciting average *expectation* and the often exciting actual *realization* of the capital gain.

The first three terms on the right-hand side of eq. (3.29) refer to the current period's earnings. I propose an expression that is as similar as possible to the corresponding first three terms of the right-hand side of eq. (3.26) for the required expected return on holding money balances. The hypothesis behind the expression

$$q_0 + q_1 \ln(py/Q) + q_2\ln(y/y^e)$$

in the equation for the required return on equity shares is that over longer periods of time the aggregate price-earnings ratio on equity shares can be approximated as a function of the quotient py/Q, the ratio between our index for nominal national income and the price index of one representative equity share. This would be a reasonable approximation if, for example, corporate earnings were a constant proportion of national income after averaging over the complete business cycle and if the dividend pay-out ratio were constant, too. Later we shall try to simulate the consequences of a price-earnings ratio that changes secularly through making the parameter q_1 a random walk over time. The term $q_2\ln(y/y^e)$ creates a channel for effects of the phase of the business cycle on corporate earnings. I have chosen the logarithmic form here – as in eq. (3.26) – in order to get convenient expressions for the effects of next period's uncertain shocks on the actual ex-post returns on currently held assets.

Now that the description of the composition of the expected returns on four different types of asset has been completed, the next set of equations, eqs. (3.30)-(3.33) follows directly. These equations explain why the ex-post rate of return will differ from the expected return. This is trivial in case of money and short-term nominal assets: only surprises with respect to next period's price level can drive the actual return away from the expected return. For long-term bonds and equity shares unexpected capital appreciation is another source of differences between expected and actual returns. B^{ue}_{+1} and Q^{ue}_{+1} represent the unexpected nominal capital gains or losses on bonds and equity shares.

The auxiliary equations (3.34) and (3.35) will help to determine the extent of such capital gains. The equations have been obtained through differencing equations (3.28) and (3.29). For simplicity, a small approximation has been made in the first term on the right-hand side of eq. (3.34).

The final set of equations, eqs. (3.36)-(3.38), connects the price-output bloc of the model to the equations that determine required rates of return. Equation (3.36) is definitional; it indicates how changes in the components of nominal wealth, together with unexpected changes in the aggregate price level, alter real wealth, W. The coefficients w_b, w_q and w_m indicate the respective proportions of long-term government bonds, shares and money in the total financial portfolio. I consolidate the complete private sector, so that no room remains for bonds issued by private entities. Government bonds are assumed to be part of the private sector's net wealth. These weights should ideally be updated over time, but this has been neglected in the analysis.

The remaining two equations, (3.37) and (3.38), relate the marginal utility of current consumption and the expected marginal utility of future consumption to earlier estimates and to current surprise changes in real wealth, real income, the rate of economic growth, and the degree of uncertainty in the economy. Figure 3.1 shows the dynamic properties that have been selected. The top panel of the figure shows how people expect a steady increase in the volume of consumption over time. But, unexpected bad news reduces consumption for time t (to keep the figure clear, continuous lines indicate the volume of consumption instead of the discrete rectangles that would be more in line with our empirical work where period averages are used). I have assumed that the bad news has either purely temporary consequences for consumption, so that consumption at time t + 1 goes back on the originally expected path, or that the shock at time t permanently lowers the optimal level of consumption for all subsequent periods. In both cases the expected growth rate of consumption after time t + 1 is not affected. But, if the news is not an unexpected *level* change in real wealth or real income, but a changed perception about the trend of future economic *growth*, gr_{+1}, the slope of the two lines in the top panel of figure 3.1 can change. Although such permanent alterations are possible, there are no slowly decaying autoregressive elements in the determination of the growth of consumption, so that the expected growth rate always remains a constant from the next period onwards. The lower part of figure 3.1 gives the corresponding picture for the marginal utility of consumption, drawn on the assumption that secular increases in the volume of consumption imply a secular decline in the marginal utility of consumption (compare Olson and Bailey, 1981). The dynamics are the same as in the top panel, with no possibility of predicting any changes beyond the next period.

The equations for the actual and expected marginal utility of consump-

Figure 3.1   Dynamics of the marginal utility of consumption
(see section 3.6 of the main text for explanatory remarks)

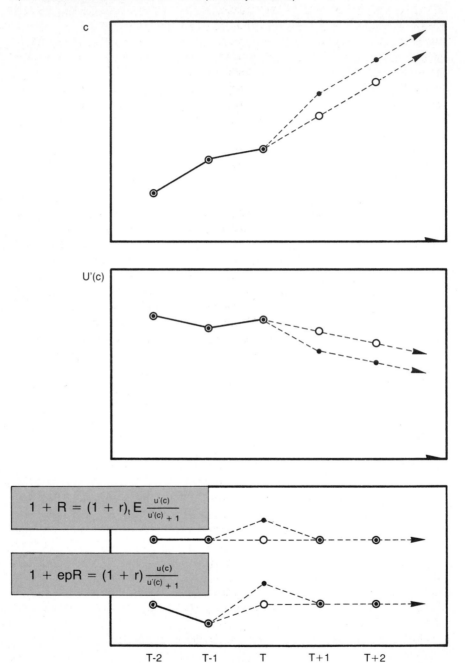

tion do not incorporate any influence for *expected* changes in wealth or income. I have not attempted to proceed beyond including the term $c_3 gr_{+1}$ in the equation for the updating of the expected marginal utility of consumption. Foreseeable changes in the rate at which wealth is accumulated therefore have to be subsumed under this term.

When combined with the simplifying assumption that the pure rate of time preference, r, is constant throughout the analysis, we get the attractive result that $1 + R$ will either be a pure random walk or at least remain constant after the next period. If $1 + R$ exhibited autoregressive elements in the form of slow adjustment after a major disturbance, or some kind of a predictable return to some 'normal' level, holders of long-term bonds or equity could look forward to long-lasting strings of future capital gains, something I wanted to avoid as it complicates consistent analysis of expectations.

In two respects equations (3.37) and (3.38) fall short of being rigorous. First, because I have considered separately what makes current consumption differ from its expected value and what determines the expected level in future periods, taking either the actual or the previously expected level of current consumption as point of departure. However, interest rates are connected to the expected value of the quotient $u'(c)/u'(c)_{+1}$, which is not the same as the quotient of $u'(c)$ and the expectation $Eu'(c)_{+1}$. It follows that the procedure up to now neglects Jensen's inequality at least once, and possibly twice. To see this, consider what happens to the intertemporal marginal rate of substitution if it becomes harder to predict future levels of consumption. First, with many common assumptions about the shape of utility functions, the expected marginal utility of future consumption will increase further above the marginal utility of expected future consumption:

$$E(u'(c)) > u'E(c)$$

The logarithmic utility function is an obvious example: the expected marginal utility of future consumption will increase, as in the case of other utility functions that have a convex first derivative. Secondly, we have to take into account that the inverse function is also a convex function, so that the expectation of $u'(c)$ divided by $u'(c)_{+1}$ is larger than $u'(c)$ divided by the expected value of $u'(c)_{+1}$. The two effects work in opposite directions: uncertainty about the future increases the expected marginal utility of future consumption, which by itself would tend to lower $1 + R$, but taking the expected value of one over this marginal utility instead of the inverse of the expectation works in the opposite direction. In the case of a logarithmic utility function, both effects cancel each other.

If the type of liquidity effect studied by Mishkin (1976, 1978a, 1978b) were important, greater uncertainty about future consumption would surely lead to a lower value for $1 + R$ and to higher (absolute) values for the covariance terms that together with $1 + R$ make up the required real rates of return on financial assets. In the analysis that follows I shall concentrate on the effects of greater uncertainty on the covariance terms, and continue to neglect Jensen's inequality.

My failure to derive a choice between consumption and investment from first principles constitutes the second reason why equations (3.37) and (3.38) for the dynamics of the marginal utility of consumption represent an easy short-cut. I have simply assumed that unexpected positive short-term changes in income and wealth increase current consumption and lower its marginal utility, whereas changes in the perceived long-term growth rate of output may either increase or decrease the long-term risk-free real rate of interest. Until now there appears to be a trade-off in the literature between either greater rigour in the derivation of the marginal utility of consumption from first principles on the one hand and variety of assumptions regarding the dynamics of money and prices on the other. I have preferred the latter at the expense of the former.

The exposition of the final model of this chapter is now complete. The following sections contain a number of thought experiments with this model, so that we can investigate whether the assumptions underlying it are sufficient to derive the required signs of the coefficients in the reduced form equations of our empirical analysis.

3.7 Monetary uncertainty and the yield gap between bonds and shares

In this and the following section the model of section 3.6 will be used for a number of experiments, first with respect to monetary uncertainty. We are now in a position to differentiate between the following questions:

– What will happen if an unexpected monetary surprise occurs at the beginning of the following period?
– What will happen if agents raise their estimate of the uncertainty surrounding long-run projections of future money growth?

I begin by looking at these questions under the simplifying assumption that the marginal utility of consumption is a pure random walk with trend. This is achieved by equating c_1 to c_4, c_2 to c_5 in eqs. (3.37) and (3.38) and by assuming that gr is constant. Inspection of equations (3.37) and (3.38) shows that this will make the quotient $u'(c)/Eu'(c)_{+1}$ and thus $1 + R$ approximately a random walk, so that agents cannot foresee any changes in expected real rates of return.

Assume for simplicity that the only source of uncertainty in the economy is the behaviour of the nominal supply of money, which has to be predicted on the basis of its own past. We may now distinguish a number of different cases.

(1) *A pure random walk for the logarithm of the money supply*

In this simple situation, the expected rate of inflation $\hat{p}^e_{+1}$ is constant at all times, which means that all nominal rates of interest are constant too. Unexpected monetary shocks change only the ex-post real rates of return on financial assets. The output bloc of the model, combined with the equation that describes the demand for money services, leads to the following expressions for the unexpected changes in prices and output that are caused by a monetary surprise:

$$p^{ue} = [m_1/(m_1 (1 + \beta) + m_2\beta)] \, M^{uc}$$

$$y^{ue} = [m_1\beta/(m_1 (1 + \beta) + m_2\beta)] \, M^{ue}$$

With such shocks occurring regularly, the covariance terms in equations (3.22)-(3.25) will be different from zero. To assess these terms we need to evaluate the following two expressions:

$$epR - R = (1 + r) \frac{u'(c)}{u'(c)_{+1}} - E (1 + r) \frac{u'(c)}{u'(c)_{+1}}$$

$$u'(c)_{+1} = Eu'(c)_{+1} - c_4 W^{ue}_{+1} - c_5 y^{ue}_{+1}$$

A positive monetary impulse, M^{ue}_{+1}, increases next period's real income, y^{ue}_{+1}, Since there are no consequences for inflation, only for the price level, real balances are bound to increase, so the liquid fraction of real wealth increases in value. Holders of short-term debt lose some purchasing power, and eq. (3.34) shows that holders of long-term debt suffer an equal loss, since the nominal market value of one bond, B, is unchanged (all other terms in this equation remain as before, so that the yield of this fixed-coupon bond has to remain constant also). Inspection of eq. (3.35) shows that Q^{ue}_{+1} must be positive as can be seen by moving this equation one period forward in time. A positive monetary surprise at the beginning of period t + 1 does not change the required return on equity shares, but it does increase the price level as well as real output permanently. Thus, the expected level of Q at the beginning of period t + 2 must be equal to its level before the monetary surprise at the beginning of period t + 1 plus an adjustment for the permanent increase in nominal national income (move eq. (3.29) two periods forward). The required real return over period t + 1 can be achieved if Q increases by such an amount that the additional dividend income is exactly nullified by the expected capital loss when Q_{t+1} decreases at the beginning of period $t + 2$ to its expected future level $E_{t+1} Q^e_{t+2}$.

The combined effect of these changes in the components of real wealth is uncertain; let us assume that real wealth either goes up or that its decrease is less important for the marginal utility of consumption during $t + 1$ than the effect of additional real income on consumption. With $u'(c)_{+1} <$ $Eu'(c)_{+1}$ it follows that $epR - R$ is positive. The covariance term $cov(r_m,R)$ is negative but close to zero; the same holds for $cov(r_s,R)$ and $cov(r_b,R)$ whereas $cov(r_q,R)$ must be positive under these assumptions. The required real rate of return on equity shares will thus be slightly higher than the required real return on long-term bonds. Since the monetary surprises have important implications for the stylized business cycle in the model but do not carry inflationary risks for bonds – it is only the price level that changes, not the expected rate of inflation – equity shares are riskier, and moreover they show a positive covariance with R.

Note that the sign of $cov(r_s,R)$ is different from section 3.4, because in the minimal model of that section there was no link between unexpected changes in prices and unexpected changes in output. A monetary surprise caused a loss in real wealth, but did not lead to increases in real output. Since wealth consisted solely of short-term nominal assets, there resulted a positive covariance between the ex-post changes in r_s and R in the earlier construction.

(2) *The rate of money growth is a pure random walk*
With the growth rate of the money supply changing permanently after each monetary surprise, the potential losses of wealth for holders of long-term bonds will be much larger. All required real rates of return remain constant as in the first case above, but the expected rate of inflation will change so that the right-hand sides of equations (3.34) and (3.35) will have to change as well. In equation (3.34) there will never be foreseeable changes in the nominal bond price B, but the actual price will change with each revision of the expected inflation rate. By contrast, in equation (3.35) the term $\Delta\hat{Q}^e_{+1}$ will adjust with each change in expected inflation (see eq. (3.29)). Since the left-hand sides of equations (3.34) and (3.35) change by the same amount if expected inflation goes up or down, whereas the term $\hat{B}$ is multiplied by the coefficient I/B that is smaller than one, the riskiness of bond holdings has increased relative to the risk attached to holding equity shares. The statement that frequent changes in expected inflation make bonds riskier relative to shares has to be qualified if shares in equity are not the perfect hedge against inflation in the long run I have assumed them to be.

Comparing this case to the simpler situation in which there were only changes in the *level* of the money stock, we see that the postulated increase in epR after a positive monetary surprise must be smaller now, and may even turn negative. This conclusion holds also for situations that are intermediate between cases (1) and (2) in which the growth rate of the money supply behaves according to the ARIMA (0, 1, 1) model: the oft-discussed case in which the adaptive expectations model is appropriate for the growth rate. The mixture of permanent shocks to the level and permanent shocks to the growth rate implies that positive monetary surprises lead to real losses on bonds and real gains on equity shares, with the net effect becoming more negative as the inflationary implications of a given positive monetary surprise become more ominous.

(3) *Changes in inflationary expectations*
At the extreme end of the spectrum that runs from case (1) through case (2), i.e. from purely temporary increases in the money stock that have no inflationary consequences to changes in the money stock that imply a permanently higher inflation rate in the future, we get the limiting case of an increase in inflationary expectations that is not based upon a factual increase in the money stock. Whilst the generally bad consequences of higher expected future inflation remain, the positive short-term effects on real output of an unexpected increase in the supply of money have evaporated. Assume, then, that inflationary expectations go up at the beginning of the following period, and that the interest elasticity of the demand for money is small, so that only a minor increase in the price level is required to restore equilibrium in the money market. In that case, the loss on real bonds will dwarf the small gains on equity shares and this negative net change in the real value of the long-term assets will be much more important than the small real losses on money and short-term nominal assets. Real wealth decreases and real income is assumed to rise by so small an amount due to the decrease in the demand for money that the combined effect on the marginal utility of next period's consumption is positive. With hindsight people are sorry that they did not consume a little less during the previous period and saved somewhat more for the less favourable times that have been ushered in by this increase in the future rate of inflation. Under these conditions the covariance $cov(r_b,R)$ is strongly positive: agents lose on their bond holdings exactly when they would appreciate financial wealth even more than expected. The other three covariance terms will be close to zero, with $cov(r_m,R)$ and $cov(r_s,R)$ slightly positive and $cov(r_q,R)$ negative. The required real return on bonds is higher now than the required real return on shares (compare Gordon and Halpern, 1976). Bonds are riskier than shares if the only source of uncertainty is the unpredictable outlook with respect to inflation and if an upturn in inflationary expectations is not associated with a significant temporary increase in real activity.

The analysis in this section has proceeded so far on the assumption that

1 + R, the ex-ante expected real risk-free rate of return was horizontal at all times. Ex-ante rates of return on financial assets could change over time, but only because of changes in the required risk premia. Ex-post real rates of return were not constant, of course, and each piece of news about the money supply or monetary uncertainty led to temporary discrepancies between the ex-ante and ex-post real rates. Figure 3.1 shows that different assumptions about the dynamics of consumption over time imply temporary changes in the expected rate of return which, if significant, require us to modify the earlier analysis. For simplicity I limit the discussion to the two extreme scenario's in figure 3.1 and assume now that the marginal utility of consumption shows a purely temporary deviation from its earlier trend after a monetary surprise (the intermediate case where the marginal utility of consumption moves as a noisy random walk with trend over time combines elements of both polar cases). Reconsider now the first example of this section: a permanent (downward) change in the level of the money stock with no inflationary consequences. Before, such an occurrence had no effect on 1 + R, but altered epR because of the associated output and wealth effects. By contrast, I now assume that a negative monetary impulse lowers consumption in the current period only, so that 1 + R increases for one period (see figure 3.1).

The model of section 3.6 does not permit a full analysis of the implications for prices, output and rates of return, since the only feedback channels from the financial to the real sector are through the demand for money function; missing are the implications of higher interest rates for investment and economic growth. A rise in 1 + R does increase the price level and the rate of output in the model so as to maintain equilibrium in the money market. More important are the effects of a higher value of 1 + R for bond and share prices. The price of the nominal long-term bond, B, has to fall so that the expected appreciation at the start of the following period plus the interest payment during the current period together produce the required higher rate of return. The value of an equity share has to fall by approximately the same relative amount. The question is whether the temporary losses in wealth caused by the adjustments in B and Q outweigh the perspective of a long-term real gain on the holdings of money and debt because of the lower future price level. The outcome would seem to depend on the interest elasticity of economic growth (zero in this model), and the extent to which firms and individuals are distressed by temporarily higher interest rates. Analysis of these issues requires a model in which the private sector is not consolidated, so that changes in the real burden of privately issued debt can affect consumption and investment (see, for example, Mishkin, 1976, 1978a, b).

(4) *Greater monetary uncertainty*

Still assuming that unexpected changes in the money supply are the only source of uncertainty in the economy, what will be the consequences if this type of uncertainty regarding the future becomes more prominent? Within the framework of our analysis the following changes will occur:

– The required risk-free real rate decreases if unexpected adverse news could be so bad that $u'(c)_{+1}$, the advantage of being a little more liquid in the next period, could turn out to be much larger than anticipated. Less informally: the absolute difference between $_tE \dfrac{u'(c)}{u'(c)_{t+1}}$ and $_tE \dfrac{u'(c)}{u'(_tE(c)_{t+1})}$ increases, so that $1 + R$ decreases holding $_tE(c)_{+1}$ fixed.

– Risk premia on assets with returns denominated in paper money will increase. Since we assume that equity shares are an inflation hedge over the long-run, this means that the inverse yield spread between shares and bonds will increase.

If share prices are thought to suffer under an increase in expected inflation, then the risk premium in the real rate on long-term bonds will have to increase more, since the potential losses in real wealth will become larger for a given degree of monetary uncertainty. In the statistical analysis of chapter 5 we shall find a significant effect of increases in an index for monetary uncertainty on long-term real rates in the U.S. The regression coefficient would increase over time if agents generally learnt that equity shares were *not* a good hedge against inflationary uncertainty.

Within the confines of the model the covariance between unexpected changes in R and unexpected changes in the real return on bonds is much larger in absolute magnitude than the other three covariance terms. All four types of assets, however, are sensitive to changes in $1 + R$, the required risk-free real rate of interest. As discussed in section 3.5, a decrease in $1 + R$ will cause an unanticipated one-time decline in the aggregate price level and in real output, as the demand for money increases. If an increase in monetary uncertainty is triggered by an unexpectedly sharp decline in money growth that makes agents wonder whether the central bank will persevere in such a stern anti-inflationary policy, or whether a downward shift in the money multiplier has had a one-time effect on the money stock, then two different sets of forces depress prices and output. First, there are the standard consequences of an unexpected negative monetary impulse: prices and output have to decline below their previously expected paths in order to equilibrate the demand for money, and if the expected rate of inflation declines there will be further effects in the same direction as the demand for money goes up. In the second place, greater uncertainty about future consumption levels may increase the expected marginal utility of fu-

Exhibit 3.2   Monetary overkill
A sharp decline in money growth may have a greater impact on economic growth than an
equally-sized surge in money

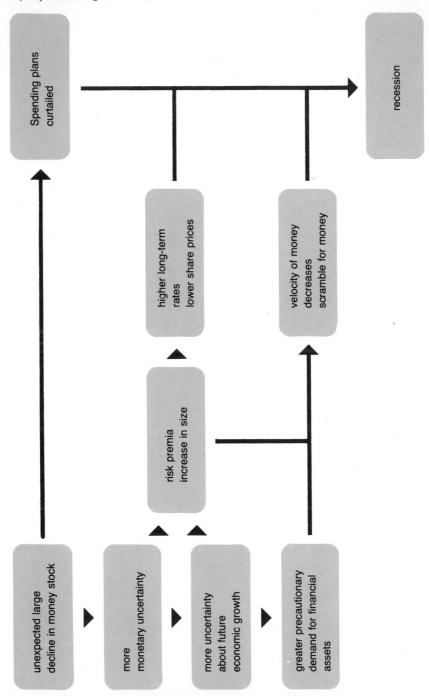

ture consumption so that the required return on holding money balances declines. Once again, the price level and the real rate of output have to adjust in a downward direction.

The two effects work in opposite directions if monetary uncertainty increases due to a positive monetary shock. In such a situation prices and output may rise a little faster due to the unexpected surge in aggregated demand, whereas the lowering of the required return on money balances has a negative effect on prices and output. The contrast may be relevant for evaluating the experiences of the early 1980's in the U.S. where monetary uncertainty – at least as measured by our index or that of Mascaro and Meltzer – did increase sometimes because of unexpectedly sharp declines in the rate of money growth. The doubly deflationary consequences for real output were bound to be more substantial than would have be expected on the basis of earlier evidence pertaining to periods when monetary surprises were on average positive (inflation was on a secularly rising trend) so that positive output effects and negative consequences of increased monetary uncertainty worked in opposite directions.

One of the major economic puzzles of the early 1980's has been the sharp fall in the income velocity of money that occurred in the United States and many other nations (see, for example, figure 4.1 below). Chapter 5 will contain some statistical evidence that increased monetary uncertainty played a role, but a more definitive assessment will have to wait until the pattern of recovery after the 1981-82 recession has become more clear. Increased monetary uncertainty can at least provide a consistent explanation why the anti-inflationary policies proved more costly in terms of output losses than was generally anticipated and why both nominal and expected real interest rates remained at surprisingly high levels for such a long time.

3.8 Monetary and real uncertainty

In addition to investigating monetary uncertainty we can use the theoretical model of section 3.6 for analysis of real uncertainty and its effects on the risk premia that make the expected real rates of return on financial assets differ from the risk-free rate $1 + R$. As before, two different types of questions need to be answered: what are the effects of unexpected changes in productivity, perceived long-term economic growth etc. on expected and realized rates of return and secondly, how are risk premia affected if these types of shocks become more or less important over time? Exhibit 3.3 shows the consequences of three kinds of real shocks on prices, output and inflation as well as on the ex-post realized returns together with similar information regarding three types of monetary news discussed already in section 3.7. Indicated also are the likely effects on total financial wealth and the differences between the ex-post values $1 + epR$ and the expectations $1 + R$.

Exhibit 3.3 Uncertainty and real rates of interest
Monetary uncertainty will raise real long-term rates; the effects of greater uncertainty about future economic growth are uncertain

	unexpected temporary increase in productivity	more optimism about economic growth	unexpected increase in business profitability	unexpected monetary impulse	surge in expected inflation	increase in monetary uncertainty
	(1)	(2)	(3)	(4)	(5)	(6)
1. Unexpected impact on the price level	−	−	o	+	+	−
2. Unexpected impact on real output	+	−	o	+	+	−
3. Unexpected effect on the trend of inflation	o	−	o	o	+	o
4. Effect on bond prices (corrected for inflation)	+	+ +	o	−	− − −	− −
5. Effect on prices of equity shares (corrected for inflation)	+	+ + +	+ +	+	+	−
6. Unexpected impact on real wealth	+	+ +	+	?	−	−
7. Unexpected impact on 1+R	+	+	+	+	−	−

In cases (2) and (5) the effect on 1+R is especially uncertain since the income and wealth effects on the marginal utility of consumption work in opposite directions.

After the extensive treatment of the different instances of monetary uncertainty in section 3.7 a few words will be sufficient with respect to the three examples of real uncertainty. Unanticipated shifts in productivity raise real output and decrease the price level for a given level of the money supply. Ex-post real returns on bonds and equity shares are somewhat higher than anticipated, real wealth increases and epR surpasses its expectation R. Due to the positive covariances $cov(r_b,R)$ and $cov(r_q,R)$, the risk premia on long-term bonds and on equity shares are both positive. These assets yield a little more when the owners need it less. This conclusion would be reversed if upward shifts in productivity were associated with important surges in investment that caused people to shift resources from consumption into business investment. In that case the marginal utility of consumption would increase, and the risk premia on bonds and shares would become negative. Without additional information about the causes of the productivity shift and a model of the consumption-investment decision it is impossible to say which of the two cases applies.

A similar ambiguity holds if the long-term rate of economic growth changes. On the assumption that the expected rate of inflation will decrease by more than the permanent increase in $1 + R$, nominal interest rates will fall and bond prices will increase. Share prices will go up also to an extent determined predominantly by the coefficient q_1 in eq. (3.29). Real wealth will increase, and I have assumed in exhibit 3.3 that the marginal utility of current consumption will decrease, so that epR exceeds its expectation.

Simpler is the case in which an unanticipated change in the coefficient q_1 in equation (3.29) occurs. Exhibit 3.3 shows how prices, output and inflation remain unchanged if q_1 increases – for example because of a tax change – with the only important effect a sudden rise in share prices. If unanticipated changes in real wealth and real income do lower the marginal utility of consumption – as hypothesized in eq. (3.38) – then epR will again go up.

To conclude this discussion I summarize a number of conclusions that follow from the theoretical model of section 3.6:

- Increased monetary uncertainty raises the required return on long-term bonds.
- Large government deficits imply a higher proportion of government debt in the future portfolio, so that the required risk premia on each unit of debt will have to increase.
- Faster growth of nominal national income implies a lower proportion of debt in the total portfolio ceteris paribus, so that the required risk premia on long-term government debt will decrease.
- Unexpected increases in the trend rate of economic growth may affect real long-term rates of interest in both ways: $1 + R$ goes up if agents

want to profit from exceptional business opportunities, but $1 + R$ decreases if people find saving less attractive since they will grow richer at a faster rate over time.

- Increased uncertainty about future real growth may therefore also affect real long-term rates in either direction: the change in the covariance term cannot be determined a priori.

Comparing the effects of different types of uncertainty leads to one additional observation. Of the six different future events displayed in exhibit 3.3, some have similar consequences for long-term bonds and equity shares, whereas in other instances bonds go up when share prices fall or vice versa. In the latter case aggregate risk on the portfolio is less than if bonds and shares move in the same direction

I submit that over the past few years the types of events that cause equidirectional changes in long-term bonds and shares have become more important relative to news that has opposite effects on bonds and shares. Monetary uncertainty has increased, as we shall see in chapter 5, and there are good reasons for assuming that uncertainty regarding long-term economic growth has increased. The two energy crises of 1973 and 1979-1980 have obliterated the comfortable notion that annual economic growth rates fluctuated around a well-defined long-term trend. Moreover, several countries in our sample plan to reduce their collective sectors which steers these economies into even more uncharted waters. With such uncertainty regarding inflation and long-term growth, the relative importance of predicting the phase of the short-term business cycle, represented in exhibit 3.3 by uncertainty about future shocks to the level of the money stock, has diminished (see Barro, 1977, the papers in Brunner and Meltzer, 1978, and Bomhoff, 1980 for evidence regarding the important role of monetary shocks in triggering the business cycle).

In earlier times, when economic uncertainty meant in the first place uncertainty about size and direction of the next unanticipated monetary surprise and thus uncertainty about the phase of the business cycle, bond and share prices were uncertain, but there was at least some negative covariation between the returns on bonds and shares. If the major uncertainties today relate to long-term economic growth and inflationary uncertainty, bond and share prices will have a greater tendency to move together. This raises the aggregate risks on the portfolio, which must result in higher risk premia on both the long-term real rate of interest and the required return on equity shares.

The argument gains additional force if the 1970's have taught investors that equity shares are not a hedge against the trend in inflation, but lose in real terms as inflation increases either because of non-neutralities in the tax system, or because high and variable inflation weakens the economy. I have assumed in the theoretical model as well as in exhibit 3.3 that shares are an inflation hedge: if this is in doubt, bonds and shares will move together even more and the required risk premia will go up further. If there is some validity to this line of argument, then the costs of inflation and the inflationary uncertainty that arrives in its wake are higher in the real world than in theoretical analyses (or econometric computer models) that neglect the importance of uncertainty.

chapter

Inflationary expectations

with Clemens J.M. Kool

"For it is not the fact of a given rise of prices, but the expectation of a rise compounded of the various possible price-movements and the estimated probability of each, which affects money rates."

J.M. Keynes, "A tract on monetary reform",
London, MacMillan, 1923, p. 22.

4.1 Money and the price level

With the actual rate of inflation depending so much on previously formed inflationary expectations, the question about the precise connections between money and the price level has to be separated into:

(1) Does money growth effect inflationary expectations?
(2) Do short-run movements in money explain the discrepancies between expected and actual rates of inflation?

Many researchers have concluded that channel (1) is more important than channel (2) (see, for example, the papers in Brunner and Meltzer, 1978, Bomhoff, 1980). Barro (1978) finds that a one per cent increase in the money supply (M1) in the U.S. has no impact at all on the price level during the initial quarter, which suggests that the prime channel through which money affects inflation is by exerting pressure on inflationary expectations. An unobservable variable, therefore, transmits the major part of the monetary message regarding future inflation, which complicates statistical analysis considerably.

In chapter 2 I tested for the incremental value of monetary data in predicting the short-run changes in economic growth by putting together summary statistics regarding previous growth and the current change in real balances together in a single regression equation. Given three explanatory variables that together summarize all the necessary information contained in the past numbers on economic growth, we found that the growth of (corrected) real money balances had incremental predictive power in forecasting the business cycle. Whoever guesses wrongly that money growth will remain stable over the next year whereas in fact money becomes more plentiful has therefore underestimated economic growth over the near term.

The counterpart to our earlier research strategy for determining the monetary effects on economic growth would be to regress the current rate of inflation on one or more previous inflation rates and perhaps on other variables plus a current measure of changes in monetary conditions. This has been more or less the approach of many so-called 'causality tests' (see Sims, 1972, for the original article, and Zellner, 1979, and Schwert, 1979, for methodological discussions).

In the context of money and prices the technique would require two restrictive assumptions: (a) no change in the nature of any relationships during the sample period; and (b) a fixed formula for computing the monetary impulse on the basis of past data on the money supply. The first restrictive assumption is counter-intuitive: current rates of price change are a much better signal of future rates of inflation at some periods than at others, depending for instance on the importance of temporary shifts in the price level because of failed harvests, higher commodity prices or sharp exchange rate movements. If there is a marginal contribution that quantity-theoretic insights can make to predicting future inflation, that contribution is likely to vary over time. The second assumption of a fixed formula for computing the monetary input in the inflation forecast says that there can be no changes over time in the relative importance of permanent and transitory changes in the growth rate of the money supply. We shall consider this issue in depth in later sections of this chapter and conclude on the basis of our statistical investigations that the assumption is falsified by the evidence.

In order to have more adaptability and more economic theory in our procedures, we decided to investigate the potential of monetary data for contributing to inflation forecasts in a spirit similar to that of the causality tests – if money is important it should have incremental predictive power – but chose a rather different statistical implementation. Two different indices of expected inflation will be developed, one that is based solely on earlier price data, and another measure of expected inflation that uses the rate of money growth within the framework of the quantity theory of money. We then compute a composite indicator of expected inflation that combines the extrapolative forecast and the quantity-theoretic formula. Which of the two components is more important in the combined measure will depend on the relative success of the two components in predicting the actual rate of inflation in the recent past. If, therefore, the weight of the extrapolative ('univariate') measure of expected inflation is almost one and the weight of the quantity-theoretic index virtually zero, we can conclude that watching the money supply is not of great importance for short-term forecasts of inflation. Some weighted average of recent inflation rates will do the job. If on the other hand we find that the extrapolative forecasts of inflation can be improved by adding a monetarist element, we have some statistical evidence that money matters also for short-term forecasts of inflation.

In the next chapter we shall use our constructed data of the expected rates of inflation for two different purposes. First, we shall investigate whether changes in our index of expected inflation have a noticeable impact on long-term interest rates. It is certain that high inflation tends to be associated with high long-term interest rates, other things equal, but it is much easier to provide supporting evidence for this statement by considering a cross-section of different countries at a given point in time, or by considering secular trends in inflation and interest rates in one country that experiences both low and high inflation over time, than to register the immediate impact of higher inflationary expectations on long-term interest rates. The statistical tests in chapter 5 will look for such short-term effects employing the measures for expected inflation to be developed in this chapter.

The second reason why we require indices of expected inflation is for computing an index of inflationary uncertainty. Many researchers have estimated the degree of inflationary uncertainty by computing the standard deviation of the actual inflation rate with respect to its average over some historical period, or by calculating the standard deviation of the *changes* in the observed rates of price change. Since both procedures work with actual data on the rate of price change, the resulting indices for inflationary uncertainty will be unable to distinguish properly between (a) the frequency and size of accelerations or decelerations in the price level that are of a more or less permanent nature and (b) the transient 'noise' introduced in the price indices because of temporary or permanent changes in the price *level* that have no long-term consequences for the maintained rate of inflation. Prices of agricultural products, raw materials or energy may change spectacularly and surely influence the aggregate price *level,* but whether such events have significant permanent effects on the rate of inflation is another matter and depends to a large extent on how unions and businessmen assess the reactions of the central bank to such one-time events (the degree of indexation in the labour market will be important here).

We have preferred to measure the degree of inflationary uncertainty by the extent to which our index for expected inflation changes from quarter to quarter; this expected rate of inflation will be constructed in such a way that purely temporary influences on the price level are eliminated as far as possible. What remains is a measure of more permanent trends in the price level, and we take the standard deviation of the first difference of this series to be a superior indicator of inflationary uncertainty, because it is computed after the temporary influences have been filtered out. At the end of this chapter and again in chapter 5 we shall compare movements in such an index for inflationary uncertainty to changes in an index of monetary uncertainty derived from the first difference of the underlying rate of money growth.

All these constructed indices purport to represent magnitudes that cannot be observed directly. There is no market-place where we can observe the expected rate of inflation and our constructed indices of inflationary uncertainty have to be taken on faith. Admittedly there are some collections of survey data on inflationary expectations, but the rationality and unbiasedness of these measures are still matter of dispute. A few words on the survey data will suffice here.

A voluminous literature has studied the 'Livingston Series' on inflationary expectations in the United States, named after Joseph A. Livingston of the 'Philadelphia Inquirer' who collected forecasts from professional economists of the rate of price change over the next six and twelve months (see Cukierman and Wachtel, 1979, Mullineaux, 1978, 1980, and Gramlich, 1983, for interesting evaluations, and Carlson, 1977, for the first major study of the data). Recently, the Statistical Office of the European Economic Community has begun to publish survey data on inflationary expectations in different E.E.C.-countries (see for example E.E.C., 1983). We have done some experimentation with these data for the four E.E.C.-countries in our sample – Germany, Holland, Belgium and Denmark – and have found the survey data inferior to the constructed index of inflationary expectations that will be developed here (see section 5.5 below).

In the next section we begin by setting out the construction of the extrapolative ('univariate') index, and show how it produces a rational forecast of the future rate of inflation based on earlier rates of price change. Section 4.3 deals with the quantity-theoretic ('multivariate') index of expected inflation that uses the equation of exchange to derive forecasts of future inflation on the basis of trends in money, velocity and output. We compare the two indices in section 4.4 and show that the extrapolative index is usually somewhat better at predicting the rate of inflation in the near future, but that the 'monetarist' forecast often has something to contribute. It follows that more monetary uncertainty means more inflationary uncertainty. Near the end of this chapter we display the constructed series for inflationary expectations together with the actual rates of price change. The technical aspects of the forecasting techniques have been relegated to Statistical Appendices 1 and 2 at the back of the book.

4.2 Extrapolating inflation with Kalman Filters

In this section we shall give the principal ideas of the so-called Multi-State Kalman Filter (MSKF) method for predicting economic time series and illustrate the technique with a practical application to one of the quarterly series on money growth that were discussed in chapter 2. Readers who are familiar with the methodology of forecasting discrete time series will want to skip the next few paragraphs and go directly to the explanation of the MSKF-method.

Systematic search for a proper way to compute forecasts of a time series on the basis of its own past have to start from recognizing that the unanticipated changes in the series which make forecasting such a hazardous experience can be of different types. Consider, for example, the two following highly stylized representations of segments from a quarterly time series:

A: 4.1 4.2 5.0 4.2 4.0 1.0 3.9 4.1 3.8 4.0 ....

B: 4.0 4.1 5.2 5.0 5.1 1.3 1.1 1.2 1.0 1.4 ....

Both series assume values between one and six, but there are important differences between their characteristics that make for radically diverse forcasting formulas. Let's assume that each period one further observation becomes available and that we wish to predict the next few observations (reading from left to right) in a rational manner. Long-time observers of series A will have noticed that the large changes occurring from time to time are of a temporary nature: each time the series reverts to a value close to 4.0. Thus, a fitting procedure to forecast series A would be to estimate the apparently constant long-term average on the basis of all the available observations and to forecast that the series will continue to fluctuate around this level. A sensible forecast for the next five observations after the ten shown above would be:

Forecasts of A: 4.0   4.0   4.0   4.0   4.0   ....

Series B is different. Most changes in the series are small, as with series A, but whenever a large change occurs, it is of a rather permanent nature. After the series has increased from approximately four to somewhat over five with the third observation shown, it remains in the vicinity of five for a few periods. Having dropped from 5.1 to 1.3 it stays very close to 1 for the remaining time. A rational forecaster would have to admit that there is no way to predict the next major change in the series, so that a reasonable forecast would take either the last observed value (1.4) or the average of the observations after the last major change (1.2) and take either of these numbers as forecast for all future periods:

Forecasts of B: 1.4   1.4   1.4   1.4   1.4   ....

or: 1.2   1.2   1.2   1.2   1.2   ....

Series A represents in its stylized way the behaviour of a stationary time series that has a long-term mean which we can compute by taking the average over as long a historical stretch as is available. Series B illustrates the behaviour of a non-stationary time series that behaves almost like a pure 'random walk' over time. There is little transient, temporary noise in this series, and all major changes in its level are permanent until further notice. To forecast this series quick learning is required and values of the series dating from before the last major adjustment in the level should be disregarded. In the extreme case of a pure random walk, the series has become a memory-less process, for which the last observed value is the only input needed for forecasting future observations.

Moving a little closer to the real world we consider next series that exhibit a mixture of permanent (B) and transitory (A) shocks. Consider series (A + B), simply the sum of series A and B above:

A:	4.1	4.2	5.0	4.2	4.0	1.0	3.9	4.1	3.8	4.0	....
B:	4.0	4.1	5.2	5.0	5.1	1.3	1.1	1.2	1.0	1.4	....
A + B:	8.1	8.3	10.2	9.2	9.1	2.3	5.0	5.3	4.8	5.4	....

The correct recipe for forecasting series A + B is:

> 'If a large change has just occurred, assume that it will be nullified for approximately 50 per cent in the next period; otherwise set all predicted future values equal to the last observed value'.

Equally appropriate would be the adaptive expectations model, in this instance with a decay parameter of approximately 0.5:

$$y_t^e = 0.5 \, y_{t-1} + 0.25 \, y_{t-2} + 0.125 \, y_{t-3} + \dots \tag{4.1}$$

By writing the forecast formula in this way, we can see without difficulty that the appropriate statistical model for series (A + B) is intermediate between the statistical models that would be suitable for series A and B separately:

$$y_t^e = 0.1 \, y_{t-1} + 0.1 \, y_{t-2} + 0.1 \, y_{t-3} + \dots + 0.1 \, y_{t-10} \tag{4.2}$$

$$y_t^e = 1.0 \, y_{t-1} + 0 \, y_{t-2} + 0 \, y_{t-3} + \dots + 0 \, y_{t-10} \tag{4.3}$$

For clarity both formulas have been cut off arbitrarily after ten lagged periods. The forecasting rule for series A has a decay parameter of 1, since all observations are equally useful for forecasting the long-term constant average of the series (approximately 4.0). Formula (4.3) provides forecasts for series B and uses a decay parameter of zero: an automatic forecasting rule cannot look back more than a single period, since otherwise the forecasts may incorporate from time to time observations that are no longer relevant for the determination of the current level of the series (informal, non-automatic forecasts would be based on all available observations after the last major movement, but this is impossible to incorporate in a linear forecasting formula).

Equation (4.1) for the sum of A + B has a decay parameter of 0.5, half-way between the extreme values of 1 (eq. 4.2) and 0 (eq. 4.3). The well-known book by Box and Jenkins (1970) shows how the optimal value of the decay parameter can be computed from the data for all time series that are similar to series (A + B), and also how more complicated statistical models with several parameters can be developed in a similar fashion. Box-Jenkins statistical models cover as special cases both the exponential smoothing models of the linear variety and the adaptive expectations model. All these statistical techniques have been designed to cope with time series that exhibit a mixture of temporary and permanent changes:

$$y_t = \bar{y}_t + \varepsilon_t \tag{4.4}$$

$$\bar{y}_t = \bar{y}_{t-1} + u_t \tag{4.5}$$

Here, y_t is the level of some economic variable, $\bar{y}_t$ the 'underlying' level that is buried to some extent under transient noise ε_t, whereas the shocks u_t indicate how the underlying or permanent level changes as a pure random walk over time. The optimal way of forecasting a series with this structure consists – as we have seen – of taking an (infinite) sum of previously observed values y_t, with weights that add to unity and decay exponentially over time. The size of the decay parameter depends on the relative importance of the transient shocks, ε_t, and the permanent shocks, u_t. If the permanent shocks are not very important, whereas the series contains a lot of transient noise, then it makes sense to utilize data from a comparatively distant past in order to optimally estimate the current level $\bar{y}_t$: the decay parameter has to be close to unity. If on the other hand the underlying level of the series changes very rapidly, then the 'rate of forgetfulness' should be high and our predictions will simply have to be based on the past few observations: heavy discounting by way of a decay parameter that is close to zero.

Using the formal representation of equations (4.4) and (4.5) we can describe series A by setting all permanent shocks u_t equal to zero and taking many small values together with a few large values for the temporary shocks ε_t. Conversely, series B will be replicated by equations (4.4) and (4.5) if we keep all temporary shocks ε_t quite small and make the permanent shocks u_t equal to zero at most times, but occasionally very large. Series (A + B) can obviously be represented also by equations (4.4) and (4.5) if we make the correct (somewhat richer) assumptions about the shock terms ε_t and u_t.

Consider next a different series that can also be described by equations (4.4) and (4.5) but is not optimally forecast by any formula of the type (4.1) − (4.3). Once again we add the original two basic series A and B, but with one important difference compared to the earlier construction of series (A + B). No longer do the major changes in series A coincide in time with the important shifts in series B. In both series the big news occurred in periods 3 and 6; we now leave series B unchanged, but construct a different realization for series A, to be called A':

A':	4.0	4.1	3.9	4.0	4.0	4.1	4.2	5.0	4.2	4.0	....
B:	4.0	4.1	5.2	5.0	5.1	1.3	1.1	1.2	1.0	1.4	....
A' + B:	8.0	8.2	9.1	9.0	9.1	5.4	5.3	6.2	5.2	5.4	....

Everything is as before, only the numbers in series A' appear five periods later than before in series A. Although the component parts are identical, the earlier recipe for predicting series A + B no longer applies to series A′ + B: instead of the 'overshooting' that went on before, we now have large changes that are either fully permanent (as in periods 3 and 6) or purely temporary (as in period 8). A sensible way to forecast series A′ + B would be the following:

> 'If nothing special has occurred over the past two periods use the best up-to-date estimate of the current level as the forecast. If a large change took place two periods ago, use the most recent observation to assess whether it was temporary or permanent and forecast accordingly. If there was a major change in the most recent period, prepare two forecasts, one on the basis that a permanent change occurred, and another on the assumption that the shock was temporary and take a weighted average of these two separate forecasts as the optimal prediction, with the weights depending on the relative importance of transitory and permanent shocks in the past'.

This is the way of the Multi-State Kalman Filter method: several different forecasting schemes are operating in parallel with the relative weight of each separate forecast for the composite prediction determined by (a) its general success over the past and (b) its relevance to the most recent two observations. Now we can cope with series that exhibit a mixture of transitory and permanent shocks under either of two different interpretations of 'mixture':

(1) each important change is partly temporary and partly permanent: overshooting occurs with each large shift;
(2) some shocks are temporary, others are permanent.

In case (1) each large disturbance is intermediate between being temporary and being permanent; statistical representations that are intermediate also between stationarity and random walk will be able to cope optimally with the mixed case. The adaptive expectations model, or more generally the appropriate Box-Jenkins model is applicable. The MSKF-method achieves an equivalent result once it has learnt that the two extreme forecasting formulas always need to be combined into a composite forecast.

In case (2) the MSKF-method will generate a combined forecast if there is not yet certainty about whether the most recent large change was temporary or permanent: it's better to make a small error each time than to be right in 50 per cent of all cases but to make twice as large an error in the remaining 50 per cent. Once the latest change has been classified, however, the combined forecast is replaced with the appropriate extreme forecast, since the computer has been able to deduce whether the latest large change was temporary or permanent. We refer the interested reader to Appendix

1 and to our earlier publications (Bomhoff, 1982, Kool, 1982, Bomhoff and Korteweg, 1983) for details.

The forecasting problem does become even more complicated if the time series to be forecast does not only exhibit a mixture of permanent (type B) and transitory (type A) shocks to its level, but if there is also a secular trend in the series that may change over time. In that case the data combine the characteristics of types A, B and C:

C: 4.0 6.1 8.0 10.2 12.3 13.3 14.2 15.1 16.3 17.4

Example C illustrates the case of a series where there are almost equally-sized increments during a number of periods, after which the 'slope' of the series changes. In this particular case the increments are approximately equal to 2.0 during the first five periods after which they decrease to approximately 1.0 per period. One of us (Kool) has extended the algorithms used in the previous publications to cope with time series exhibiting a mixture of all three different characteristics over time; we can distinguish between large and small changes that are purely temporary, between large and small changes that are permanent to the level of the series and between large and small changes that have permanent effects on its growth rate. In the case of an index for the aggregate price level, for example, these three categories of shocks would correspond to transient shocks to the level of the series, caused for example by sudden changes in agricultural markets, permanent shifts in the level of the price index, due for instance to a drop in the real effective exchange rate of the currency, and permanent increases or decreases in the trend of the series over time, corresponding to persistent changes in the rate of inflation.

Moreover, the learning mechanism that is built into the MSKF-method allows for changes in the relative importance of the three types of disturbance over time. The advantage of the MSKF-method over Box-Jenkins modelling is thus twofold: the method can deal with cases where purely temporary shocks alternate with purely permanent changes. whereas Box-Jenkins models and other time series techniques are designed for series where *each* disturbance is a mixture of temporary and permanent elements; secondly, instead of having to re-estimate the statistical representation after each fresh observation (or using one fixed model for each and every time) the Bayesian approach to updating the prior probabilities of the separate filters ensures that intelligent learning occurs if the characteristics of the time series evolve over time. In both respects, therefore, the Multi-State Kalman Filter method resembles better the actual formation of forecasts by business firms and individuals who, too, will try to improve their forecasting technique over time.

Table 4.1 Forecasting the Swiss money supply

	Actual (SF billions) (1)	Predicted (SF billions) (2)	log actual (3)	log predicted (4)	error (per cent) (5)	growth rate actual (6)	estimated (7)
1973I	51.5	51.9	3.942	3.949	−0.8	1.7	2.1
II	51.6	52.7	3.943	3.964	−2.1	0.1	2.0
III	51.7	52.6	3.946	3.963	−1.7	0.3	0.8
IV	53.2	52.2	3.975	3.956	1.9	2.8	2.2
1974I	53.4	54.4	3.977	3.996	−1.9	0.3	0.8
II	54.0	53.9	3.989	3.987	0.3	1.2	1.0
III	53.8	54.5	3.985	3.998	−1.3	−0.4	0.3
IV	53.1	54.0	3.972	3.989	−1.7	−1.3	−0.3
1975I	52.5	53.0	3.960	3.971	−1.1	−1.2	−1.0
II	51.8	52.0	3.947	3.951	−0.5	−1.4	−1.2
III	50.8	51.2	3.928	3.935	−0.8	−1.9	−1.5
IV	50.6	50.1	3.924	3.914	0.9	−0.4	−1.2
1976I	51.1	49.9	3.934	3.911	2.3	1.0	−0.7
II	51.5	50.7	3.942	3.925	1.8	0.9	0.9
III	52.7	52.0	3.965	3.951	1.4	2.3	1.7
IV	54.4	53.5	3.996	3.980	1.6	3.0	2.7
1977I	55.5	55.7	4.016	4.020	−0.4	2.1	2.5
II	57.6	56.9	4.053	4.042	1.1	3.7	2.8
III	59.2	59.0	4.082	4.078	0.4	2.9	2.9
IV	58.4	60.9	4.067	4.110	−4.2	−1.5	−0.9
1978I	59.8	57.9	4.092	4.058	3.4	2.5	2.2
II	63.6	61.2	4.153	4.114	3.9	6.1	4.3
III	64.0	66.1	4.159	4.191	−3.2	0.7	2.6
IV	67.5	66.1	4.212	4.191	2.1	5.3	3.7
1979I	70.0	69.8	4.248	4.245	0.3	3.6	3.8
II	69.9	72.6	4.247	4.285	−3.8	−0.1	2.9
III	70.5	72.9	4.255	4.289	−3.3	0.8	1.8
IV	70.6	72.4	4.257	4.282	−2.5	0.2	0.7
1980I	71.9	71.4	4.275	4.268	0.7	1.8	0.9
II	71.8	72.4	4.273	4.282	−0.8	−0.2	0.7
III	71.9	72.5	4.276	4.283	−0.8	0.3	0.5
IV	72.7	72.5	4.287	4.284	0.3	1.1	0.6

For a practical illustration of the Multi-State Kalman Filter method, we take a segment from one of the time series in chapter 2, namely the quarterly series on the (corrected) money supply in Switzerland. The first column of table 4.1 shows the development of the Swiss money supply (M1) between 1973 and 1980 and column (2) shows the forecasts as computed by the MSKF-method. Each forecast is printed on the horizontal line corresponding to the quarter to which it applies; the forecasts are computed on the basis of all the data up to and including the average level for the previous quarter. Column (3) gives the natural logarithms of the actual quarterly averages in column (1); this series of logarithms has been the input for the forecasting process. The resulting composite forecasts are shown in column (4); these numbers have been transformed into the equivalent monetary amounts in column (2). Subtracting columns (3) and (4) and multiplying the differences by a factor 100 gives the forecast errors as a percentage of the actual level (column 5). Finally, columns (6) and (7) relate to the rate of growth of the Swiss money supply, with column (6) giving the actual quarter-to-quarter rate of growth and column (7) the corresponding estimate of the 'underlying' rate of growth as computed by the algorithm.

The picture of this series in chapter 2 reveals how its characteristics change during the 1970's with near-stationarity between 1973 and 1975, moderate growth in 1976 and 1977, rapid growth in 1978 and a return to a modest, positive growth rate in 1979 and 1980. During the transitions between these four sub-periods large errors occur as the algorithm tries to cope with the unexpected changes in behaviour and adjusts the weights on the individual filters. To provide some insight into the workings of the algorithm, we shall look at the successive transitions from stagnation to growth and vice versa.

At the beginning of 1973 the Swiss money supply has grown at a rate of 2 per cent per quarter (over 8 per cent per annum) for the past two years. Since there is almost no change in the money stock between 1973I and 1973III the estimated 'underlying' or permanent rate of growth is reduced from 2 per cent per quarter to 0.8 per cent per quarter. At the end of 1974 the underlying growth rate turns negative and the forecasts go below the most recent recorded level, whereas in 1973 they used to be 1-2 per cent above the last observed level.

It is interesting to note that up to 1978 the underlying growth rate in column (7) changes less 'nervously' from period to period than the actual growth rates; one can say that the underlying growth rate offers a smoothed estimate of the longer-term rate of growth. A clear example is the period between the first acceleration in early 1976 and the second transition into a higher 'gear' in late 1977. The estimated underlying growth rate accelerates from -0.7% (1976I) to 2.7% (1976IV) and remains in the 2.5%-3% range until 1977IV. By contrast, the actual growth rate fluctuates between 2%

and 3.7% during these quarters. When the observations for 1977IV and 1978I come in, it becomes clear that the long-term growth rate must have changed, since extrapolation of a quarterly growth rate of approximately 2.5% results in enormous forecast errors for these two quarters. One of the six component models in the Multi-State Kalman filter algorithm is designed to accommodate important changes in the underlying growth rate. The importance of this model is increased automatically, and as a consequence the estimated underlying growth rate begins to follow more closely the changes in the actual growth rate. Note that in 1978I and 1978II the changes in the actual growth rate are incorporated to a much larger extent into the underlying growth rate than, for example, between 1976IV and 1977IV.

At the beginning of 1979 some confidence about the underlying growth rate has returned, but the erratic changes during 1978 have increased the estimated importance of shocks to the *level* of the money supply. It takes a while therefore until the underlying growth rate has reverted to a value below 1.0% per quarter when the money supply stops growing in 1979. During the transition some large forecast errors are made in 1979II, 1979III and 1979IV. The interested reader can inspect additional statistics on the changing importance of the component forecasting models in Statistical Appendix 1 at the end of the book.

As can be been in table 4.1 the algorithm produces an estimate of long-term growth in the money supply that is smoother than the actual quarter-to-quarter growth rate, but does succeed in learning after approximately two quarters about major changes in the speed at which money is supplied. Once confidence about the long-run rate of growth has returned, the algorithm assigns responsibility for large forecasting errors to temporary or permanent changes to the level of the money supply, until (as in 1977IV) it becomes apparent that the previous long-term growth rate no longer applies.

We have applied the Multi-State Kalman filter method to all time series for the quarterly average value of the gnp (gdp) deflator and consider the estimated underlying rates of growth – as in column (7) of table 4.1 for the Swiss money supply – to be an approximation of the expected rate of inflation. In the following section we shall develop a multivariate prediction for the expected rate of inflation based on the quantity theory of money and subsequently proceed to a comparison in section 4.4.

4.3 Monetarist predictions of inflation

Since the aggregate price level is an index of the purchasing power of money over goods, it is worthwhile to investigate whether predictions of the price level can be based fruitfully on the respective speeds at which the supplies of money and goods increase. If $\hat{M}$ indicates the rate of growth of the money stock, and $\hat{y}$ the growth rate of real output, then the difference

$$\hat{M} - \hat{y} \tag{4.6}$$

indicates the relative scarcity of money and goods. A high positive value for $\hat{M} - \hat{y}$ means that money is becoming relatively more plentiful so that the price of goods must increase. A low value for $\hat{M} - \hat{y}$ implies that money is becoming more scarce, so that its own price, the inverse of the aggregate price level, has to increase: i.e. downward pressure on the aggregate price index.

Forecasts of inflation based on this principle generally use the framework of the quantity theory of money,

$$M \cdot V = p \cdot y \tag{4.7}$$

and make a simplifying assumption about the behaviour of the income velocity of money. Equal year-over-year changes in velocity, for example, because of increased efficiency in the payments mechanism would give the following simple forecasting formula for inflation:

$$\hat{p} = c + \hat{M} - \hat{y} \tag{4.8}$$

Symbols
M money stock
p aggregate price level
y rate of real output
c constant growth rate of velocity
^ logarithmic rate of growth

Equation (4.8) with its assumption of constant growth in velocity is more appropriate for investigations of long-term secular patterns in inflation than for short-run analysis. Velocity is quite likely to depend on the phase of the business cycle, and short-run accelerations or decelerations in the money stock contribute to significant short-run movements in V. Even the long-term trend in velocity appears to change over time in virtually all the countries studied in this book. Figures 4.1 and 4.2 provide a visual impression of the degree to which the growth rate of velocity fails to be constant over our sample period. The graphs show the estimated underlying growth rates of the money supplies, as computed with the MSKF-filter (see section 4.2) together with the underlying growth rates of nominal national income ($\hat{p}^e + \hat{y}^e$). The vertical differences between the two lines in the graphs therefore indicate the quarter-to-quarter underlying growth rate of the income velocity of money. (Vertical distances between the lines would have been

Figure 4.1   The velocity of money in the U.S.
The fall in U.S. velocity in 1982 was out of line with the experience of the 1970's

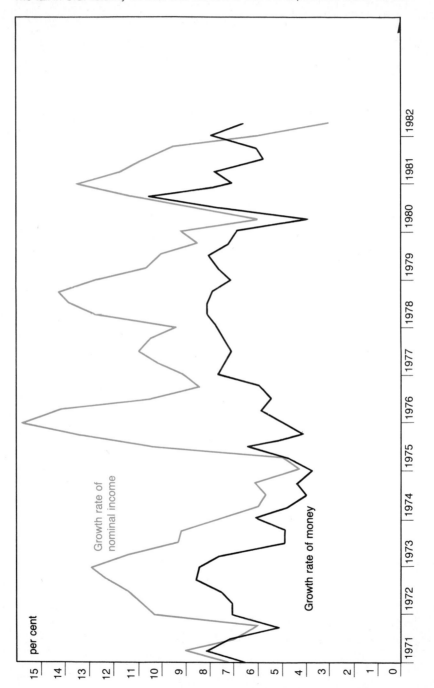

Figure 4.2 The velocity of money in Holland
The variability of velocity seems to be related to the variability in money growth

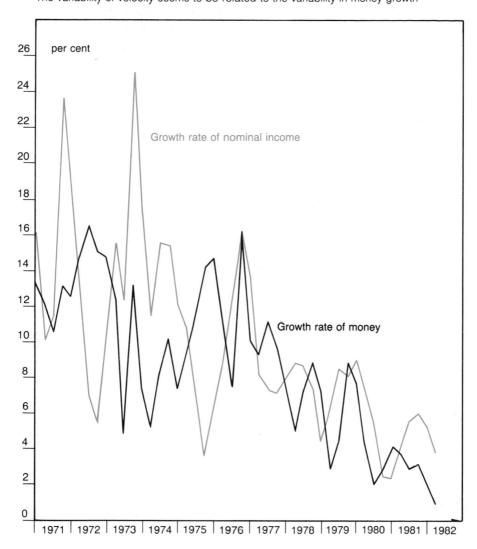

The vertical distance between the annualized rate of growth of nominal gnp and the rate of growth of M1 indicates the (annualized) rate of growth of the income velocity of M1. All rates of growth have been filtered with the MSKF-method in order to eliminate temporary "noise".

identical if we had depicted changes in $\hat{M} - \hat{y}$ and $\hat{p}$, but graphs of the expected inflation rates are provided already elsewhere in figures 4.3-4.9.)

As is clear from the graphs, the two series are strongly connected to each other but the vertical distances are far from being constant. Formal tests of the stability of quarterly changes in underlying velocity show that our corrections to the money supplies (see chapter 2) have decreased to some extent both the short-term and the long-term (trend) variation in velocity, but neither quarter-to-quarter changes in underlying velocity, nor their annual averages are constant. The graph for the U.S., for example, shows how the underlying growth rate of velocity turns negative in 1982I for the first time in many years.

We have tried to develop a statistical method that could produce consistent estimates of the underlying growth rate in prices, money, output, and velocity, whilst allowing for short-term as well as long-term movements in velocity. Statistical Appendix II at the end of the book describes the technique which is a further refinement of the Recursive Prediction Error Method used in Bomhoff (1982). We have used an identical specification for all seven countries with the following channels between prices, money, output and velocity:

(1) The expected level of real output depends on its previously expected level plus the estimated underlying growth rate with adjustments for output effects of changes in expected velocity growth.
(2) The underlying growth rate of real output changes over time as a function of the underlying rate of growth of the money stock.
(3) The expected level of velocity depends on its previous expected level plus the computed underlying growth rate in velocity with adjustments for the effects of economic growth on velocity.
(4) The underlying growth rate of velocity changes if the underlying rate of growth of the money supply accelerates.

Forecasts for the levels of money, output and velocity are combined into a prediction of the future level of prices. For each period the computer compares the predicted levels of output and prices to the realizations. The forecast errors are introduced immediately into the four prediction formulas (1) − (4) according to the Kalman Filter methodology.

Since all the parameters in the equations of the Kalman filter are computed adaptively, the forecasts for prices and output and their underlying rates of changes are based exclusively on current and past observations of money, prices and output. As in the case of the MSKF-filter of section 4.2 the forecasts have been computed ex-post by us in early 1983, but do not employ any information that would have been unavailable when the forecasts had to be made during our historical sample period. We exploit the

Figure 4.3   Inflation in the U.S.
The persistent upward trend in U.S. inflation between 1976 and 1979 was contrary to
experience in many European countries

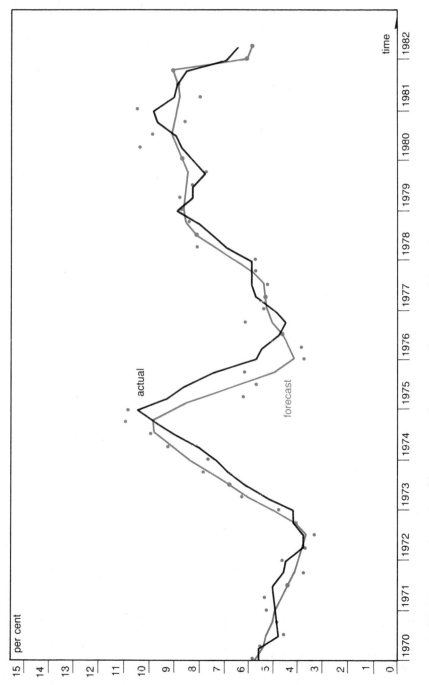

Actuals are percentage rates of increase over the corresponding quarter of the previous year.
Realizations and forecasts relate to the index for the general price level of national income. The
forecasts have been plotted in the quarter when they can be computed.

Figure 4.4   Inflation in Germany

Inflationary uncertainty in Germany could decline to a very low level after 1976

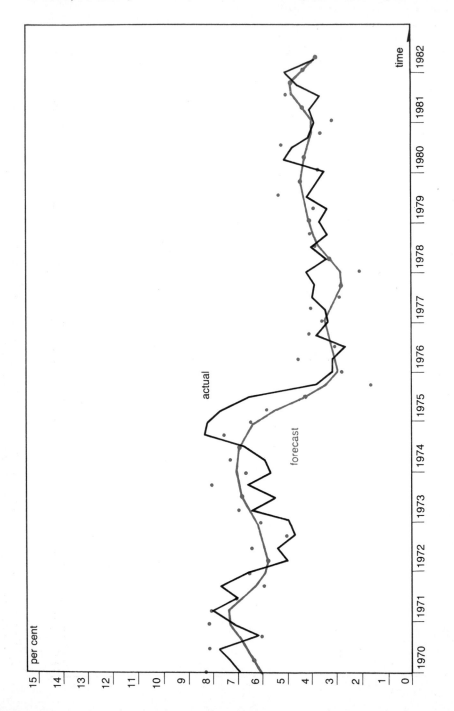

Figure 4.5   Inflation in Holland

Year-to-year variability in inflation has been larger in Holland than in Germany

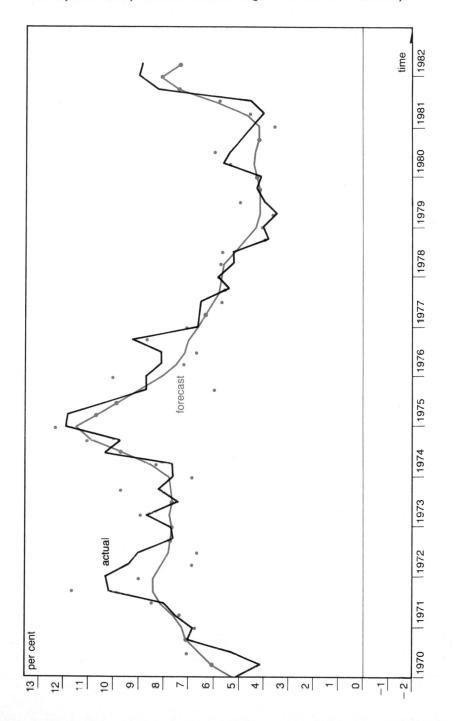

Figure 4.6 Inflation in Switzerland

Inflation peaked much earlier in Switzerland than in other Western countries, because the
Swiss monetary authorities were the first to prove their anti-inflationary resolve

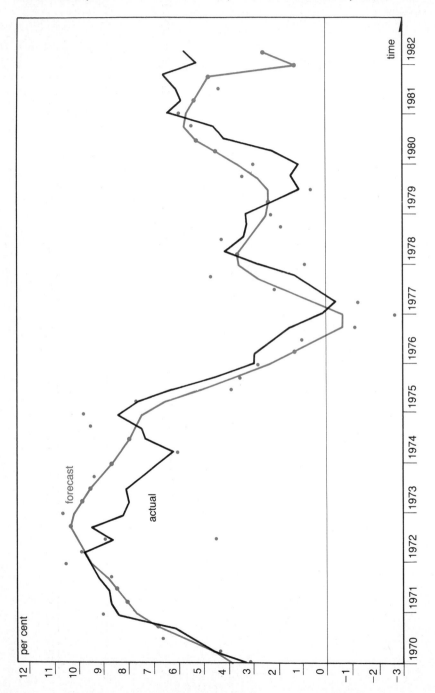

Figure 4.7 Inflation in Belgium

After 1976, inflation in Belgium did not differ much from inflation in Holland; more important for interest rates (and exchange rates) are differences in economic structure and government finances

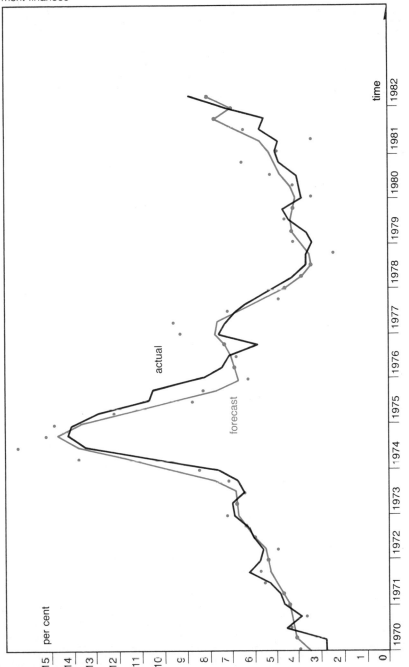

Figure 4.8   Inflation in Austria
Inflation in Austria has not diverged much from inflationary trends in Germany

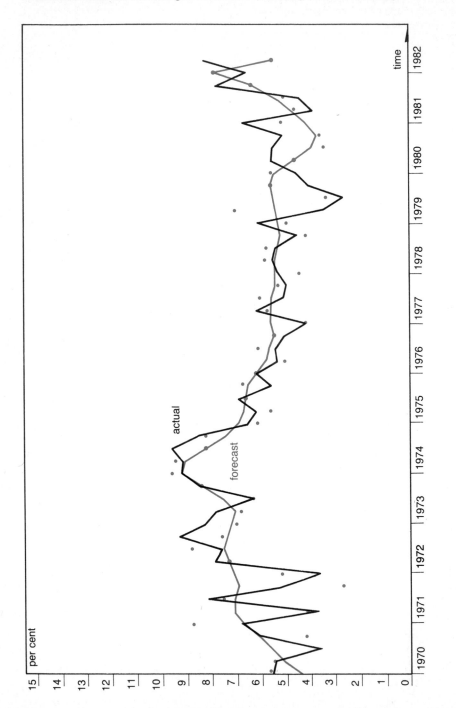

Figure 4.9 Inflation in Denmark

According to our estimates the expected rate of inflation in Denmark never went belov
per cent after 1970

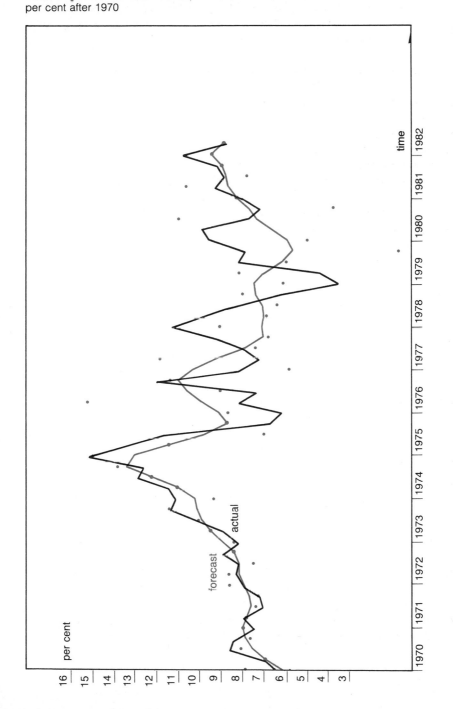

important advantage of Kalman filter methods over ordinary regression techniques in allowing random-walk type behaviour for the 'constant term' in the model. Instead of assuming that the growth rate of velocity is constant (see, for example, Karnosky, 1976), c in eq. (4.8) can change secularly over time if this is indicated by the data.

4.4 Combining the extrapolative and the monetarist forecasts of inflation

Having computed two measures of the expected rate of inflation, our remaining task is to find a sensible way of combining them. It is likely that in some countries and periods the extrapolative forecast will be more useful, whereas on other occasions the quantity-theoretic forecast should carry more weight. We have therefore constructed a composite forecast to which the two separate forecasts contribute with varying weights over time. We have tested two alternative formulas for computing the weights on the extrapolative and monetarist forecasts, namely the simple formula for combining forecasts that takes the ratio of the variances of the forecast errors and a more involved expression that takes account also of the covariance between the two separate forecasts (see Granger and Newbold, 1977, chapter 8). The simple formula worked better, in agreement with Granger and Newbold's verdict 'in favour of the combining procedures that ignore correlation over those that attempt to take correlation into account' (p. 75). The weights on the two forecasts are thus simply proportional to the variances of the respective forecast errors.

Both the extrapolative and the monetarist forecast try to distinguish between the predicted rate of price change that takes into account how temporary factors affect the price level, and the underlying rate of inflation estimated after these temporary effects have been eliminated: the Kalman filters estimate the underlying inflation rate in such a way that it is representative not only for the next quarter but also for all longer time horizons.

The relative success of the extrapolative and the monetarist forecasts in predicting inflation can thus be measured in different ways depending on the forecast horizon. At one extreme we can compare the one-quarter-ahead forecast errors and compute the weights in the formula for the composite forecast accordingly. Conversely, we could assume that the estimated underlying inflation rates will continue to hold over the next ten years, consider the forecast errors as far as data availability on actual inflation allows and use these ten-year forecast errors for computing the weights in the composite forecast. Good long-term inflation forecasts would be welcome for the analysis of long-term rates of interest in chapter 5, but our sample period is much too short to allow for a realistic calculation. Actual rates of inflation exhibited cyclical patterns in many countries, so that the errors in long-term forecasts of inflation showed extreme changes from one year to the next.

Figure 4.3 for the expected and actual rates of inflation in the U.S., for exanple, shows that the estimated underlying rate of inflation in early 1970 was not much different from the average rate of inflation realized over the 1970's, and the estimates for 1973III and 1973IV were virtually equal to the average rate of price change between 1973 and 1982. All this is true in hindsight but not useful for assessing the accuracy of long-term inflation forecasts. Even for a two-year horizon we found that the size of the forecast errors for each individual forecasting scheme changes erratically over time and cannot serve as basis for computation of the weights in the composite forecasts.

We have preferred to use the one-year ahead forecast errors to gauge the accuracy of the extrapolative and monetarist forecasting schemes. A geometrically weighted average of the last 16 squared forecast errors (decay parameter 0.9) was used to compute an adaptive estimate of the variance of these one-year ahead forecast errors. Table 4.2 shows the ratio of the estimated variances of the extrapolative and monetarist forecasts at both end-points of our sample period for the interest rate regressions in chapter 5 and at three intermediate points. The numbers in the first column may be low in some cases because the parameters in the quantity-theoretic model are still ill-determined. The potential contribution of the monetarist forecast varies considerably but is larger than 30% at least some time in all countries.

According to the numbers in table 4.2 forecasters who neglected completely the potential contribution of the quantity theory in predicting future inflation did so at their peril. Increased monetary uncertainty, defined as a greater variability in the underlying growth rate of the money supply does appear to have a bearing on inflationary uncertainty, defined as a greater variability in the underlying inflation rate. We have attempted to find statistical evidence for the monetarist hypothesis that the comparative strength

Table 4.2 Weight of the quantity-theoretic forecast

	1971-I	1974-I	1977-I	1980-I	1982-II
U.S.A.	0.08	0.35	0.49	0.46	0.43
West-Germany	0.09	0.31	0.31	0.13	0.04
The Netherlands	0.04	0.05	0.10	0.13	0.33
Switzerland	0.25	0.36	0.26	0.24	0.51
Belgium	0.11	0.07	0.38	0.20	0.29
Austria	0.18	0.21	0.25	0.34	0.12
Denmark	0.04	0.03	0.39	0.35	0.08

Weight of the quantity-theoretic forecast:

Variance of the extrapolative forecast/(variance of the extrapolative forecast plus variance of the quantity-theoretic forecast). This constrains the weight to lie between 0 and 1.

of quantity-theoretic forecasts of inflation increases if the forecast horizon grows longer, but our sample period proved to be too short for a reliable comparison of the accuracy of short-term and long-term inflation forecasts.

Figures 4.3-4.9 show the composite forecasts together with the actual inflation rates for the period 1970I-1982II. To mitigate the impact of transitory impulses on the graphs, we have applied smoothing procedures to both time series in figures 4.3-4.9. Actual rates of price change are depicted by rates of growth that cover the last four quarters: shown for 1982II for example is the growth rate between 1982II and 1981II. The composite forecasts have been smoothed by an error detection scheme based on cubic spline coefficients (see IMSL library, volume 2, routine ICSMOU, 1980).

The smoothing procedure for the expected inflation rates leaves many numbers unchanged, but replaces others by an estimate that draws on the adjacent data on both sides. Thus, the procedure introduces an ex-post element into the expected rates of inflation. We have therefore performed all the analyses for interest rates in chapter 5 with both the smoothed estimates of expected inflation and the unsmoothed composite forecasts and show the latter (as dots) together with the smoothed series in figures 4.3–4.9. The smoothing routine is anchored on the first and last three observations which affects the final observations in the graphs; we have started the procedure in 1969 so that the left-hand margin of the graphs is not similarly affected.

When inspecting the figures it should be remembered that the apparent effectiveness of the weighted forecasts to predict future movements in actual inflation is largely due to the use of four-quarter rates of price change. If the actual rate of price change behaves as a random walk, rates of changes measured over four quarters will to some extent be predictable, which helps explain the visual success of the series for expected inflation in tracing out actual price patterns.

Additional information with respect to the different forecasts may be found in table 4.3. Shown are the summary statistics about the differences between the actual rates of price change over four-quarter periods – exactly as depicted in figures 4.3-4.9 – and the expected underlying growth rates as estimated at the start of each four-quarter span:

$$100 \times (\log(p)_t - \log(p)_{t-4}) - {}_{t-4}E(\hat{p}^e) \tag{4.9}$$

Recall that the expected underlying rates of inflation are different from the expected rate of price change which also takes temporary and permanent changes in the price *level* into account. Only the underlying growth rates behave as pure random walks over time and are suitable candidates, therefore, for inclusion in equations for long-term interest rates. When temporary (or permanent) shocks to the level of prices are important relative to changes

Table 4.3 Differences between actual and underlying inflation

RMSE's for four-quarter ahead differentials.

	univariate	multi-variate	combined forecast	after smoothing with spline functions
United States	2.02	2.33	1.80	1.51
West-Germany	1.42	2.97	1.48	0.95
The Netherlands	2.59	6.33	2.27	1.99
Switzerland	2.39	3.76	2.76	2.60
Belgium	1.83	4.51	1.82	1.66
Austria	2.13	3.72	2.05	1.81
Denmark	2.65	7.54	2.88	2.45

in the underlying growth rate, the latter may be too low or too high for protracted periods of time, which affects the RMSE's in table 4.3.

The first three columns of the table show the discrepancies between actual and underlying inflation rates for the univariate, monetarist and combined forecasts, respectively. The final column relates to the RMSE's for the smoothed version of the combined forecast. The errors of the combined forecasts are approximately two percentage points in five out of seven countries, and close to three percentage points in Switzerland and Denmark. The smoothing procedure reduces these average errors considerably in some cases, so that the average for the seven countries goes below 2 percentage points. The spline functions do introduce some ex-post elements into the 'forecasts' however.

Distinctly poor are the results of the quantity-theoretic predictions of underlying inflation for the Netherlands and Denmark. In both countries the problem is not systematic over- or underestimation of the actual inflation rates, but a few episodes during which rapidly changing growth rates of money (or output) perturb the estimated growth rate of velocity and lead to wild forecasts of the underlying inflation rate. In addition, the Recursive Prediction Error algorithm with its dozen of adaptively estimated parameters and automatic initialization requires some time to produce reasonable estimates for the parameters. We plan to continue looking for ways to make the RPE-method converge more rapidly.

chapter 5

Monetary Uncertainty and long-term rates

with Paul T.W.M. Veugelers

"The pluralist control of the state which emerged from the struggle of workers, farmers, and business groups has produced the disintegration of the earlier structure of property rights and replaced it with a struggle in the political arena to redistribute income and wealth at the expense of the efficiency potential of the Second Economic Revolution. Moreover, this resultant struggle has not led to a new ideological social fabric that resolves the organizational tensions. The erosion of the gold standard since 1914 and especially since the 1930s has eliminated the nominal anchor of the money supply and therefore the forces that limited changes in the price level. In consequence manipulation of the money supply by contending interest groups is a major destabilizing force in the modern world."

Douglas C. North : "Structure and change in economic history", W.W. Norton & Company, New York and London, 1981, p. 185.

5.1. Changes in long-term interest rates.

Our aim in this chapter is to identify some of the factors influencing long-term interest rates on government bonds in the United States, West-Germany, Holland, Switzerland, Belgium, Austria and Denmark over the period 1971I – 1982II. Specifically we are interested in measuring the contribution –if any – of monetary uncertainty, defined as the likely margin of error surrounding forecasts of future growth rates of the money supply, to the surprisingly high nominal and real interest rates of the early 1980's.

One basic assumption about the behaviour of long-term interest rates has dictated much of the style of our research, namely the assertion that short-term changes in long-term interest rates must be largely unpredictable. For, if investors could foresee with confidence how long-term rates would change over the next few days or weeks, short-term capital gains would lead to excessive short-term rates of return which would violate the postulate of efficient markets. When looking back, investors in the long-term bond market will remember exceptional rates of return over some periods, but the market as a whole could not have been able to predict these record rates of return in advance.

In our view, four guidelines to interest-rate research follow from the assumption that short-term movements in long-term interest rates are practically unpredictable :

1. The proper magnitude to investigate is the period-to-period change in the long-term rate, rather than its level over time. With imperfect researchers working in a non-deterministic world, no investigation into interest rates is ever going to provide a 100 % explanation of their movements over time. Some unidentified factors will remain important, and these hidden causes themselves will have to change unpredictably over time ; otherwise, so-called technical analysis would provide a means of forecasting future interest rates. But, if the unidentified factors in a statistical model do not fluctuate around a constant mean value over time but behave like random walks, it is imperative that changes in economic magnitudes rather than their levels are subject of the research, unless very specialized statistical techniques are employed (see Bomhoff, 1982, for further discussion).

2. The best variable to explain is the (change in the) nominal interest rate, rather than the (change in the) real rate of interest. In the very long run economic mechanisms work to eliminate persistent differences in (risk-corrected) real rates of return on different financial or real assets. But, to conduct an investigation into short-term

movements of interest rates in real terms would require an almost perfect measure of the expected rate of inflation. We have seen in chapter 4 how difficult it is to construct adequate indices for expected inflation, especially for longer time horizons. Computation of a real rate of interest with the help of an imperfect proxy variable for expected inflation produces measurement errors of unknown amplitude in the estimated real rates. The danger then exists that the research identifies determinants of the interest rates that are fully dependent on the particular way in which expected inflation has been measured. This risk is not eliminated, but at least reduced, if the nominal rate of interest is regressed on the expected rate of inflation plus other explanatory factors.

3. The explanatory variables must exert their influence on long-term rates in such a way that short-term changes in the interest rate remain virtually unpredictable. This requirement is necessary, because otherwise interest rates could be predicted via forecasts of one or more important determinants. If, for example, an investigation concluded that the growth rate of world exports was important in explaining long-term interest rates in open economies such as Germany and Holland, then long-term interest rates would become predictable to some extent, unless next quarter's growth in world trade or domestic exports would be completely unknown at all times. We have taken a double precaution to prevent successful interest rate forecasting through the route of predicting their fundamental determinants : first, we have separated statistically all the potential explanatory variables into foreseeable and unforeseeable elements. Only the unforeseeable changes in world trade, government deficits, money growth etc. are allowed a role in the statistical equations which explain changes in long-term interest rates. To the extent that changes in the explanatory variables could have been predicted in advance with confidence, they should have had their effects already on the current rate, since otherwise the next change in the interest rate would be predictable.

Not only did we replace measured changes in the explanatory variables by unexpected changes, we also limited the time delays with which unexpected changes in budget deficits, money growth etc. would affect long-term rates to at most one time period (two periods in the case of uncertainty indices - see below). Since we try to explain changes in quarterly averages of long-term rates on the basis of unexpected changes in quarterly averages of world trade, deficits, money growth and other variables, an "overspill" of one period is unavoidable (see Working, 1960). Longer delays in the transmission of changes in a fundamental factor to actual changes in long-term rates would mean that fundamental analysis provided a means for the market as a whole to forecast interest rates. If no long lags appear in the empirical analysis and if all explanatory variables have been purged of their predictable elements, then the statistical findings do not provide any evidence against the hypothesis that the only way to apply fundamental analysis to interest rate forecasting is to have opinions on future deficits, money growth etc. which diverge from the market's average expectation and to be proved right by subsequent events.

4. Small-scale econometric technology is more appropriate for explaining changes in long-term interest rates than traditional large-scale econometric models. For, all three previous requirements are easily satisfied if we regress changes in long-term rates on different combinations of potential explanatory variables : so-called reduced form analysis. Our research in this chapter will take the form of such single equations for explaining changes in long-term rates. Current large-scale models, however, are less likely to pay full respect to the postulate of market efficiency and its consequences (1) – (3) above. In some sectors of the real economy, for example home building or investment in new plant, the national accounts data on installations which are used in the econometric models are the result of decisions taken many quarters or even years before. Substantial lags between causes and effects are thus legitimate in some parts of a national or international econometric model, but since interest rates are partly determined within the equations that exhibit these lags, it will be very difficult, if not impossible, to have long-term interest rates behaving like random walks without predictable future changes.

A brief comparison with some other recent empirical work on interest rates in the United States may provide additional perspective on the four principles guiding our research in this chapter. Table 5.1 gives some of the main features of four academic studies of short and long-term interest rates on U.S. government obligations.

Wilcox and Mishkin terminate their analysis in 1979, Makin in 1980, whereas Mascaro/Meltzer and Bomhoff c.s. cover at least a part of the very recent period of exceptionally high real rates of interest. There is rather more variation in the starting points of the regressions, with Mishkin and Wilcox incorporating most of the 1950's, Makin beginning in 1959, and the last two studies starting around 1970. All work with quarterly data, apart from Wilcox who uses semi-annual observations.

In spite of the considerable overlap with respect to the period of

Table 5.1 Research on U.S. interest rates

Author(s)	Mishkin	Makin	Wilcox	Mascaro/Meltzer	Bomhoff/Veugelers
Interest rate explained;	3 month T-bill	3 month T-bill	one year T-bill	90 day bankers acceptance/10-year government bonds	20-year government bonds
approximate coefficient on expected inflation	0.7	0.4-0.8	1.0	0.7-1.0/0.2	0.2
measure of expected inflation	actual rate of price change as observed afterwards	Livingston survey data on price expectations	Livingston survey data on price expectations	statistical proxy (fixed model)	statistical proxy (adaptive model)
level of interest rate of first difference explained?	level	level	level	level	first difference
money surprises important?	no	yes	yes	yes	probably not
real factors important?	none identified	yes	yes	yes	yes
risk factors important?	–	discussed, not yet in equations	–	yes	yes

estimation, there are important differences in specification between the five studies. Mishkin works with the actual rate of price change during the holding period of the treasury bill instead of some measure of the expected rate of inflation as it was anticipated when the bills were priced. This procedure is out of the question for long-term interest rates, as it requires specific assumptions about the discrepancies between the actual and expected rates of price change. It is no problem to make a restrictive assumption about the forecast error with respect to the rate of price change over the next few months, but it does not seem feasible to distinguish in the regressions between factors that influence long-term interest rates as determined in today's market and factors that cause errors in long-term inflation forecasts, as observed ex-post ten or twenty years from today.

Two of the remaining four studies use survey measures on price expectations. Both Makin and Wilcox work with the series that have been collected by Joseph Livingston of the Philadelphia Inquirer. The Livingston data have been scrutinized by many researchers (see Pearce, 1979, for a critical evaluation), and their suitability as a proxy for the market expectation of the short-term rate of price change is still matter of dispute.

Survey measures of expected inflation in some European countries are available for a much briefer historical period, and we report below on some econometric experiments with survey data. The limited coverage of the survey measures precludes their general use in our work, so that we have preferred to used the computed indices of expected inflation which were developed in the previous chapter.

The Mascaro/Meltzer paper offers an important lesson regarding the influence of changes in the expected rate of inflation on interest rates. Their measure of expected inflation works very well for the short-term rate, but its coefficient drops to 0.2 in the equations for the 10-year government bonds. There are at least two alternative explanations : either real long-term rates of interest do indeed decline almost one-for-one when the expected rate of inflation increases, because of non-neutralities in the tax system or for other reasons ; or the coefficient is hardly different from zero because the expected rate of inflation is measured in such a deficient manner. The period of analysis is much too short with respect to the life of the bonds both in the Mascaro/Meltzer study and in our own work to settle this issue. It seems likely on theoretical grounds that at least a large part of the explanation has to be provided by the errors-in-variables hypothesis since 0.2 is so much smaller than the 0.7-0.8 range for this coefficient in the case of short-term interest rates to which the same non-neutralities should apply in principle.

In our econometric work for the United States the coefficient on 20-year government bonds is also close to 0.2, but since we estimate equations for the change in the nominal interest rate, the errors-in-variables argument applies with even greater force. To obtain a coefficient of 1.0 on the variable that measures expected inflation would require a perfect substitute for the market's expectation with respect to both size and timing. In our first-difference specification even small leads and lags between changes in the market's expectation and our proxy for it will drive the coefficient to zero.

Probably for this reason, all the research in table 5.1 apart from our own was done for levels of interest rates rather than first differences. Many researchers used to feel that real rates of interest were either stationary or moved within a narrow band so that a regression of the level of the nominal interest rate on a proper measure of the expected rate of inflation plus other variables would result in well-behaved residual errors. Recent interest-rate experience has thrown considerable doubt on that hypothesis. We have tested extensively whether one can still estimate equations for the *level* of the long-term U.S. bond rate, but have found for each specification that the unexplained part of the interest rate behaved like a random walk over time. As explained above, this is but natural if the interest rate itself moves approximately like a random walk ; it has led us to conclude that the proper specification is in terms of first differences.

In addition, explaining a non-stationary variable as a combination of several other non-stationary variables means that the coefficients on the explanatory variables will be very sensitive to the presence or absence of other explanatory variables. As a consequence, the statistical significance of any one of these causal factors – for example monetary uncertainty – becomes less than fully convincing. Nominal interest rates were much higher at the end of the period than at the beginning, and so were numerous other economic variables, including our index of monetary uncertainty. It is hard to discriminate between the potentially large number of candidate variables if what the computer needs is a rough tracing out of the level of the long-term interest rate. More convincing in our opinion will be the failure to reject the hypothesis that changes in an index of monetary uncertainty, for example, have nothing to contribute to an explanation of the quarter-to-quarter changes in the long-term interest rate.

Hence one more reason to prefer a specification in terms of changes in the rates of interest. The chance that variables are wrongly included in the equation is reduced, but the price to be paid is that meaningful relationships between broad long-run trends in the time series may get lost : a first-difference specification emphasizes correlations at the "high frequency" end of the spectrum and neglects links at "low frequencies".

Since our aim in this chapter is to test different hypotheses about the fundamental determinants of long-term interest rates, we have employed standard statistical techniques, which allow for precise conclusions regarding the statistical significance of monetary uncertainty and other explanatory factors. All regression equations have been estimated by ordinary least squares augmented with the so-called Cochrane-Orcutt technique to cope with serial correlation in the residuals. We list the explanatory variables in the next section, after which section 5.3 contains our preferred regression equations. Sections 5.4 and 5.5 provide information about some alternative specifications ; section 5.6 contains some summarizing remarks.

5.2. Fundamental determinants of interest rates.

In this section we discuss the fundamental factors that will be included in the regression equations of the following section. Because of our decision to work throughout with first differences, we study the effects of *changes* in fundamental factors on *changes* in nominal rates of interest, but to avoid using the word "change" in every sentence, we omit mention of this fact where there is no danger of confusion.

Long-term rates of interest.

We try to account for changes in long-term interest rates on government bonds in the U.S., Germany and five smaller European Countries. We allow for one-way influences running from American interest rates to all interest rates in Europe, and again from German interest rates to interest rates in the smaller European countries. All potential feedback channels remain closed : we assume that changes in Dutch, Swiss, Belgian, Austrian and Danish interest rates do not influence the German long-term rate and that changes in the European rates have no impact on interest rates in the United States. We have not attempted to test whether these assumptions are appropriate.

Expected rate of inflation.

Chapter 4 contains an account of the computation of our composite index for expected inflation. We have explained in the previous section why we include this variable on the right-hand side of our equations for nominal interest rates. Section 5.5 provides information about some alternative tests with a survey measure of expected inflation in the E.E.C.

Real rates of interest.

These are computed by subtracting the expected rate of inflation from
the nominal interest rate. We discuss several problems regarding this
procedure in the following section. The resulting real rates of interest are
ex-ante, and will be different from the actually realized real rates of
return on long-term investments. We test whether changes in real interest
rates in the United States have an impact on German nominal rates, and
whether changes in U.S. and German real rates have effects on nominal
interest rates in the smaller European countries.

Liquidity effects.

Equilibrium in the macroeconomic money market requires that all
changes in the nominal supply of money have effects on one or more of
the determinants of the demand for money balances. In the short term
the aggregate price level will usually not change rapidly enough to reflect
the most recent money surprises, so that changes in interest rates may be
required to maintain equilibrium between actual and desired real money
balances. As our measure of this liquidity effect on interest rates we use
the quarter-to-quarter change in the estimated underlying growth rate of
the money supply. All these changes in the underlying growth rate are
unpredictable, because of the way in which it is computed with the
Multi-State Kalman filter (see chapter 4). Statistical Appendix 1 explains
how each unexpected movement in the money stock has implications for
both the estimated underlying level and the estimated underlying growth
rate. We prefer changes in either of these two variables to the observed
unexpected changes in the actual numbers, since the Kalman filter will
have eliminated at least part of the purely temporary and thus irrelevant
"noise". Changes in the underlying growth rate fit our specification
better than changes in the underlying level; the latter would need to be
deflated by changes in the expected price level (see chapter 2), and that
would be impractical in the present context were the expected rate of
inflation is included already as one of the other explanatory variables.

Budget deficit.

We subtract (seasonally adjusted) revenues from (seasonally adjusted)
expenditures and divide the resulting deficits by the expected rate of
nominal national income for the same quarter. This deficit-to-income
ratio behaves much like a random walk as shown by the fact that the
Multi-State Kalman filter produces estimates of the expected deficit-to-
income ratio which are generally close to the most recent value of the

Figure 5.1 The volume of world exports

Positive changes in this index have an upward effect on interest rates in many trading nations

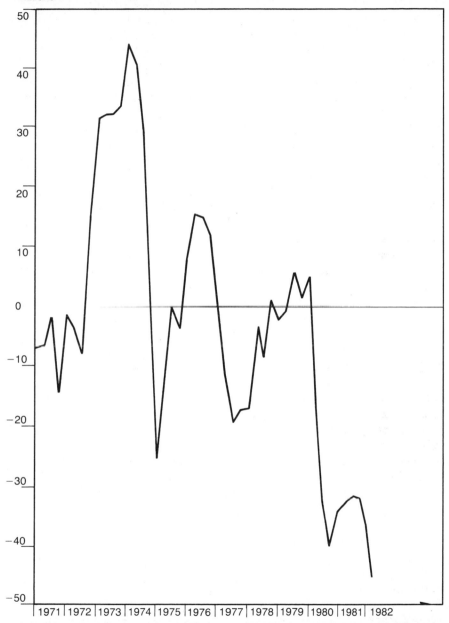

This index for the volume of world exports has been transformed so that its quarterly changes are statistically unpredictable. Now that the index moves as a random walk, it has become useful for interest-rate analysis.

ratio. Since the expected levels performed slightly less well in the
regressions, we decided to use changes in the actual deficit-to-income
ratio in our preferred equations. Section 5.4 has an extensive discussion
of this variable.

The world business cycle.

The International Monetary Fund publishes a series on the volume of
world exports. That index does not have the characteristics of a random
walk over time, implying that its direct inclusion into our regressions
would introduce an element of predictability in long-term interest rates
(see the previous section). We have therefore computed unexpected
changes in the index with the help of the Multi-State Kalman filter
method and test whether such unpredicted movements in the strength of
the world business cycle have an impact on long-term rates of interest.
Figure 5.1 shows the cumulated sum of these unexpected changes, in
order to facilitate inferences from the state of the world business cycle to
the *level* of nominal interest rates.

Prices of imported energy.

We use the dollar price of oil on the Rotterdam spot market as an
indicator of energy prices. Again, our regressions employ the unexpected
changes in this variable.

Monetary uncertainty.

Our measure of monetary uncertainty is derived from the computed
underlying growth rates of the money supply (see chapter 4 and
Technical Appendix 1). The first difference of this quarterly time series
was used to measure the liquidity effect ; an adaptively computed
estimate of its variance (decay parameter 0.9) serves as our index of
monetary uncertainty. Figures 5.2 and 5.3 show the levels of monetary
uncertainty for the U.S., Germany and Switzerland. Note how monetary
uncertainty in the U.S. reaches very high levels in 1980-1981. More
about this variable in section 5.3, where we compare its behaviour to
that of an alternative measure of uncertainty regarding future price
levels :

Inflationary uncertainty.

We estimate inflationary uncertainty by computing the variance of the
first difference of our composite index for expected inflation (see chapter
4), again with a decay parameter of 0.9.

Figure 5.2   Monetary uncertainty in the U.S.

According to our estimates, the increase in monetary uncertainty during 1980 added approximately 200 basis points to U.S. long-term rates

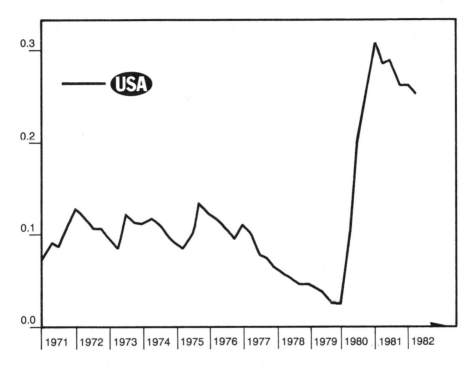

This index of monetary uncertainty relates to the variability in the quarterly rates of growth of M1.

Figure 5.3   Monetary uncertainty in Germany and Switzerland

This index of monetary uncertainty in Switzerland increases tremendously in 1977, but the Swiss monetary authorities had proved already their anti-inflationary stance (compare figure 4.6)

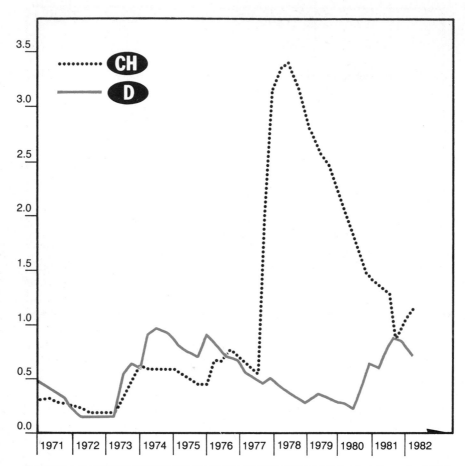

The indices of monetary uncertainty relate to the variability of the quarterly rates of growth of M1 in Germany and Switzerland.

Uncertainty regarding the world business cycle.

This index is based on the underlying growth rate of world exports, as computed with the Multi-State Kalman filter. Technically, its construction is similar to that of the indices for monetary and inflationary uncertainty.

Discarded explanatory variables.

We have computed indices of uncertainty regarding the deficit-to-income ratio and with respect to energy prices. General lack of statistical significance led us to drop these variables from our preferred regressions. Budgetary uncertainty, however, could well be important in explaining high interest rates, if budgetary uncertainty and monetary uncertainty are related (see section 5.4 for further discussion).

The theoretical exposition of chapter 3 provides guidance as to the correct signs of some explanatory variables in the regressions.
Greater uncertainty about the future rate of inflation, measured by an index of monetary uncertainty or an index of inflationary uncertainty, should raise the required ex-ante real rate on long-term debt. If higher budget deficits indicate reliably that long-term debt will figure more prominently in the future portfolio, then such news should increase the absolute value of $cov(r_b,R)$, implying that any existing positive risk premia on long-term debt will increase further. In other words, if high monetary uncertainty puts a substantial risk premium into long-term rates, then a more unfavourable perspective for the budget deficit will increase this risk premium. We have not attempted, however, to combine indicators of the risk per unit of debt (such as monetary uncertainty) with indicators about the future supply of debt (such as the budget deficit in relation to national income) ; instead, changes in monetary uncertainty and changes in the deficit-to-income ratio have been included as separate explanatory variables to facilitate statistical testing of their relative importance.

Since the model of chapter 3 relates to a closed economy, it is not helpful with respect to the likely coefficients on changes in foreign nominal or real rates of interest. In this study we do not attempt to build a theory about exchange rates, but assume that integrated world capital markets imply that real interest rates exhibit joint movements across countries to at least some extent. In view of the difficulties connected to measuring expected rates of inflation, we have experimented with both changes in nominal foreign rates and changes in real foreign rates ; any significant coefficients should be positive. We tried without success to measure the impact on European rates of changes in the risk-free U.S.

long-term rate ; further analysis will be required to decide whether changes in market-determined real U.S. rates or changes in real rates after correction for risk have most impact on interest rates in other countries.

The theoretical model of chapter 3 bears on all the other explanatory variables listed above, but gives equivocal conclusions regarding their signs in the interest rate regressions. Chapter 3 contained an extensive discussion of the liquidity effect on long-term rates ; in the empirical analysis we find no significant liquidity effects on long-term rates in the U.S., and small negative effects in a few specifications for European rates. If changes in the index for the volume of world exports contribute to an explanation of long-term rates, the coefficient is always positive. In an IS-LM analysis changes in world trade would imply an outward shift of the IS-curve so that interest rates would rise. In the model of chapter 3, however, a specific assumption about the dynamics of the marginal utility of consumption is required to obtain this result.

In the model of Wilcox (1983) negative real supply shocks drive down real and, ceteris paribus, nominal interest rates. We fail to obtain significant coefficients on unexpected changes in the dollar price of oil. According to the theoretical analysis of chapter 3 purely temporary negative shocks to productivity could lead to higher real rates of interest. Energy crises with adverse effects on medium-term economic growth should cause a drop in real interest rates.

As discussed in chaper 3, uncertainty about future economic growth, based for example on uncertainty regarding the world business cycle, may affect long-term rates both ways, depending on the assumptions about the dynamics of the marginal utility of consumption. According to the empirical analysis, changes in the index have a negative effect on U.S. rates, a positive effect on German rates and a positive effect on interest rates in Belgium. Since this index is a constructed proxy for an unobservable variable, more research will be required before one can attach much weight to these findings.

5.3. The results.

In this section we present our findings regarding the determinants of changes in long-term interest rates on government debt. First, we introduce statistical tables 5.2 – 5.7 which contain the estimated regression equations ; then we draw some conclusions about the main theme of this book : monetary uncertainty and its harmful effects. Our analysis of long-term interest rates will continue in section 5.4 with information about the importance of budget deficits on interest rates, and in section 5.5 which has more to say about the treatment of

Table 5.2 Long-term interest rates in the United States, 1971-I to 1982-II.

Dependent variable:
Δi_b; government bond yield with constant 20-year term to maturity

Explanatory variables:	(1)	(2)	(3)	(4)	(5) USA
c constant term	.146 (.056)	.145 (.058)	.148 (.061)	.148 (.062)	.153 (.060)
$\Delta\hat{p}^e_{+1}$ expected rate of inflation	.188 (.088)	.192 (.191)	.165 (.091)	.175 (.092)	.190 (.091)
$\Delta\hat{M}^e_{+1}$ expected rate of growth of the money stock (M1)		.023 (.047)		.038(-1) (.042)	
ΔDef deficit as a proportion of gnp	.171(-1) (.070)	.162(-1) (.071)	.116(-1) (.066)	.120(-1) (.067)	.110(-1) (.066)
Trade^{ue} unexpected changes in world trade	.010 (.006)	.0098 (.0060)	.0090 (.0057)	.0090 (.0057)	.0091 (.0056)
Poil^{ue} unexpected changes in energy prices					-.0010 (.0008)
$\Delta\sigma_M$ index of monetary uncertainty	7.79(-2) (2.41)	7.81(-2) (2.48)	7.14(-2) (2.43)	6.63(-2) (2.51)	6.94(-2) (2.40)
$\Delta\sigma_{trade}$ index of uncertainty with respect to world trade			-.047 (.016)	-.047 (.016)	-.047 (.016)
ϱ Cochrane-Orcutt parameter for first-order serial correlation	-.170 (.147)	-.142 (.148)	.0025 (.149)	.011 (.149)	-.019 (.149)
R^2 percentage of variation explained	.31	.31	.42	.43	.44
S.E.E. standard error of estimate	.432	.436	.403	.404	.400
D.W. Durbin-Watson coefficient for first-order serial correlation	2.1	2.1	2.0	2.0	2.0

– Standard errors are printed below each coefficient
– lags (in quarters) are indicated after the corresponding coefficient.

Table 5.3   Long-term interest rates in Germany, 1971-I to 1982-II.

Dependent variable:
Δi_b; public authorities' bond yield

Explanatory variables:		(1)	(2)	(3)	(4)	(5)
c	constant term	-.026	.0079	-.015	.063	.067
		(.071)	(.0693)	(.077)	(.081)	(.075)
$\Delta \hat{p}^e_{+1}$	expected rate of inflation	.258	.358	.276	.718	.690
		(.193)	(.193)	(.201)	(.243)	(.240)
Δi_{US}	long-term government bond yield in the U.S.	.532	.361	.519		
		(.137)	(.132)	(.139)		
Δr_{US}	real rate of interest in the U.S.				.281	.212
					(.088)	(.088)
ΔDef	deficit as a proportion of gnp			.049		
				(.052)		
$Trade^{ue}$	unexpected changes in world trade	.025(-0.5)	.025(-0.5)	.026(-0.5)	.028(-0.5)	.027(-0.5)
		(.008)	(.008)	(.008)	(.008)	(.008)
$\Delta \sigma_M$	index of monetary uncertainty	.663	.880		.797	.952
		(.543)	(.585)		(.560)	(.589)
$\Delta \sigma_{trade}$	index of uncertainty with respect to world trade	.048		.049	.035	
		(.016)		(.016)	(.015)	
ϱ	Cochrane-Orcutt parameter for first-order serial correlation	.121	.022	.187	.248	.149
		(.148)	(.149)	(.146)	(.144)	(.147)
R^2	percentage of variation explained	.59	.51	.59	.55	.49
S.E.E.	standard error of estimate	.378	.412	.381	.397	.417
D.W.	Durbin-Watson coefficient for first-order serial correlation	1.9	1.9	1.8	1.8	1.9

–   Standard errors are printed below each coefficient
–   lags (in quarters) are indicated after the corresponding coefficient.

Table 5.4 Long-term interest rates in the Netherlands, 1971-I to 1982-II.

Dependent variable:
Δi_b: weighted average yield of three latest government bond issues — NL

Explanatory variables:		(1)	(2)	(3)	(4)	(5)
c	constant term	-.0089 (.0506)	-.012 (.048)	-.010 (.067)	.022 (.049)	-.015 (.073)
$\Delta\hat{p}^e_{+1}$	expected rate of inflation					.158 (.124)
Δi_{US}	long-term yield in the U.S.	.262 (.121)	.277 (.117)	.486 (.122)		
Δi_G	long-term yield in Germany	.557 (.126)	.587 (.100)		.740 (.095)	
Δr_G	real rate of interest in Germany					.600 (.148)
$\Delta\hat{M}^e_{+1}$	expected rate of growth of the money stock	-.034 (.017)	-.030 (.017)	-.034 (.018)	-.035 (.018)	-.052 (.020)
ΔDef	deficit as a proportion of gnp	.028(-1) (.028)			.046(-1) (.028)	.041(-1) (.030)
$Trade^{ue}$	unexpected changes in world trade	.0066(-0.5) (.0068)		.023(0.5) (.007)		.0168(0.5) (.0084)
$Poil^{ue}$	unexpected changes in energy prices	.00089 (.00071)	.00086 (.00069)		.00094 (.00073)	.0015 (.0009)
$\Delta\sigma_M$	index of monetary uncertainty	.585(-2) (.333)	.532(-2) (.320)	.543(-2) (.420)	.571(-2) (.347)	.502(-2) (.441)
ϱ	Cochrane-Orcutt parameter for first-order serial correlation	-.073 (.149)	-.136 (.148)	.068 (.149)	-.068 (.149)	.128 (.148)
R^2	percentage of variation explained	.67	.65	.50	.62	.52
S.E.E.	standard error of estimate	.331	.332	.393	.344	.397
D.W.	Durbin-Watson coefficient for first-order serial correlation	2.0	2.0	2.0	2.0	1.9

– Standard errors are printed below each coefficient
– lags (in quarters) are indicated after the corresponding coefficient.

Table 5.5 Long-term interest rates in four European countries, 1971-I to 1982-II.

Dependent variable:
Δi_b: long-term government bond yield

Explanatory variables:		CH	B	A	DK
c	constant term	-.027 (.054)	.083 (.055)	.041 (.070)	.100 (.148)
$\Delta\hat{p}^e_{+1}$	expected rate of inflation	.103 (.046)	.058 (.054)		
Δi_{US}	long-term yield in the U.S.	.108 (.077)	.250 (.120)		.317 (.276)
Δi_G	long-term yield in Germany	.276 (.077)	.165 (.102)	.185 (.084)	
$\Delta\hat{M}^e_{+1}$	expected rate of growth of the money stock	-.0070(-1) (.0076)			-.040(-1) (.019)
ΔDef	deficit as a proportion of gnp				.353(-1) (.283)
Trade^{ue}	unexpected changes in world trade				
Poil^{ue}	unexpected changes in energy prices	.00077(-1) (.00045)			.030(-0.5) (.016)
$\Delta\sigma_{trade}$	index of uncertainty with respect to world trade		.029 (.013)		
ϱ	Cochrane-Orcutt parameter for first-order serial correlation	.326 (.141)	.166 (.147)	.391 (.137)	-.176 (.147)
R^2	percentage of variation explained	.57	.43	.28	.19
S.E.E.	standard error of estimate	.235	.287	.287	.897
D.W.	Durbin-Watson coefficient for first-order serial correlation	2.0	2.0	1.9	2.0

– Standard errors are printed below each coefficient
– lags (in quarters) are indicated after the corresponding coefficient.

Table 5.6 Long-term interest rates in four European countries, 1971-I to 1982-II.

Dependent variable:
Δi_b: long-term government bond yield

Explanatory variables:	CH	B	A	DK
c — constant term	-.017 (.078)	.089 (.072)	.034 (.080)	.146 (.145)
$\Delta\hat{p}^e_{+1}$ — expected rate of inflation	.111 (.052)	.132 (.073)	.056 (.081)	
Δr_{US} — long-term yield in the U.S.		.115 (.077)		
Δr_G — long-term yield in Germany	.197 (.082)	.135 (.106)	.123 (.088)	
$\Delta\hat{M}^e_{+1}$ — expected rate of growth of the money stock	-.0076(-1) (.0076)			-.037(-1) (.019)
ΔDef — deficit as proportion of gnp				.382(-1) (.286)
$Trade^{ue}$ — unexpected changes in world trade	.0087(-0.5) (.0061)			.034(0.5) (.016)
$Poil^{ue}$ — unexpected changes in energy prices	.00077(-1) (.00046)			
$\Delta\sigma_{trade}$ — index of uncertainty with respect to world trade		.020 (.011)		
ϱ — Cochrane-Orcutt parameter for first-order serial correlation	.503 (.129)	.358 (.139)	.440 (.134)	-.154 (.147)
R^2 — percentage of variation explained	.49	.37	.25	.17
S.E.E. — standard error of estimate	.257	.303	.296	.900
D.W. — Durbin-Watson coefficient for first-order serial correlation	2.0	2.1	2.0	2.0

– Standard errors are printed below each coefficient
– lags (in quarters) are indicated after the corresponding coefficient.

Table 5.7   Interest differentials vis-à-vis Germany, 1971-I to 1982-II.

Dependent variable: $\Delta i_b - \Delta i_{b,G}$		NL	CH	B	A	DK
Explanatory variables:						
c	constant term	-.015 (.052)	-.110 (.052)	.019 (.056)	-.053 (.059)	.097 (.144)
$\Delta i_{US} - \Delta i_G$	interest rate differential U.S. vis-à-vis Germany	.333 (.102)	.498 (.125)	.596 (.132)	.528 (.139)	.924 (.307)
ΔDef_G	German deficit as a proportion of gnp			-.058 (.051)	-.095 (.055)	-.247 (.129)
$\Delta \sigma_{M,G}$	index of monetary uncertainty in Germany		-.534 (.461)			
$Trade^{ue}$	unexpected changes in world trade		-.015(-0.5) (.007)	-.012(-0.5) (.007)	-.026(-0.5) (.008)	
$\Delta \sigma_{trade}$	index of uncertainty with respect to world trade		.022 (.016)	.046 (.017)	.025 (.018)	.048 (.043)
$\Delta \hat{M}^e_{+1}$	expected rate of domestic money growth				-.032(-1) (.014)	-.044(-1) (.019)
ΔDef	domestic deficit as a proportion of gnp	.029(-1) (.027)				
$Poil^{ue}$	unexpected changes in energy prices	.563(-2) (.354)	.00063(-1) (.00066)			
$\Delta \sigma_M$	index of domestic monetary uncertainty					
R^2	perc. of variation explained (corrected for degrees of freedom)	.25	.44	.42	.48	.22
S.E.E.	standard error of estimate	.342	.333	.361	.379	.931
D.W.	Durbin-Watson coefficient for first-order serial correlation	2.2	2.0	2.1	1.9	2.4

–   Standard errors are printed below each coefficient
–   lags (in quarters) are indicated after the corresponding coefficient.
–   In the case of Austria the change in expected money growth is set equal to zero in 1979-I and II

inflationary expectations. Figures 5.4 – 5.7 contain graphs of the long-term bond rate for all seven countries, and for the United States, Germany and Holland we also provide visual information about the main determinants of changes in long-term bond rates.

Table 5.2 contains five representative equations for changes in the long-term government bond yield in the U.S. Tables 5.3 and 5.4 refer to Germany and Holland respectively. Both to economize on space and because the results are less satisfactory, we present fewer equations for the remaining four countries. Switzerland, Belgium, Austria and Denmark are represented by one equation containing one or two nominal foreign interest rates as explanatory variables in table 5.5 and by an alternative equation with foreign real rates of interest instead of foreign nominal rates in table 5.6. Finally, table 5.7 shows equations for the differentials between long-term rates in the smaller European countries and in Germany ; we discuss this table separately below.

Our search for the "best" regression equations has been guided by the following principles :

- Generally explanatory variables were included in one or more of the alternative specifications, if they could reach a statistical significance level of 0.10 or above in at least one of the specifications. We have tried to present alternative specifications with and without certain marginal variables so as to enable the reader to draw his own inferences.

- Since all explanatory variables have either been constructed explicitly as first differences of random walks, or exhibit behaviour similar to that of a serially uncorrelated variable, multicollinearity is not much of a problem in general. A notable exception is the coefficient on changes in the expected rate of inflation in table 5.3 for the German long-term rate, which is very sensitive to whether a nominal or a real American rate is included in the equation. Similarly equations (3), (4) and (5) in table 5.4 for the Netherlands show that excluding long-term rates in the U.S. or Germany from this equation makes a difference to the coefficient of the other foreign interest rate and to the coefficient on the expected rate of domestic inflation in Holland, which becomes marginally significant only if both nominal foreign interest rates are omitted.

- We have included the current values only for the expected rate of inflation and the nominal or real foreign interest rates. With respect to all other explanatory variables some lagged effect has been allowed. Changes in the two indices for uncertainty, monetary uncertainty and

Figure 5.4   Long-term government bond yield in the U.S.

Karl Brunner and Allan Meltzer have maintained that monetary uncertainty did more to keep interest rates high in 1981-1982 than budget deficits. Our findings support their hypotheses

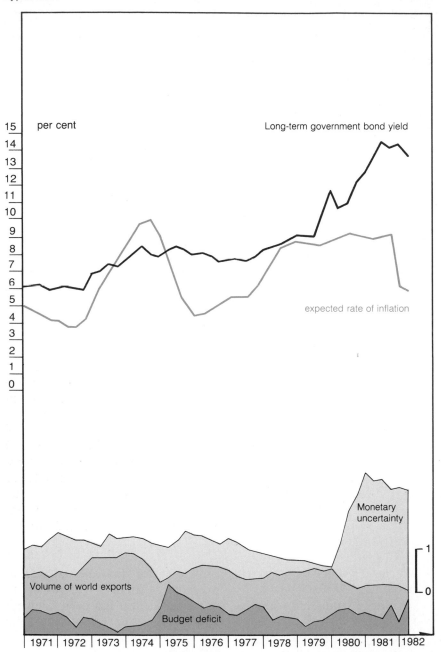

Figure 5.5   Long-term government bond yield in Germany
Changes in the volume of world trade together with changes in real U.S. rates are important
in Germany

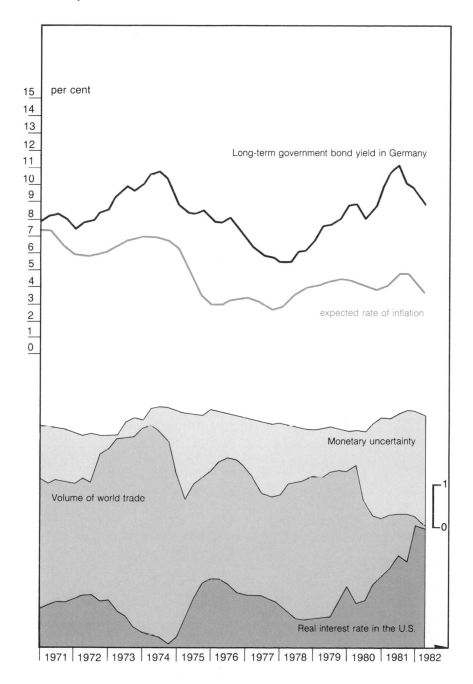

Figure 5.6   Long-term government bond yield in Holland

So far, Dutch long-term rates have stayed close to German rates and domestic Dutch factors have not been very important (but see table 5.7 for evidence about the influence of U.S. rates)

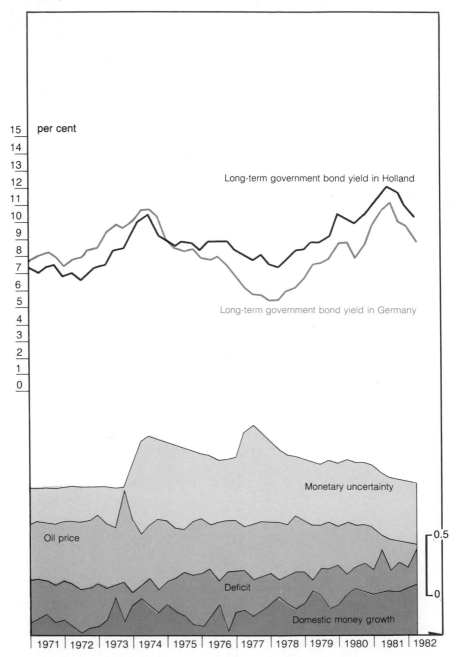

Figure 5.7   Long-term rates in four smaller countries

The synchronous peaks and troughs in 1974 III/IV and in the second half of 1978 underline the importance of German rates for interest rates in the smaller economies

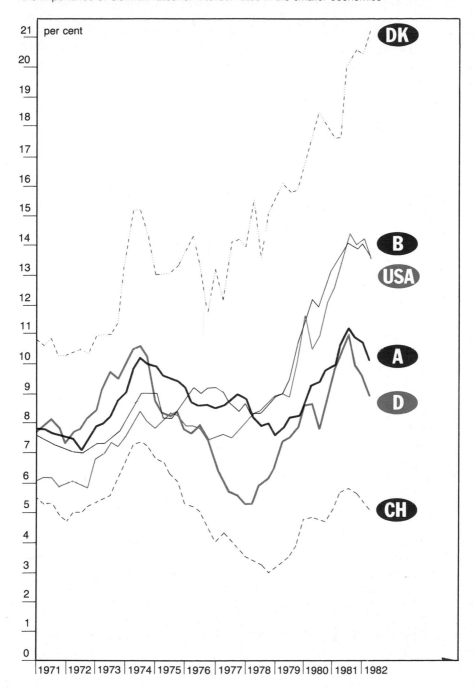

uncertainty regarding the volume of world trade, were included either current, or lagged one and two quarters. The current value of these indices incorporates all the news about the current quarter, and can thus be computed only after the correct value for money growth or world trade in the current quarter has been observed. We do not know whether the adaptively computed estimates of uncertainty properly reflect the learning that must go on in reality with respect to the degree of macroeconomic uncertainty. In view of the experimental character of the indices for uncertainty, we have allowed for slightly longer lags than elsewhere. Changes in the indices for uncertainty with respect to budget deficits and energy prices were tested also both in current form, and delayed one or two quarters, but did not contribute significantly to explaining interest rates.

• All remaining explanatory variables were included either currently, or lagged one quarter, or as the average of the current and once-lagged observations. The notation (-0.5) refers to this intermediate case.

• All regression equations in tables $5.2 - 5.6$ have been estimated with a Cochrane-Orcutt parameter for first-order serial correlation in the residuals. Many of these equations contain the expected rate of inflation as an explanatory variable and since we have preferred the smoothed index for the regressions, a moderate amount of positive serial correlation may have crept into the equations. The regressions in table 5.7 do not include expected rates of inflation among the explanatory variables ; for these alternative regressions we have omitted the Cochrane-Orcutt parameter. Our use of period averages may have caused also some serial correlation, but the results suggest that serial correlation in the residuals – if it occurred – had economic rather than statistical causes. The Cochrane-Orcutt parameter is never significant in the equations for the U.S., Germany or Holland, but often reaches significance at the 0.05 level in the four smaller countries. The behaviour of long-term interest rates in these smaller markets apparently can deviate more from the random-walk model.

Three separate figures illustrate our findings for the U.S., Germany, and Holland, the countries where our statistical research has been most satisfactory. The top panel of figure 5.4 shows the nominal long-term rate on government bonds (constant 20-year maturity) in the U.S. together with our smoothed index of expected inflation over the coming 3 months. As noted above, the influence of changes in expected inflation on nominal interest rates depends both on the term to maturity of the asset and on the way in which expected inflation is measured. Our estimate of approximately 0.2 for the smoothed measure of expected inflation corresponds to the findings of Mascaro and Meltzer, but may still be much too low because of the poor quality of our index for expected inflation.

The figure shows that the lows of expected inflation in 1972III and 1976I were slightly in advance of corresponding lows in the nominal interest rate. A meaningful comparison between the dates of the peak in expected inflation in 1974IV and the peak in interest rates in 1975III probably is less insightful because of the important temporary effects of changing energy prices on economic activity and the price level. Our smoothed index of expected inflation stays high until the beginning of 1982, so that the ex-ante real rate of interest reaches its maximum value near the end of the period under review.

The lower panel of figure 5.4 indicates the contribution of changes in three important explanatory variables to interest rate changes in the U.S. The effects of budget deficits, the world business cycle, and monetary uncertainty have been drawn on the same scale, so that the reader may compare their relative importance according to the first equation in table 5.2. Disregarding the sensitivity of the real rate of interest to changes in expected inflation, hard to measure on the basis of an 11-year long sample period, the biggest single shock to the long-term rate was caused by the increase in monetary uncertainty during 1980-1981. Less important, but clearly significant according to normal statistical criteria, were the changes in budget deficits. As in the case of expected inflation, the estimated coefficient may be too low as an indicator of the true impact of a permanent rise in the budget deficit, mainly because so little is known about the way economic subjects interpret changing budget deficits as signals of higher or lower future burdens of the national debt.

For figure 5.5 relating to the long-term government bond rate in Germany, we have chosen equation (5) in table 5.3. The top panel of the figure shows the nominal German rate together with our measure of expected inflation in Germany. The estimate of the coefficient on the expected rate of inflation equals 0.69 with a fairly wide standard error, so that we cannot reject the hypothesis that changes in expected inflation have a one-to-one effect on German long-term rates. We have been unable to understand why the coefficient on expected inflation in Germany is more than three times as large as the coefficient on the corresponding variable in our equations for the U.S. All our indices for expected inflation have been computed in exactly the same manner, but only in the case of Germany do changes in expected inflation appear to have almost a one-to-one effect on long-term interest rates.

Three explanatory variables are depicted in the bottom panel of figure

5.5 : the real rate of interest in the U.S., the world business cycle as measured by our random-walk type cumulated index for world exports, and monetary uncertainty in Germany. In the regression equation the variable for monetary uncertainty is significant at approximately the 0.10 level, but the real rate in the U.S. and the state of the world business cycle are clearly significant at high levels. Each of the latter two variables contributes to explaining major movements in German long-term rates, with the 1973 surge in world trade explaining much of the rise in German real rates during 1973-74 and the high real rates in the United States during 1981-82 more than compensating for the depressed state of the world economy during the final quarters of our estimation period. The index for monetary uncertainty in Germany exhibits a range of approximately 0.7 percentage points after multiplication with its coefficient in equation (5) of table 5.3, so that changes in monetary uncertainty as measured by us were not a very important factor in explaining German long-term interest rates.

Finally, figure 5.6 illustrates the findings of equation (4) in table 5.4 for the long-term interest rate on government bonds in the Netherlands. The upper panel of figure 5.6 indicates the high cohesion between long-term rates in Holland and Germany. Both rates peaked in 1974III, reached lows in the first half of 1978 and climbed to a new peak in 1981III.

In the illustrated regression equation, the coefficient on changes in the German rate equals 0.74, but we assume that the exact value of this coefficient depends on the precise specification of the relationship between German and Dutch rates. Somewhat different values are likely to be found if we replicate the research with end-of-quarter data instead of our quarterly averages, or if different periods are used. As long as the guilder remains closely tied to the D-mark, both in the short-term and over the longer run, the impact of changes in German rates on Dutch interest rates is bound to remain very substantial.

The lower part of figure 5.6 illustrates the scaled contributions of the four remaining explanatory variables in equation (4) of table 5.4. The regression shows that changes in underlying money growth, news about budget deficits and changes in monetary uncertainty were statistically significant at the 0.10 level whereas unexpected changes in energy prices had a weak and ill-determined effect on Dutch interest rates. None of the potential explanatory factors was of major importance in explaining those changes in Dutch interest rates not yet accounted for by changes in the German rate.

Tables 5.2–5.6 offer alternative specifications for the three countries depicted in these figures, and also for changes in long-term rates in Switzerland, Belgium, Austria and Denmark. Comparison of tables 5.5

and 5.6 shows that interest rates in the smaller countries can be somewhat better explained if nominal foreign interest rates are included among the explanatory variables than if real foreign rates are used. The coefficients on the nominal foreign rates are generally somewhat more significant.

Table 5.7 shows our preferred equation for each of the five smaller countries when we assume a priori that the domestic long-term rate in each small country goes up by 100 basis points if long-term rates in both the U.S. and West-Germany increase by a like amount. Since our "free" estimate of the effect of an equal increase in U.S. and German rates on the Dutch long-term bond rate was over 0.8, it stands to reason that the regression equation for the Netherlands in table 5.7 is as good as any of the equations in table 5.4.

The regressions show how important changes in U.S. interest rates are for the interest rate differential between Holland and Germany. If American rates go up with respect to German rates, then Dutch rates will have a tendency to rise above their German equivalents. Over the period 1971-1982 changes in U.S. rates over German rates had greater explanatory power for explaining the differences between German and Dutch rates than domestic Dutch (or German) developments.

For Switzerland, Belgium and Austria it is more doubtful to assume that domestic long-term rates incorporate fully any simultaneous increases in U.S. and German rates. Long-term rates in these three countries appear to move more independently from any weighted average of U.S. and German rates than long-term rates in the Netherlands.

The negative coefficients in table 5.7 for the index of the world business cycle confirm our earlier finding that if long-term rates in Germany increase because a boom in German exports increases competition for funds in the German capital market, rates in Switzerland, Belgium and Austria do not follow in step. Dutch long-term rates, by contrast, appear to be as susceptible to the state of world exports as German rates. Regrettably, we can say little of interest about interest rates in Denmark, since the regressions explain so little. Changes in American interest rates appear to be more important than German interest rates, and monetary expansion has a very modest negative effect on Danish long-term rates.

The Durbin-Watson coefficients for first-order serial correlation show that none of the equations in table 5.7 suffers from long strings of positive and negative residuals. Since all the constructed explanatory variables behave like random walks, and it is equally safe to assume that the interest rate differential between the U.S. and Germany behaves like a random walk also, it follows that the interest differentials between domestic long-term rates in the five smaller countries and Germany are like random walks also. This conclusion is particularly relevant for the Dutch interest rate, since the prominent influence of German interest rates on Dutch rates means that forecasts for Dutch rates are often made conditional on forecasts for German rates. Within such a context, the neutral assumption regarding the interest rates differential between Holland and Germany is one of no change, rather than a reversal to some "normal" long-term average.

Interesting also is the confirmation of the earlier finding that quarterly changes in (seasonally adjusted) budget deficits bear no easily discernible relationship to contemporaneous changes in long-term interest rates. We are unable to identify a direct "flow" effect running from greater thirst for funds from the collective sector to higher long-term rates. The reader should recall, however, that the link between measured deficits and long-term prospective ratio's between government debt and other assets is tenuous, that perhaps we should have attempted to correct the deficits for cyclical influences and that there may be connections between deficits and either money creation or monetary uncertainty, both variables that are included in their own right.

The statistical research suggests quite strongly that monetary uncertainty has become a major influence on long-term interest rates. Figure 5.4 showed how the sharp increase in the U.S. index for monetary uncertainty in 1980 and 1981 contributed slightly more than 2 percentage points to the rise in the real interest rates, taking the effects of the surge in the index between its low in 1980I and its maximum in 1981I. The average level of the long-term government bond yield in the U.S. over the period 1980IV – 1982II was approximately 1¼ percentage points higher than the average for 1971 – 1976 due to this increase in monetary uncertainty. Our estimates are very similar to the findings of Mascaro and Meltzer (1983) who employed a ten-year bond rate instead of our twenty-year rate and computed their index of uncertainty regarding the growth rate of M1 in a different way.

Changes in the index for inflationary uncertainty, a measure of variability of the constructed time series for expected inflation, never were significant in the U.S. regressions. It appears that variability in the quarterly underlying growth rates of the money supply provides more insight in the uncertainty regarding long-term inflationary expectations than the variablility of short-term inflation forecasts as computed in chapter 4.

If most changes in the underlying rate of growth of the money supply are of a permanent nature – as hypothesized in chapter 4 – whereas the actual and expected rates of inflation are subject to many transitory influences over the short-term, then the finding that increases in monetary uncertainty have greater effects on long-term interest rates is not surprising. The only country where changes in inflationary uncertainty were slightly more useful in the regressions than changes in monetary uncertainty was Holland, where the first difference of the computed index of inflationary uncertainty achieves a t-statistic of 2.27 if it replaces the index of monetary uncertainty (t-statistic 1.76) in equation (1) of table 5.4. Because of the near universal inferiority of the index for inflationary uncertainty, we have preferred to use the index of monetary uncertainty to represent long-term inflationary risks. In what follows we limit ourselves, therefore, to discussion of the coefficients on monetary uncertainty. In a similar vein Mascaro and Meltzer (1983) find that changes in their index of monetary uncertainty perform better in the interest rate regressions than combinations of monetary uncertainty and uncertainty about the growth rate of the income velocity of money.

The effects of increased monetary uncertainty on long-term interest rates in Germany are hard to assess, since the coefficient on our index is determined with less precision (highest t-value 1.62 in equation (5) of table 5.3 which is almost significant at the 0.10 level). The recent increase in the index between 1980III and 1981IV could have contributed approximately 0.5 percentage points to the long-term German rate of interest.

Nowhere does our index for monetary uncertainty increase as dramatically as in Switzerland. The Swiss experience in 1978 has been discussed in section 2.5 ; here it is sufficient to note that we could not find an impact of monetary uncertainty in Switzerland – at least as measured by our index – on Swiss long-term rates of interest.

Domestic monetary uncertainty played a modest part perhaps in Holland, where changes in the index are statistically significant at the 0.10 level in some regressions. Nowhere, however, does this variable achieve the statistical significance which it obtains in the U.S. One can argue, therefore, that the index of monetary uncertainty happens to fit the U.S. data well, but that the index represents much more than just monetary uncertainty. Other risk factors increased also in the early 1980's and uncertainty about future rates of inflation is but one element of the uncertain outlook for long-term bonds. More research will be needed to elucidate this issue ; in the next section we shall stress how difficult it is to measure budgetary uncertainty in an adequate manner and the same may be true for other kinds of macroeconomic uncertainty. Nevertheless, the present research at least does not disprove that monetary uncertainty has been an important cause of high real interest rates in the early 1980's.

5.4 Interest rates and budget deficits.

We have tested for all seven countries whether increases in the government budget deficit as a portion of gnp have an immediate upward effect on long-term rates of interest. Instead of inserting the actual quarterly changes in the deficits as a potential explanatory variable, we computed seasonally adjusted series for expenditures and revenues of the government sector and employed the differences of these two adjusted series. One can make a case for taking out not only the seasonal fluctuations but also the cyclical influences on expenditures and revenues. Especially in the U.S., economists have tried to construct a "full employment deficit", a hypothetical measure of the deficit after correction for the fact that expenditures will be higher and revenues from taxation lower if the economy operates at less than economic capacity. Such cyclical adjustments are not hard to execute if a consensus exists about the normal rate of economic growth and the economy oscillates around this well-defined trend line. After the first oil price crisis of 1973-74 economists have become much more uncertain about economic growth (see Tatom, 1979, Rasche and Tatom, 1977). In addition, the thorough extensions of the welfare state have altered the working of the labour market, both on the supply side where disability pensions or unemployment benefits make out much higher fractions of blue-collar wages than before, and on the demand side where firms have witnessed sharp increases in the real cost of labour, so that old estimates of "full employment" based on a leaner labour market no longer apply. We have declined to correct the deficit numbers for cyclical influences because of these uncertainties regarding long-term growth and "full employment", but this negative decision has equally left us with an imperfect signal of the likely future proportion of long-term government bonds in the aggregate portfolio.

Measured after separate seasonal adjustment of expenditures and revenues, but without adjustment for cyclical variation, the deficits are important only in the case of the U.S., where they are statistically significant at the 0.05 level. According to the estimate of equation (1) in table 5.2 the deficits contributed almost 1 percentage point to the increase in interest rates between 1973 and 1975, and added approximately ½ percentage points to the long-term rate between 1979 and 1982II. The severe measurement problems relating to the use of quarter-to-quarter changes in the seasonally adjusted deficit as an indicator of the long-term abundance of nominal debt suggest that the estimates are biased towards zero, and that the true impact of a permanently higher budget deficit on long-term interest rates is somewhat higher.

Comparing the importance of the two financial variables, monetary uncertainty on the one hand and budget deficits on the other, our results suggest that monetary uncertainty contributed far more to the high U.S. interest rates of the early 1980's than the measured budget deficits.

Changes in the budget deficit contribute slightly to an explanation of German long-term rates but the coefficient is three times smaller than in the U.S. and not significant statistically. The coefficient has a similar modest size in the equations for Holland, but its statistical significance is rather larger (best t-value 1.64 which is significant at the 0.1 level). Other research on Dutch long-term interest rates for slightly different periods resulted in much higher effects of growing deficits on long-term rates. All such estimates, including our own, are highly uncertain, in part due to measurement problems, but more fundamentally since the link between budget deficits and real long-term rates is an indirect one in our view. High deficits signal a preponderance of nominal debt in the future portfolio, but the reliability of this signalling function depends on assumptions about future economic growth, inflation and government expenditure. Since the link between deficits and real interest rates is so hard to measure from time series for a single country, it is not surprising that many popular discussions of this issue rely on informal cross-country comparisons.

Long-term rates in Switzerland, for example, have been below the corresponding German rates for the past ten years and many commentators regard the virtuous Swiss budgetary policy as one of the reasons. Similarly, the high levels of Danish and Belgian long-term rates are attributed in large part to the debt explosions in these countries. Figure 5.7 confirms that long-term rates are highest in those countries where the ratio of government debt to national income has risen most. A formal cross-country analysis would require a precise theory about exchange rates, incorporating assumptions about the international diversification of risk. In this area much work remains to be done.

For the sake of completeness we have experimented with two alternative measures of the deficit-to-income ratio. Instead of the actual ratio we inserted a Kalman filter estimate of the expected level of the deficit-to-income proportion. Since the deficit as a proportion of national income moved approximately as a random walk during the period under review, this substitution made no significant difference to the equations for interest rates. Our second alternative measure was a smoothed estimate of the deficit-to-income ratio.

The smoothing operation with the cubic spline functions (see section 4.4 above) does make a difference to the results. We discuss the different countries in the order of tables 5.2 – 5.7 :

- U.S. – in the specification of equation (1) of table 5.2, the coefficient on the deficit increases from 0.17 to 0.24 after smoothing, but its standard error goes up at the same time from 0.07 to 0.13.

- Germany – in equation (3) of table 5.3 the deficit variable becomes completely insignificant after smoothing.

- Netherlands – in equation (1) of table 5.4 for the Dutch bond rate the deficit variable drops out after smoothing.

- Switzerland – the smooth version of the deficit-to-income ratio (lagged one quarter) features with a coefficient of 0.29 (standard error 0.19) in the equation for Swiss long-term rates, where the unsmoothed variable for the deficit proved insignificant. The coefficient of determination in the Swiss equation increases to 0.60, the Cochrane-Orcutt parameter goes down to 0.30 and none of the other coefficients in the equation is adversely affected.

- Belgium – smoothing makes the deficit-to-income ratio also a useful variable for explaining long-term rates in Belgium. The coefficient on the smoothed variable (lagged one quarter) is 0.29 with a standard error of 0.15. With the help of the smoothed variable for the deficit, the fit of the Belgian equation increases from 0.43 to 0.48, and the Cochrane-Orcutt parameter decreases to 0.14. The coefficient on changes in the American long-term rate goes down to 0.18 from 0.25 ; the other coefficients in the equation are not affected significantly.

- Austria – no help from smoothing : the coefficient on the Austrian deficit remains insignificant.

- Denmark – in our preferred equation for the Danish interest rate, smoothing of the deficit variable increases its coefficient to 0.40 with a standard error of 0.32, so that its statistical significance remains as before.

Considering together the coefficient estimates for the original and the smoothed versions of the deficit variable, we note that these coefficients, if statistically significant at the 0.10 level or better, are concentrated in the range between approximately 0.2 and 0.4. A reasonable inference from our research would be that higher deficits do cause significant upward pressure on long-term interest rates, and that deficits to the order of 5-10 percent of national income increase long-term rates by some 100-200 basis points above where they would be if deficits did not increase beyond levels which can be sustained over the longer term.

5.5 Alternative measures of expected inflation.

As a check on our specifications we have searched also for the best interest rate regressions with the unsmoothed composite index of inflationary expectations instead of the smoothed index that was used in tables 5.2 – 5.6. This substitution does not greatly affect the size or statistical significance of the coefficients on the remaining explanatory variables, but since the tracking ability of the regressions decreases with the use of this rougher index of inflationary expectations, the outcomes are generally somewhat poorer. In the equations for the U.S., for example, the standard error on the coefficient for monetary uncertainty increases by approximately 10 % over the 2.4 – 2.5 range in table 5.2. In the equations for Germany the highest coefficient on the U.S. nominal rate now becomes .31 (standard error 0.13). In the remaining countries, changes in inflationary expectations as measaured by our smoothed index are not very important anyway, so that it makes little difference whether the smoothed or unsmoothed composite index is employed.

Smoothing the computed index for inflationary expectations does make an important difference to the computation of ex-ante real rates of interest. The smoothed series – used in tables 5.2 – 5.7 and in all the figures of this chapter – lead to quarterly series for real interest rates that vary much less from quarter to quarter than if the unsmoothed index is used. If the real rates of interest are computed with the unsmoothed series for inflationary expectations, they are nowhere significant in our regressions, by contrast to the outcomes in tables 5.2 – 5.6 where the U.S. real rate contributes significantly to explaining the German bond yield, the German real rate is highly significant in explaining Dutch and Swiss interest rates, long-term rates in Belgium may well depend on both U.S. and German real rates, and Austrian interest rates may be connected to the real rate in Germany also. None of these channels can be made visible if the real rates in the U.S. and Germany respectively are measured with an unsmoothed estimate of expected future inflation. The finding suggests that the smoothing procedure based on cubic spline functions (see section 4.4) does enhance the informational value of the computed series for inflationary expectations and eliminates some of the severe measurement errors in the computed index. Admittedly the smoothing technique introduces an ex-post element in the representation of expected inflation, but the superior functioning of the smoothed estimates in our regressions, both as a direct explanatory variable and through an indirect presence in the computed series for real interest rates, makes us prefer the smoothed versions.

As a further alternative, we have estimated regression equations for Germany, Holland, Belgium and Denmark, with a survey measure of real-life inflationary expectations instead of our computed index of expected future inflation. The European Economic Community coordinates consumer surveys in the member countries, which include questions about current inflation and about the likely trend in the aggregate price level over the next twelve months. The respondents are not asked to provide numerical answers, but have to choose one out of five possible answers to the question about current and future price trends : more rapid increase (+1), same increase (+½), slower increase (0), stability (−½), fall slightly (−1). Three times each year the EEC publishes the average responses for each country in the form of numbers between −100 and +100 ; we have used these series as basis for our alternative computations.

First, we substract the index number for the current rate of inflation from the index for the expected rate of inflation over the next twelve months. This difference between predicted and perceived inflation, multiplied by the actual rate of price change over the most recent year, serves as explanatory variable in regressions for the difference between the actual rate of price change over the next year and the observed rate of inflation over the most recent twelve months. We perform three regressions : one for the January survey data in Germany, Holland, Belgium and Denmark, one for all the May data and one for the October observations. Taking the average of the three regression coefficients, we then compute numerical estimates of the expected rates of inflation over the next twelve months and transform these numbers into quarterly average data.

Introducing the survey-based measure of inflationary expectations in our regressions for long-term interest rates produces poor results that are very similar to the outcomes when the unsmoothed computed index is used. In Germany the coefficient on the expected rate of inflation reaches a value of 0.07 (standard error 0.10) in the specification of equation (2) in table 5.3. In all other instances the coefficient is either positive, but even less statistically significant, or insignificant and negatively signed. However, the regressions were only executed for the period 1974II − 1982II, because the first observation for Belgium relates to May 1974 (data for Germany, Holland are available from October 1973 onwards ; the series for Denmark begins in January 1974). It is worth nothing that the survey-based index of inflationary expectations is significantly related to our computed composite index, as shown by the coefficients of determination for a simple regression of changes in the computed index on changes in the survey based index. On average, approximately 25 % of the variation in our computed index could be explained by changes in the survey measure. We have noted by how much the contribution of changes in inflationary expectations to an explanation of changes in long-term interest rates improves if we apply a smoothing procedure to the series for expected inflation ; it is possible that more refined statistical operations on the survey data – for which longer stretches of data should be required – will result in a greater role for the survey index as well.

5.6 Conclusions

Fresh evidence has been presented in this chapter for one as yet controversial channel through which the course of the money supply can affect long-term rates of interest : if the authorities create greater monetary uncertainty, risk premia in long-term rates may increase. A steady and predictable policy of lower rates of money growth, by contrast, contributes to keeping the risk premium for monetary uncertainty low. Our estimates confirm the earlier results of Mascaro and Meltzer, who found that extreme monetary uncertainty in the early 1980's added something to the order of 2 percentage points to long-term rates in the U.S. Nevertheless, contributing a substantial part of the high real rates in 1981 – 1982 to monetary uncertainty remains controversial since there are at least four alternative hypotheses. Our research obviously is far from definitive, but provides at least some additional evidence regarding the relevance of the following theories why real U.S. rates were high in the early 1980's :

- *Government deficits keep real rates in the U.S. high.* We discussed this hypothesis in section 5.4, and concluded that it receives little support from our comparative work on seven developed economies.
  However, our estimates for the influence of budget deficits may well be too low because of conceptual and measurement problems.

- *A liquidity crunch of unprecedented severity has driven real rates to record levels.* The hypothesis that U.S. monetary policy simply became extremely restrictive in 1980 so that extreme real rates of interest were required to equilibrate the macroeconomic demand for money gets minimal support from our statistical work. More importantly, it appears without support from the facts, because intermittent periods of very high money growth kept the longer-term average growth rate of M1 at a level not far below its trend over the late 1970's. Between 1979IV and 1982II, for example, the narrow money supply increased at a 6.3 percentage annual rate, as compared to an 8.2 % annual rate of growth between 1976III and 1979III. In our view, the key characteristic of U.S. monetary policy since 1979IV has been unpredictability rather than severity.

● *Real rates of interest decline when unexpected inflation increases so that real rates have to go up if inflation comes down.* To investigate this hypothesis, we can consider the coefficient of the expected rates of inflation in equations for nominal rates of interest. Table 5.1 indicates that the coefficient is generally unity in equations for short-term rates, but declines considerably for longer-term interest rates. Wilcox (1983) finds a coefficient of 1.0 for a one-year rate, and the work by Mascaro and Meltzer as well as our own points to a coefficient in the vicinity of 0.2 for 10 and 20 year terms-to-maturity respectively. The question is : how much of this effect is due to the mis-match between a 10- or 20-year interest rate and a measure of the expected rate of inflation over the following quarter or year, and how much is the true negative dependence of the real ex-ante rate of interest on the expected rate of inflation over the term of the bond ? As discussed in section 5.1 our data base is much too short and limited to solve this issue. Quite possibly, the expected rate of inflation over the next ten or twenty years does not behave like the pure random walk we have supposed it to be ; but even if an increase in the one-year rate of inflation does not translate fully into a similar rise in the expected rate of inflation over the long-term, because people still assume that bad news about inflation is somehow temporary and will be followed by more cheerful developments, it would be an unwise government that attempted to use inflation as a deliberate instrument to reduce real rates of interest. Such a policy is bound to increase monetary uncertainty which by itself puts upward pressure on real rates, and who knows for how long people will continue to believe that today's league of moderate-inflation countries will never see some of its members downgraded ?

● *Finally, risk premia may indeed have been the main reason for high real rates in the U.S., but uncertainty about future inflation was not the main worry for investors.* Two other sources of uncertainty which potentially merit a risk premium in the long-term rate proved insignificant in our analysis : neither budgetary uncertainty, nor uncertainty about the world business cycle helped to explain the rise in long-term U.S. rates. Time will show whether the hypothesized relationship between variability in the rate of money growth and real long-term rates holds outside our sample period.

chapter 6

Can big computer models forecast long-term rates?

"The experience of the past ten years, however, has revealed serious flaws in standard macro theory shaped by the Keynesian tradition. Keynesian theory did not present adequately the working of fiscal or monetary policy and neglected the interaction between the two sets of policies. The role of expectations was barely recognized, and important channels linking shifting policy patterns with capital markets or price behavior on output markets were neglected also. All this does not establish the bankruptcy of macroeconomics, but means that macroeconomics moves beyond the Keynesian phase of the 1950s and 1960s."

uit : Karl Brunner and Allan H. Meltzer, "The problem of inflation", in : Karl Brunner and Allan H. Meltzer (eds.) :"The problem of inflation", Carnegie-Rochester Conference Series on Public Policy, Volume 8, Amsterdam North-Holland 1978, p. 2.

"New talent is not attracted to refining and developing Keynesian economics. This is what we mean by the "death" of a scientific idea."

uit : Robert E. Lucas Jr. "The death of Keynes", in : Thomas J. Hailstones "Viewpoints on supply-side economics", Richmond, Robert F. Dame, Inc. 1982, p. 5.

6.1 Big is blemished

During the 1970's a remarkable trend became visible in economics that ran counter to normal developments in other sciences. Economic researchers started using more and more simple techniques to investigate the outstanding issues in macroeconomics. Thus, at a time when ever larger computer models or laboratory installations were ordered by scientists in other fields, a seemingly retrograde movement occurred in economics. Back-of-the-envelope calculations once again could vie for attention with the large-scale econometric computer models. When, in the winter of 1974, an aide to President Gerald Ford asked Arthur Laffer to explain his supply-side theory, a paper napkin was sufficient for the single parabola that said it all. This legendary example may be extreme, but there is no doubt that the large econometric models are no longer the arbiters of different economic theories they used to be until the early 1970's.

Perusal of the academic journals on economics shows how little impact the large-scale econometric models make on the course of current professional research. The last twelve months' issues of the 'Journal of Monetary Economics', for example, contain one sole article out of over forty published which reports on research done with a large econometric model, developed at the Board of Governors of the Federal Reserve in Washington. Some other articles report work with systems comprising 5–10 estimated statistical equations, but the great majority of the research reports in this leading journal rely on small systems with 1–5 different equations. The articles relate to current debates on economic policy: What were the effects of the oil price shocks of the 1970's on inflation, economic growth and exchange rates? Can expansionary monetary policy reduce unemployment? How does U.S. monetary policy influence foreign interest rates? Are budget deficits ominous for future inflation? How important are the weekly M1 numbers in the U.S.? Illumination of these and similar questions does not require reference to the large econometric models, although the operators of the large models have their numerical answers to such questions. Ten years ago, by contrast, the professional academic journals reported extensively on the outcomes of policy experiments with large-scale econometric models.

Many of the highlights in the debate on 'crowding out', for example, consisted of elaborate simulation experiments with large econometric models which were relied upon to provide information about the question of how much of a fiscal stimulus occurs at the expense of private investment. What happened in this type of research was that the analyst took one of the major computer models, implemented a change to a more expansionary fiscal policy and studied the subsequent behaviour of interest rates and investment, as provided by the computer print-out.

Such experiments were, of course, highly hypothetical and could never be

definitive, since in the real world one cannot observe the effects of an increase in government expenditure in isolation from the innumerable other
shocks that impinge incessantly on a real-life economy. Economists do not
have at their disposal a laboratory in which controlled experiments can be
conducted in the absence of other disturbances. Nevertheless, if a number
of simulation studies with different econometric models led to comparable
results, this was widely regarded as reliable evidence with respect to the real
economy. Often, the enthousiastic econometricians tended to forget that all
the large models were constructed on the same methodological principles,
so that evidence from one model could not really qualify as an independent
corroboration of the outcomes of some other model. One of the few experts
to voice a strong warning was Allan H. Meltzer:

> 'There does not seem to be very much difference between being a lit-
> erary economist and having the prior beliefs in one's head or being an
> econometrician and having the prior beliefs written down in the form
> of four hundred equations'...
>
> Meltzer concluded by claiming that Klein's and Modigliani's models
> represent largely, if not completely, a denial of the scientific procedure
> of evaluation.'

in: Karl Brunner (editor) 'Problems and Issues in current econometric practice,' College of Administrative
Science, the Ohio State University, Columbus, 1972,
p. 282.

Meltzer's warning went unheeded at the time, and he, together with Karl
Brunner and Milton Friedman (all monetary economists) belonged to a
small minority that remained sceptical vis-à-vis the large econometric
models. The majority of the profession, however, regarded simulation experiments with large computer models as admissible evidence on how the
real economy works, and was scornful of the much more modest computations that were performed in the monetarist camp.

The controversy about the 'St. Louis equation' illustrated the once influential position of the large-scale models. In November 1968 two researchers
at the Federal Reserve Bank of St. Louis published a statistical relationship
that predicted nominal national income in the U.S. on the basis of earlier
values for the money stock (M1) and different measures of fiscal policy.
Leonall Andersen and Jerry Jordan found that changes in the money stock
have substantial predictive power in foreshadowing changes in national income, whereas changes in government expenditure or taxes – for a given
path of the money supply – have short-term effects that dissipate over the
longer run. The relative impotency of fiscal policy ran counter to the major-

ity view at that time, which was based on Keynesian-type analysis of the income-expenditure flows and had received clear support from the large-scale econometric models. Quite a few contributions to the ensuing scholarly debate consisted simply of repeated policy simulations with large-scale models as if such evidence was sufficiently strong to settle the issues. One of the first commentators on the Andersen-Jordan piece, for example, wrote:

'The first thing I want to note about the St. Louis equation is that it portrays a world in several respects *sharply at variance with the expectations of most of us*...The fiscal multipliers are virtually zero... At no point do these multipliers rise above unity, and after four quarters they have returned essentially to zero. Multipliers taken from the recent Federal Reserve Board staff-Massachusetts Institute of Technology structural econometric model..., by contrast, *correspond roughly* to expectations, rising to over 3 after a year.'

> Richard G. Davis, How much does money matter? A look at some recent evidence in: Monetary Economics, Readings on Current Issues, William E. Gibson and George G. Kaufman, McGraw-Hill, Inc. U.S., 1971, p. 134-135.

Two other prominent academics concluded a critical analysis of the St. Louis study by suggesting:

'We would like, in conclusion, to encourage the use of the Federal Reserve-MIT model as a framework for resolving these puzzling differences among estimates of monetary and fiscal policy effects.'

> Frank de Leeuw, Edward M. Gramlich, 'The channels of monetary policy' in: Monetary Economics, Readings on Current Issues, William E. Gibson and George G. Kaufman, McGraw-Hill, Inc. U.S., 1971, p. 167.

The findings of a single equation had to be less reliable than the simulation results with models containing hundreds of equations, at least according to the majority view.

The main reason why confidence in the large-scale econometric models is much less today than it was ten years ago is the large gap between predictions of the models and the reality of the 1970's.

'As recently as 1970, the major U.S. econometric models implied that expansionary monetary and fiscal policies leading to a sustained infla-

tion of about 4 per cent per annum would lead also to sustained unemployment rates of less than 4 per cent, or about a full percentage
point lower than unemployment has averaged during any long period
of U.S. history. These forecasts were widely endorsed by many economists not themselves closely involved in econometric forecasting.
Earlier, Friedman and Phelps had argued, purely on the basis of the
observation that *equilibrium* behavior is invariant under the units
change represented by sustained inflation, that *no* sustained decrease
in unemployment would result from sustained inflation. In this instance, the policy experiment in question was, most unfortunately, carried out, and its outcome is now too clear to require detailed review.'

> Robert E. Lucas Jr., Understanding Business Cycles
> in: Carnegie-Rochester Conference Series on Public
> Policy, Volume 5, Amsterdam 1977, pp. 7–29 (foot-
> notes omitted in the quotation).

Lucas does not criticize the models for lack of success in short-term forecasting. A poor forecasting record does not necessarily reflect adversely on
the economic competence of the forecasting organization, but may be due
simply to surprising changes in policy at home or abroad that were unforeseeable when the forecast was made. The argument works in the opposite
direction also: the much-noted improvement in short-term ability to forecast
during the 1960's took place at a time of fixed exchange rates, stable (since
1956–57) energy prices and moderate business cycles, factors that make
macroeconomic forecasting easier. At the time the proprietors of the large-
scale models credited the improvements in forecasting technology to ever
larger models and longer stretches of historical data; in 1983 they are more
modest when reflecting on another year of poor predictions in 1982:

'I've been forecasting 15 years, and last year was the worst.'

> Lawrence Chimerine, chairman of Chase Econome-
> trics, Wall Street Journal, February 21, 1983.

The senior vice-president at Data Resources, another of the big three forecasting firms in the U.S., admits that unexpected changes in policy do not
provide a complete excuse, but that the big computer models can be faulted
also:

'For two decades, we let businesses, the media and the public think
that models were perfect crystal balls. Well, they're not. And maybe
now we're paying the price.'

> idem.

Apportioning the blame for poor forecasts to erratic policies and defective computer models is a difficult matter, but a clear indictment is in order with respect to the policy advice given by the large-scale models. Lucas does not criticize the models for missing turns in the business cycle, but for being theoretically unsound. For example, in the quotation above, he recalls one glaring example: the built-in assumption that a moderate increase in inflation would permanently lower unemployment. Milton Friedman's opposing view (1968) was derived from the theoretical argument that systematic attempts to make money more plentiful relative to goods would indeed lower the value of money but remain without lasting effects on production and employment for which 'real' rather than 'nominal' things would have to change. Neither Friedman, nor Phelps (1968) took recourse to econometric models in support of their theoretical reasoning: it was an intellectual battle of man against machine and although the computer models were unanimous, history proved them wrong.

The computer models continue to play a role in the political debate on economic policy, as politicians will always be grateful for outside analyses supporting their positions. Econometric models are still used in support of facile policies aimed at painlessly reducing unemployment by way of nominal stimulus. Continuing political demands for scientific-looking evidence about questions of economic policy help the large models stay in business, but they seem to have lost their earlier impact on the scientific quest for economic knowledge. Experiments with the large-scale models are no longer considered by most academic researchers as admissible evidence regarding the true structure of the economy. The way of doing advanced research in economics has changed from technological complexity towards greater emphasis on clarity and consistency with well-established economic observations and principles. Whereas the large econometric models are built and maintained by teams of economists, statisticians and computer personnel, virtually all the innovative scientific research in economics is done by individual researchers who test their hypotheses in a much less grandiose, but – let us hope – more precise manner.

Faulty advice on economic policy caused much harm to the standing of the large-scale models. But equally crucial were two mutually connected developments in economic science. The search for a theoretically consistent explanation of the business cycle – initiated in 1970 by an influential book by Phelps et al. – called into question the Keynesian multiplier-accelerator mechanisms for neglecting many insights about the behaviour of business firms and individual consumers. Earlier emphasis on the multiplier-accelerator interaction had pushed the model builders towards more and more disaggregation of consumption and investment, but statistical modeling of the numerous channels between these components of total aggregate demand had always been very much ad hoc; the computer was free to determine the dynamic characteristics of the large-scale models according to the criterion of best possible 'fit' over some historical period. Changes in inventories acted with complicated time lags on investment, for example, and consumers changed expenditure patterns according to perceived changes in total income. Multitudes of mathematical equations connected the different sectors of the economy, but one could only hope that the complete computer model still made economic sense.

Most academic researchers became dissatisfied with this uncontrollable approach and went back to more basic investigations of the causes underlying the business cycle (see, for example, Lucas 1972, 1975, 1981). Macroeconomics started to look for a sound theoretical foundation in what is known about markets, business firms and individuals. As a consequence, the crumbling of the Keynesian multiplier-accelerator constructs coincided with much greater attention on the role of expectations about the future in determining economic behaviour, both in relation to the determination of business investment and with respect to price setting in financial markets. Since business investment must be determined by expected future profits, any econometric model that mechanically relates investment decisions to past changes in inventories, retained profits or other variables, must be suspect. In the same vein, computer models that predict with confidence how long-term interest rates will exhibit oscillating movements over time are hard-pressed to reconcile this view with the efficient financial market model where such nice foreseeable opportunities to make capital gains are automatically eliminated. Economists began to require that computer models of national economies not only satisfy statistical criteria of being able to trace the historical developments, but also be consistent with what we know about the importance of expectations and efficiency of markets:

- events that increase expected future profits should be positive for business investment, even if the multiplier-accelerator mechanism has not yet managed to digest the good news and to produce an increase in total demand;
- events that increase long-term rates of interest should very likely do so without delay, as systematic but gradual increases in long-term rates produce excessive total returns for bond holders and contradict the assumption that financial markets are efficient.

Requirements of this type are very hard to satisfy with large-scale econometric models of the current variety. A proper treatment of expectations regarding the future is feasible in small computer models such as those used in this book but has not yet proved possible for large-scale econometric models (see, for example, Bomhoff 1980, chapter 5). The great stress on the multiplier-accelerator mechanism with its call for maximum disaggregation means that good or bad news has to travel between the many equations of the model resulting in the oscillatory movements for many variables, including long-term interest rates, as are so typical of large-scale econometric models.

The major econometric models have parted ways with most academic researchers: the model builders make continuous adjustments to their jerry-built constructs but continue to rely on strongly disaggregated modelling of the multiplier-accelerator mechanism for producing economic dynamics, whereas the scientific journals report on research that investigates a few variables only but models their interactions with greater emphasis on the role of expectations and market efficiency. Admittedly, there have been occasions when the academic researchers overlooked problems of learning and adjustment that plagued the real-life economies during the troubled 1970's, so that their predictions were at least as far off the mark as those of the traditional econometric models; a real danger exists that theoretical purity leads to sterility. Nevertheless, the upkeep of the large-scale models has become so isolated from most active research in economics that their impact on the collective search for more insight into the way real economies behave is likely to remain minimal for some time to come.

In the remaining pages of this chapter I shall try to illustrate some of the points made above by way of a practical example. We shall see how the long internal lines of communication within the large-scale econometric models inhibit the correct dissemination of important economic news and contribute to curious dynamic characteristics. The discussion will help to put into perspective some informal evidence in section 6.3 regarding the interest rate forecasts of some large models. A short concluding section terminates this chapter.

6.2 How economic news journeys through a large econometric model: an example

Dinosaurs never were famous for their speedy reactions to changes in the environment: long internal lines of communication apparently prevented speedy transmission of sensory messages inside the giant animals. Problems of size also affect large-scale econometric models. They are best discussed by way of an example, for which purpose I shall use the most recent available macroeconometric model of the Dutch economy, published in April 1977. ('Een macro-model voor de Nederlandse economie op middellange termijn' Vintaf-II, Occasional Paper No. 12, Central Planning Bureau, The Hague, 1977). This annual model is not particularly large with 112 equations, but it serves to show the type of problem that arises from the attempt at large-scale modelling of the economy.

One of the pivotal equations in the model explains the volume of exports of Dutch goods. According to the formula, exports will increase in step with world trade, but the exact relationship depends on two other factors. One of these additional determinants is the ratio of average prices in the Dutch exporting sector to the average price level of Holland's international competitors. If Dutch exports become relatively cheaper, then the Dutch share in world imports will increase.

Assume, for example, that a sudden change in the foreign value of the guilder makes Dutch exports 5% more competitive in the international market-place. The devaluation will increase the prices of imported goods, but I abstract from that here. In this model, Dutch exports will eventually increase by an additional four percentage points, but the expansion in exports is not immediate. It takes approximately one year for the improvement in the competitive position to make its way into the volume of exports.

The surge in the Dutch exports will generate additional employment and income in the exporting sector of the economy. According to the model, increases in consumers' income are translated directly into higher consumption expenditures. It follows that the one-year delay between an improvement in the competitive position and the rise in exports is also a good estimate of the time lag between the initial devaluation and the induced rise in consumption.

Not only will consumption grow, the general buoyancy of the economy will cause an increase in business investment. Once again, a certain delay occurs, this time between the upsurge in the economy and the subsequent increase in business investment. The equation for business investment in the Dutch model tells us that this delay lasts on average 1 ½ years since average retained profits over the previous two years are one of the principal determinants of business investment in the current year.

Adding the time lag between good news about Dutch competitiveness and the subsequent increase in Dutch exports to the delay between the upturn of the economy and the induced increase in investment, results in an economic chain-letter that covers 2 ½ years. But that is not all. With exports, consumption, and investment all higher than before, capacity utilization in the economy will improve, with the usual consequences for wages and prices. Real wages will increase and put upward pressure on the price level, so that Dutch products become less competitive. Such secondary effects are bound to cause continuing fluctuations in investment, exports, consumption and other economic variables. Computer simulations with this econometric model of the Dutch economy do show indeed that investment and many other important economic magnitudes show slowly damped oscillations around their trends that last for more than ten years after some initial piece of good or bad news.

And why not, one might ask. Is it not possible that the jerry-built constructions of the Keynesians do approximate the way in which the real economy works? The difficulty with that hypothesis is that the computer model, as a whole, has these characteristics of slowly damped oscillations around trend, resulting in periods of adjustment after each shock that last over a decade, which are at variance with the assumptions that underly the different parts that together make up the complete model. Take for example the equation that determines business investment. According to that formula business firms monitor retained profits and adjust their investment plans according to changes in that variable, with a 1½ year lag between changes in retained profits and instalments of new plant and equipment. That may be a reasonable assumption as long as retained profits are a valid indicator of the general stance of the economy and of the expected future profitability of current investment opportunities.

However, the model as a whole shows clearly that other economic variables are highly relevant for business investment, too. A favourable shift in international competitiveness is one example of news that does have a significant impact on investment. But, since a measure of competitiveness is absent from the formula that determines business investment, the good news about the exchange rate has to travel through the computer in order to reach the investment equation. It is a journey in two stages, whereby the news travels from the export equation (greater competitiveness → higher exports) through the consumption equation (more exports = higher national income → greater consumption → more sales) to more investment. Precisely because news about international competitiveness makes its way into the model through the export equation, it takes 2½ years before such news has an effect on business investment. For statistical reasons the model builders are forced to select a very few types of news only for incorporation into each component equation of the model. In the case of the investment equation, changes in competitiveness were excluded, simply because not everything that affects investment can be included into a single formula.

The implications of this compartmentization of news for the dynamics of the model as a whole are obvious. It is as if exporters, consumers, and executives who decide about new business investment all live their separate lives, unaware of economic news that affects the other categories until it shows up in the few variables that have been selected for inclusion in the equation that governs their own behaviour.

The more disaggregated and detailed the model the more serious this problem becomes. Large-scale econometric models are in danger of begetting a characteristic of the slow-witted dinosaur: reacting too slowly when something important occurs.

Each year, many different types of economic news require actions by consumers and business firms. In the current generation of large econometric models the speed of response depends on whether the news happens to be included in the small set of variables that affects decisions about consumption or business investment directly, or whether the news has to 'reach'

Figure 6.1   Lack of communication between different sectors
One reason why large-scale econometric models contribute so little to scientific knowledge
is because they are based on a segmented view of the national economy

Traditional large econometric models sub-divide total spending into numerous categories. Important
economic news may affect several areas of the economy at the same time, but the impact of changing
expectations on total spending are not well captured in the big national computer models.

the different decision makers through a circuitous route. In our example, news about international competitiveness took 2½ years to reach the investment sector, not because such news is not immediately relevant to investment plans, but because a year is lost before the news has been able to affect one of the variables that happen to be included in the equation for business investment.

A change in the exchange rate that improves international competitiveness may well require a year to fully work its way into the volume of exports; however, changes in the exchange rate do not have to wait for next year's newspapers to become known nationwide. The model extends the period of adjustment that may be required to translate a more favourable business climate into investment plans with a period of adjustment in the exporting sector.

The irrational barriers that hamper the free flow of information through the economy do not necessarily make a large econometric model incapable of tracing out the historical experience. Taking up, once more, the example of the equation for business investment in the Dutch 'Vintaf'-model, it may be quite adequate to specify an equation that relates such investment to retained profits and a few other variables, but leaves out changes in international competitiveness. Statistical tests of the equation for business investment will only issue a clear warning that an important variable has been omitted if such a variable happens to be more or less perpendicular to all the variables that have been included already. If during the period of investigation, the time series on changes in international competitiveness happened to be moving similarly to some weighted average of all the time series that are included in the equation for business investment, statistical tests of the investment equation are unlikely to show that international competitiveness has been wrongly excluded.

However adequate the model may appear in predicting the past, it is clearly unreliable with respect to computer simulations of future changes in policy or external conditions. Such policy simulations profess to indicate the effects of a particular change in policy, and abstract from all the unforeseeable future events that may perturb the economy at the same time. If one asks the computer to perform a simulation experiment with respect to a change in international competitiveness, e.g. through a change in the exchange rate, then thát is the only 'news' that occurs during the forecast period. We have seen how the speed with which such news affects different sectors of the economy depends vitally on the question whether the relevant variable has or has not been included in all the major equations of the model. Success of the model in predicting the past does not provide a guarantee that the news reaches all the equations in proper time, and therefore the computer simulations are not a reliable indicator for what might happen in the real world.

Smaller reduced-form models have more solid foundations in this respect. Often, all the important sources of news (the exogenous variables) will be present in each and every estimated equation, so that the news never has to travel through the model. There are no irrational barriers to information; instead all the news reaches each sector directly. At the current state of the art, therefore, policy simulations with reduced form models are more reliable than experiments with the large structural models that were popular during the Sixties and Seventies.

Internal consistency suffers also when models of national economies become too large. Economics, being the science of choice, requires a careful modeling of aggregate consumption with attention to the rewards of alternatives to consumption. It is standard practice therefore, to allow for an effect of (real) rates of interest on current consumption: if the reward for saving goes up, many people will feel inclined to consume somewhat less and save a little more. The presence of interest rates in formulas for predicting aggregate consumption does serve to signal that at the margin consumption has to be as attractive as saving.

Traditionally, other components of aggregate demand are described with much less attention paid to the dilemmas of choice. What do exporters do, for example, if the equation for business exports tells them that exporting has become less promising. None of the large computer models that I have seen allows for the fact that high (real) rates of interest not only make saving more attractive compared to consumption, but equally increase the attractions of financial investment relative to producing for export.

The large-scale econometric models assume that detailed disaggregation of total aggregate demand into different categories of consumption, investment, exports and government expenditure is vital for understanding the dynamics of the business cycle. But, in practice disaggregation leads to neglecting one of the most basic insights of economics: different courses of action should be equally attractive at the margin. The partial way in which changes in interest rates are incorporated into the large models fails to reflect the assumption of rational choice among alternative actions.

If rates of interest do appear at all in equations describing exports, for example, it may well be because of cost considerations, e.g. exports decline when export credits become more expensive. Changes in interest rates should be relevant also because they indicate how attractive financial investment has become as an alternative to exporting goods or services. Large models that incorporate such considerations in selected instances only suffer from inconsistency between their different equations: some formulas take alternatives into account that are overlooked elsewhere. If saving is a relevant alternative to consumption, why not to exports?

6.3 Some evidence regarding interest rate forecasts

The size of many econometric models prevents intelligibility; often it is impossible to diagnose an econometric model otherwise than to inspect its forecasts and policy simulations. I shall not be able, therefore, to make positive suggestions for improvement on the basis of the evidence about interest rate forecasts. Diagnosis of what exactly should be changed in the model is particularly difficult in the case of interest rates, since their determination does not take place in a single, well-defined market. If some econometric model produced weird forecasts for the price of bananas, one would look at the supply and demand equations for bananas as likely causes of the defective forecasts; by contrast, interest rates reflect the value of waiting with added compensation for various uncertainties (see chapter 3 and the references therein), which complicates apportioning the blame for counter-intuitive forecasts of interest rates to specific sections of the econometric model. Misspecifications with respect to consumption, investment, the demand for money, the dynamics of the exchange rate or the behaviour of the banking system may all be responsible.

Even though the evidence on recent forecasts of interest rates in the United States does not lead to additional insights into the econometric models which generated the forecasts, it serves to illustrate one of the major points of the previous two sections: much disaggregation plus cavalier treatment of expectations easily results in oscillatory patterns for the predictions. Ask any large-scale econometric model to forecast interest rates four quarters ahead, and the answer may well exhibit at least one change of direction.

A useful source of evidence are the surveys of business forecasts published each year by the Federal Reserve Bank of Richmond. The surveys do not include the three best-known econometric forecasting organizations, Chase Econometrics, Data Resources and Wharton Econometric Forecasting, but present a good sample of professional forecasts, the majority of which rely on a combination of econometric model results and judgmental forecasts.

The compilation of economic forecasts for 1983 made by the Federal Reserve Bank of Richmond, for example, presents 50 forecasts for different interest rates in the U.S. by 14 different professional forecasting organizations. The predictions relate to the four quarters of 1983, so that the forecasters have to predict three quarterly changes that will occur during the forecast period. (I disregard the predicted change between the 1982IV values and the 1983I forecasts, because these changes depend on the exact moment during the final quarter of 1982 when the forecasts are produced).

Out of 50 forecasts made in late 1982, 17 foresee continuous declines in interest rates between the first and second, second and third, and third and final quarters of 1983. Another 7 forecasts incorporate systematic increases in interest rates during these quarterly periods. The remaining 26 forecasts show one or two reversals in the direction of interest rate changes during the forecast year. Five forecasts, for example, assume that interest rates will increase between the first and second quarters, but decline during the second half of 1983. There is no reason, of course, why interest rates could not exhibit such behaviour, the question is whether one can predict future changes in interest rates with enough confidence to foresee future highs or lows. As we have seen, fifty per cent of the professional forecasts for 1983 pretend to see interest rate peaks or valleys beyond the horizon. Moreover not a single forecaster believes that the safest prediction for interest rates is to remain at current levels.

As all the professional forecasters are familiar with the medium-term forecasts from the large econometric models, they have become accustomed to seeing projections which exhibit one or more changes of direction during the forecast period. Only small monetarist or neoclassical models generate predictions that are 'flat' over time: no further changes of direction after the forecast period has started. Economists in the Keynesian tradition who have been exposed to many oscillating forecasts may find such 'flat' term structures of expectations over-restrictive.

Unfortunately there are no laboratory experiments to settle the issue, but we can consider some evidence of forecasting power (or lack thereof) and judge how well tops and bottoms over the horizon can be sighted. The annual surveys of the Federal Reserve Bank of Richmond over the past five years contain four continuous forecasts of long-term U.S. rates. Two series of forecasts relate to high-grade utility bonds; the other two series of forecasts are for rates on high-quality corporate bonds. All forecasts are made during the final quarter of each year; I consider the predictions for the average levels of the long-term rate in the second and final quarters of each forecast year.

A naive forecast for the utility bond rate in the second quarter that predicted no change from the average level during the fourth quarter of the preceding year would have resulted in an average forecast error of 0.94 percentage points over the years 1978–1982. The two banks in the Richmond studies that predicted this interest rate made their predictions in December (often during the final week of the quarter when the quarterly average could have been estimated with near-perfect accuracy), but produced average forecast errors of 1.04 and 1.40 percentage points. Four-quarter ahead forecasts for the final quarter of the forecast year were also inferior to those of the same naive no-change model. Predictions of unchanged rates on new utility bonds would have caused an average forecast error of 2.52 percentage points; the two professional forecasting groups missed by an average of 3.06 and 3.09 percentage points.

The remaining two five-year series of forecasts for the corporate bond rate have to be considered separately. One professional forecaster releases his forecasts around the beginning of November; I have compared his success to that of a naive model that held the corporate bond yield fixed to its average level of October. The standard error of the naive model is 1.04 percentage points for the forecasts relating to the second quarter and 2.40 percentage points for the forecasts relating to the final quarter of the forecast year, as against 1.64 and 2.45 percentage points for the professional forecaster. The final series of forecasts is published during December of each year; our naive model starts from the average level during the fourth quarter. The no-change predictions win for the two-quarter ahead forecasts (0.67 versus 1.04 percentage points) and tie with the professional forecasts for the four-quarter ahead predictions (1.98 percentage points in both cases).

Over the past five years the four professional forecasting organizations in this sample were clearly not superior to the naive forecasts that long-term interest rates will remain at current levels. A study by Stephen K. McNees of the Boston Federal Reserve Bank (1981) indicates that the same conclusion may hold for the forecasts of short-term interest rates. McNees presents average absolute errors of forecasts relating to the 90-day Treasury Bill Rate for various forecast horizons. The four-quarter ahead predictions, for example, have an average error of 1.4 percentage points for the most successful forecaster (late-quarter forecast by DRI) and a 2.4 percentage points average absolute error for the worst forecaster over the period investigated (early-quarter forecasts by Chase Econometrics). A naive forecast which puts the average Treasury Bill Rate in any future quarter equal to the average value during the current quarter would result in an average absolute error of 1.58 percentage points for four-quarter ahead forecasts, which is below the average of the eight series of forecasts studied by McNees. (Early-quarter forecasts by Chase Econometrics, Data Resources, the University of Michigan Research Seminar on Quantitative Economics, and Wharton; mid-quarter estimates from the Kent Economic and Development Institute and Wharton; late-quarter predictions from Chase and Data Resources).

The report by McNees relates to the years 1975–1980 and other periods may produce results that are less flattering for the naive no-change model. Also, the professional forecasting organizations may become more successful in predicting long-term bond rates than they were over the 1978–1982 period. The comparisons are in no way conclusive, but at least they do not contradict some of the assumptions underlying the research in this book:

- news affects interest rates with very short lags. Therefore, we have constructed indices for world trade, energy prices and budget deficits, for example, that behave like random walks for use in the interest rate regressions of chapter 5.

- no 'normal' long-term level exists for nominal interest rates. If return-to-normalcy elements were important, the large models should be able to do better than the naive no-change model which is based on the assumption that interest rates follow pure random walks.

6.4 The market for large-scale computer models

The informal review in the previous sections of this chapter pointed towards some lines of criticism directed at the large-scale econometric models in the Keynesian tradition:
(1) problems of size: the slowness of the econometric dinosaurs.
(2) internal inconsistency: different assumptions underlying different parts of the model.
(3) irrational expectations: the future implications of current news are represented by arbitrarily chosen averages of data from the past, without investigation whether such extrapolations are relevant.

I have argued that the three sets of problems mentioned above have not yet been resolved in a satisfactory manner. For the time being, it is more prudent to think small, therefore. A lot of allocative detail will be lost unavoidably, but we do know at least how to construct small or partial econometric models that are internally sound, whereas we are as yet unable to put together a large econometric model that satisfies the twin requirements of consistency and proper treatment of expectations with respect to the future.

Although most academic researchers seem to feel this way, the large macroeconometric models remain in business. One important reason has been alluded to before: there is a strong political demand for scientific studies which can be used in the political debate on economic policy. In addition the models sometimes sing seductive sirensongs. Part of the attractiveness and longevity of the Keynesian paradigm – as opposed to much political advice from Keynes himself, see for example, Keynes (1923) – rests on the promise of a politically easy way to combat unemployment. Bigger government outlays make the bureaucrats happy, increase the discretionary power of politicians to build coalitions and court new supporters and may even temporarily reduce unemployment. The criticism that some 'supply siders' made unrealistic promises about another costless method to reduce unemployment – simply cut taxation and the surge in economic growth will automatically eliminate the initial budget deficits – is in order, but does it not equally apply to many policy advisers in the Keynesian tradition? Policy simulations with large econometric models exude confidence about the scope for 'fine-tuning' the economy, which suits many politicians and bureaucrats. By contrast, much research in the neoclassical and monetarist tradition leads to great caution with respect to continuously adjusting instruments of economic policy.

The new research focusstresses the contribution stable policies make to a perspicuous economy and thus to a healthy investment climate. Great variability of monetary policy, for example, would make economic trends harder to interpret which raises long-term interest rates and depresses the economy. I have presented some relevant evidence on the adverse consequences of greater economic uncertainty in chapter 5. Also, as discussed in the first chapter, the large models tend to neglect the impact of greater uncertainty on economic behaviour which, together with their apparent mastery of detail, produces an automatic bias in favour of 'fine-tuning'.

In addition to the general prejudice in favour of interventionist policies, the combination of heavy disaggregation and a limited role for expectations regarding the longer-term future results in a particular form of bias, embedded in the official models of the Dutch economy and possibly elsewhere, that is attractive to many politicians. The incentive effects of lower taxes are underestimated, because reduced rates of taxation have their favourable effects on liquidity all-right but fail to have their full effects on the supplies of labour and capital. The decisions of suppliers are insufficiently sensitive to changes in expected future rates of return (the Dutch model is an extreme case in that no attempt is made to find expressions for any expected real rates of return, so that only the favourable short-term effects on costs remain). On the other hand, direct subsidies to business receive favourable treatment when modelled as pure additions to the streams of expenditure. In simulations of economic policy with the Dutch model the amount of the subsidy is added to the right-hand side of the equation that describes business investment. Such models easily imply that we can bribe ourselves with our own money: the positive effects of subsidies and other forms of government expenditure are included in the summing-up of all the components of aggregate demand, whereas their potential negative influences on expected future rates of return receive less attention. Society has to pay interest on the national debt, or needs to levy additional taxes, but such negative influences on future rates of return are much harder to incorporate into the econometric models.

There are more reasons, however, for the commercial survival of the large-scale econometric models. Karl Brunner has emphasized the influence of a descriptivist attitude towards progress in scientific understanding.

'A descriptivist attitude reflects the view that an understanding of any process or phenomenon is fostered by a massive attention to all possible observational detail. It conditions, for instance, the view that no understanding of inflation can be achieved without systematic attention to all the detail of price setting among the variety of suppliers or demanders'.

In: J. Kmenta and J. B. Ramsey (editors)
'Large-Scale Macro-Econometric Models', Amsterdam, North-Holland, 1981, p. 131.

In the case of inflation it has become commonplace again to agree that inflation is a monetary phenomenon and that detailed attention for price setting behaviour of different types of business firms contributes only to shortest-term forecasting but offers few lasting insights and is positively harmful when used to recommend price-freezing policies to combat inflation.

Brunner insists that the descriptivist ideal of ever more detailed computer models is inappropriate also for many other questions in economics:

> 'Major scientific advances are achieved by disregarding the injunction that "everything depends on everything else" with a felicitous simplification. The classical program (in economics) clearly expressed this attitude. It more or less implicitly separated global and allocative aspects of an economy. The program essentially asserts that major global phenomena, as for instance the inflation rate, can be adequately explained without invoking a host of allocative processes'.

idem, pp. 137–138.

Perhaps the increasing technological complexity of research in the medical and natural sciences has led many to believe that in economics also big problems require big computers. Until now, however, there is no evidence that the accuracy of economic forecasts increases with model size, and there is massive evidence that policy advice from the large models was faulty in the past and has failed for approximately a decade now to reflect the concerns of many researchers regarding expectations and market efficiency. In my view the descriptivist attitude – if a 1000-equation model does not work satisfactorily, let's construct a 2000-equation model – has not been fertile in macroeconomics. But, as stressed by Brunner, this is an interim judgement. The rule that well-founded simplifications are more helpful in understanding economic processes than ever-increasing complexity may have been true for the recent past, but could be successfully falsified in the future:

> 'And if it is, so be it; we would have gained an interesting hypothesis. Large-scale modelling has offered so far no useful evidence suggesting that we abandon the rule. The problems associated with this particular

econometric practice and conditioned by its underlying vision still indicate to me, at least in the range of our cognitive endeavors, the viability, if not superiority, of the classical program'.

idem, p. 138.

chapter 7

Indexation of government debt

"I think the debt management policy is deplorable. The Secretary of the Treasury would be well advised to pay much more attention to his own policies than he does to the Federal Reserve's policies. He could do a great deal to help lower interest rates by improving debt management, including the use of index-linked bonds, or getting out of the long-term debt markets, much as private corporations do when rates are temporarily high. Corporations do not saddle their stockholders with 15- or 16- percent rates of interest. I don't understand why an administration that believes it's going to reduce the rate of inflation is saddling the taxpayers with 15- or 16-percent rates for 30 years. This sends out the wrong signals. They are betting against their policies. The Congress ought to be leaning hard on the Secretary of Treasury to improve debt management policy."

"I would like indexing to be available to everybody, including the small savers who are in the most need of protection from inflation because they have the least knowledge about what their opportunities are."

Allan H. Meltzer, speaking at a hearing for the Joint Economic Committee, Congress of the United States, on October 6, 1981, p. 98, 106.

7.1 Betting against inflation

If monetary uncertainty pushes interest rates upwards, there follow important implications for the management of the national debt. A simple numerical example will clarify this point: assume that investors feel that there
is a fifty per cent chance that the current rate of inflation of five per cent
per year will also be the average rate of inflation over the next ten years,
whereas there is also a fifty per cent chance, as they see it, that the rate of
inflation will quickly go up to ten percent per year. If the Treasury attempts
to sell ten-year government debt, then the rate of interest that investors
require will have to incorporate an inflation premium that is consistent with
these expectations. Since the price level is thought to increase by 5-10%
over each of the next ten years, a reasonable assumption would be that
investors require an inflation premium of some 7-8 per cent on top of the
required real rate of interest. The nominal rate of interest will reflect the
average expectation in the financial markets, and each investor who buys
a long-term bond takes a heavy gamble on the future course of inflation. If
the average rate of inflation does indeed turn out to be closer to five than
to ten per cent per year, the holders of long-term debt gain; if inflation ends
up near the higher end of the range, then the ex-post real rate of interest is
lower than the average investor anticipated it to be.

Once the investors have placed their bets by buying long-term debt, the
monetary authorities determine the outcome through their choice of monetary policies. The choice for an anti-inflationary monetary policy is de-
manding for myopic short-term operators such as many politicians are and
requires perseverance on their part under all circumstances because smal-
ler-than-anticipated increases in nominal aggregate demand will temporarily
depress real output and employment. But, if many creditors have placed
their bets with respect to future inflation and gain from a lower-than-expected price level, there is more to an anti-inflation policy, since where creditors gain, debtors must lose. The real burdens of their debts increase by
more than was anticipated, which is just as troublesome for governments
as it is for private debtors. The government of the Netherlands, for example,
issued large amounts of long-term debt in 1980 and 1981 at interest rates
around 10 12 per cent. At the moment of writing (April 1983), the actual
rate of inflation in Holland is down to 2 per cent on an annual basis, which
makes the service of these instruments much more expensive than was anticipated. The U.S. government has contracted to pay 14-15 per cent on
some of its long-term obligations until the beginning of the next century,
giving investors a spectacular real return on their money if the price level
is stabilized sooner.

The investors' gain is the government's loss; a matter of some irony when
the same government professes its determination to reduce the rate of in-

flation and keep it low. On the one hand the authorities try to convince the public that they are serious in their abhorrence of inflation; on the other hand they try to sell long-term debt that incorporates a full compensation for the public's scepticism with respect to their anti-inflation resolve and that will be more of a real burden for the taxpayers the more successful the anti-inflation policy becomes.

> 'The administration is selling bonds to the public at rates of interest which bet against the policy the administration has announced. No private corporation – no major private corporation – is willing to sell long-term bonds at current rates. The administration does so every month. It creates a set of circumstances which I believe are harmful to the achievement of its policy and which bet against the success of the policy. I believe Congress ought to hold hearings on the question of debt management. It ought to lean very hard on the Secretary of Treasury to improve debt management. Better policies are available.'

> (Allan H. Meltzer, 1981a, p. 16; see also Bomhoff 1981).

In this chapter I shall discuss one better policy: indexation of the government's long-term debt. The following section will contain a numerical illustration of the advantages for long-term financial contracts, of indexation where the principal amount of the loan is indexed against future rises in the price level (ordinary long-term loans with a variable interest rate that is pegged to a short-term rate are sometimes described as 'indexed'; I do not follow this usage). In section 7.3 the recent experience with indexed government debt in the United Kingdom will be reviewed. Section 7.4 tries to draw some conclusions about the proper management of the national debt in times of inflationary and budgetary uncertainty.

7.2 Index-linked mortgages

The British experience with index-linked government debt – about which more below – has been a stimulus for the introduction of other indexed financial instruments. 'Target Life Assurance' started to offer index-linked pensions in 1982 with a value which is guaranteed to rise each year in line with the general price level. The development of a market in index-linked government securities with different maturities enabled this Company to advertise: 'you don't have to be a civil servant to have an index-linked pension'. Since pensioners will indeed value their pensions for the real purchasing power they confer, it would appear that under normal assumptions about the characteristics of the claimant's other assets and liabilities an index-linked pension would be valued more highly than a pension in nominal terms with the same expected total discounted value. A range of long-term government bonds that are indexed against inflation enables pension funds or life insurance companies to offer index-linked pay-outs in return for fixed nominal contributions.

If the authorities do not themselves operate a scheme for small savers – as they do in the U.K. – then a market for index-linked debt would also enable financial institutions to offer inflation-proof savings deposits. All such developments reduce the need for people to place heavy debts on the future course of inflation if they are not so inclined. Why would society require the aged or the private savers to bet their money on a specific future course for the price level? As long as there exists no institutional anchor for the price level, people run the risk that unforeseen inflation will destroy the real value of their nominal assets. Since national governments are chiefly responsible for keeping inflation under control it seems appropriate if the authorities also help the private sector to make inflation-proof agreements.

In the absence of a well-developed market for indexed government debt, the main area where the private sector can achieve results in reducing the costs of inflationary uncertainty is the market for long-term mortgages on real estate. The twin reasons are that the collateral for a loan can be expected to appreciate more or less in line with the general price level over the long run and that the servicing of the loan will generally come out of incomes that can also reasonably be expected to increase with inflation.

If both these conditions hold, then an index-linked mortgage becomes very attractive because assets and liabilities – both current and projected – match so much better than if a nominal loan is taken out to acquire a piece of real property. Not only is a real asset paid for by assuming a real liability, but the expected stream of interest and repayments also corresponds much better to the expected stream of future income provided by the building. In theory only the first point matters, since one could always take out additional loans to flatten the profile of the repayments over time; in practice this would involve high transaction costs, so that index-linked mortgages also have a real advantage in offering a prospective debt service ratio that is much flatter over time.

Table 7.1, taken from the documentation of the 'Index Linked Mortgage And Investment Company Limited' provides a nice illustration of the attractions of indexed long-term loans. Column (1) of this table shows the terms of an ideal contract for an ideal world. If the price level remains absolutely stable over the complete term of the loan, and if the lender agrees to fix the nominal interest rate on the mortgage once and for all, then an annuity will imply a constant real burden for the borrower and a constant real source of income for the lender. In the numerical example of table 7.1

Table 7.1 A £ 100,000 first mortgage over a term of 20 years

	0% inflation		10% per year inflation for 2 years, 8% per year thereafter		
	(1)	(2)	(3)	(4)	(5)
Year	Monthly Repayment (Real Money) £ pm	Amount Outstanding (Real Money) £	Monthly Repayment (Paper Money) £ pm	Amount Outstanding (Paper Money) £	Amount Outstanding (Real Money) £
1	770.00	96,988	770.00	107,149	97,408
2	770.00	93,780	847.00	114,525	94,648
3	770.00	90,363	931.70	119,745	91,632
4	770.00	86,725	1,006.24	124,782	88,421
5	770.00	82,850	1,086.74	129,565	85,003
6	770.00	78,723	1,173.68	133,940	81,364
7	770.00	74,328	1,267.57	137,767	77,489
8	770.00	69,647	1,368.98	140,869	73,365
9	770.00	64,662	1,478.50	143,034	68,974
10	770.00	59,353	1,596.78	144,008	64,300
11	770.00	53,699	1,724.52	143,493	59,324
12	770.00	47,677	1,862.48	141,134	54,027
13	770.00	41,264	2,011.48	136,515	48,388
14	770.00	34,434	2,172.40	129,143	42,384
15	770.00	27,160	2,346.19	118,443	35,993
16	770.00	19,413	2,533.88	103,738	29,189
17	770.00	11,163	2,736.59	84,235	21,946
18	770.00	2,376	2,955.52	59,009	14,235
19	770.00	0	3,191.96	26,979	6,026
20	0	0	3,447.32	0	0

Source: Index Linked Mortgage And Investment Company Ltd. (1982, p. 3).

the real rate of interest has been chosen to be 0.53% per month, and the fixed nominal payment of £ 770 per month enables the borrower to repay the complete loan after 18 years and a few months.

It is only under the extremely unrealistic assumptions that both the price level and the nominal rate of interest will be constant for such a long period of time that the column of identical numbers in table 7.1 signifies a real burden for the borrower that is also constant over time. If interest rates or the price level or both change, then ordinary level repayment mortgages will imply a real burden that changes over time. The purpose of indexing the mortgage is to alter the terms of the contract in such a way that the real burden of the mortgage (and therefore the real income for the lender) remains unchanged over the course of the contract, even though the actual rate of inflation may be high, variable, and unknown in advance.

The third column of table 7.1 shows the monthly repayments for an indexed mortgage, on the assumption that the rate of inflation will no longer be zero (as in column 1), but will be 10% per annum during the first two years, and 8% per annum during the remaining term of the loan. The amounts in column 3 are computed for any year by taking the required amount for the previous year and multiplying by one plus the rate of inflation over the past year. In year 2, for example, the price level went up by 10%; therefore the stipulated monthly repayment for year 3 will be $847 \times \dfrac{110}{100} = 931.70$ pounds per month. In real terms the monthly repayments remain unaltered, apart from slight, temporary deviations produced by accelerations or decelerations in the rate of inflation. Since the monthly repayments are reset once a year on the basis of the observed rate of increase of the price level over the previous 12 months, the capital is repaid slightly more slowly in the case of column (3) than in the case of column (1) if the inflation rate is positive. It now takes almost 20 years for the loan to be repaid, as against 18¼ years with zero inflation. These are minor differences: the main point is that indexation is a way of safe-guarding a constant real burden under conditions of variable inflation.

Taking a different perspective on the contract may help to illuminate its characteristics. After one year the borrower finds himself approximately in the position of someone who has borrowed 110,000 pounds and has fulfilled his obligations for the first year of a 20-year level repayment mortgage. The required monthly payment on such a contract would be 847 pounds per month. The borrower now enters the second year of a 'normal' annuity for 110,000 pounds and pays this sum (847 pounds) in each month of year two. At the close of the second year his position is similar to that of someone who has borrowed $100,000 \times (1,1)^2$ pounds and has completed the first two years of a level repayment mortgage for that principal sum. The normal payment for such a mortgage would be $770 \times (1.1)^2 = 931.70$ pounds per month, which equals the amount set for the next 12 months. Beginning with year 3 the price level increases by 8 instead of 10 per cent per year and therefore the monthly amount in year four will have to be increased by that percentage, but the basic principle remains unchanged: a level repayment mortgage designed for zero per cent inflation is translated into an annuity that is appropriate for variable inflation rates.

Since the institutional investors who are invited to invest in such index-linked mortgages will generally like to sell inflation-proof policies, they should have a natural preference for investments that promise a rate of return that is approximately known in real terms at the beginning of the contract period (see also Lazard, 1982). Similarly, many classes of borrowers would find an index-linked mortgage attractive, as it stipulates a financial burden that grows in step with the aggregate price level. If the assets that are acquired with the mortgage also offer streams of future income that are easier to predict in real than in nominal terms, then indexation of the mortgage on the property will result in a better matching of future proceeds and future obligations (see Siegel and Warner, 1977, for a discussion of alternative assumptions that can qualify these statements).

7.3 Indexed government debt in the U.K.

Although the Treasury was forced to sell its indexed stock against the stream – since the first issue in March 1981 inflation in the U.K. has been on a decreasing trend until the time of writing (April 1983) – nevertheless an ever increasing proportion of the long-term government debt is issued in index-linked form. After the budget of March 1982 there are no restrictions on holdership and the Bank of England Quarterly Bulletin (December 1982) reports a widening of the market for these securities.

The most difficult episode so far has been the selling of the second indexed stock (2%, I.L., July 1981) because the market required a rather higher real rate of return than was offered by the authorities. An eloquent leading article in the Financial Times of July 9th, 1981 offered solace for both borrowers and lenders by repeating the advantages of index-linked government debt:

> 'We have long favoured, and continue to favour, a role for indexed stocks in Government funding on grounds which have nothing to do with day-to-day movements in the market. They should be of help to the authorities, because the guarantee of a real return should ensure demand at a time when expectations are uncertain and demoralised. Further, they imply a known cost in fiscal terms – the yield of a penny of income-tax will move closely in line with the yield on indexed stocks; and they do not, in their early years, involve large disbursements of

cash which must promptly be borrowed back to maintain monetary control.

From the point of view of the investor, the availability of a stock which offers a known, if modest, real return is a valuable alternative to more speculative securities – for when inflation is high and variable the real yield on conventional stocks is quite unknown after a few years. An indexed stock, in a well conducted market, should fill exactly the same role as Consols did for the Victorians – a holding especially suitable for widows, orphans, and trust funds.

It also seems right that indexed retirement incomes should be available in the private sector at a realistic price – a price which could be determined from an adequate spread of indexed stocks. Finally, the availability of a security of a known real maturity value could offer an important alternative to foreign securities at times when confidence is shaky.

The problems of managing the economy are sufficient without adding to them that of managing flights of capital such as are a feature of past crises in Italy and recent political events in France. Indexed securities could in short be a source of stability in quite a broad sense.'

Financial Times, July 9, 1981.

During that month the required real rate of return rose to approximately 3% per annum, but subsequently the required real rate of return has fallen back to 2–2½% per annum.

The arguments in favour of indexation are expressed well in the article quoted above:

● *Getting the inflationary risk premium out of long-term interest rates*

Perhaps it took economic agents some years to realize that current institutional arrangements for printing paper money in a world of flexible exchange rates make the future long-term rate of inflation very much an unpredictable variable. Even though some claims that inflation has shifted into a higher gear may have been premature – see for example Parkin (1975) who mistakenly assumed that inflation under Labour could only be worse than inflation under the Conservatives – it certainly is true that the monetary gear-box is well-greased, since there is no institutional anchor on the speed at which new money is produced. In my opinion a prolonged period of financial rectitude, or different institutional arrangements, will be required before investors in the high inflation countries of the 1970's will lose their 'once bitten – twice shy' attitude with respect to the risk of accelerating inflation.

Since nobody can predict with any accuracy what the value will be in ten or twenty years' time of the pound in one's pocket or of all the world's other paper monies, long-term investors will require a compensation for such uncertainty about the future purchasing power of their nominal investments. Our statistical analysis in chapter 5 has indicated that there may indeed be a substantial risk premium in long-term interest rates which adds to the real burden of the national debt. If the authorities offered a purchasing power guarantee on their long-term debt they could avoid paying these risk premia to the holders of the debt.

Not only would indexation result in a reduction of the real burden of the debt, day-to-day management of the debt would become much easier also. It is a fact of financial life that participants in the financial markets sometimes are particularly nervous about the interest rate outlook. Such fickle market sentiments complicate the management of the long-term debt. The Dutch government, for example, decided in November 1981 to issue a large long-term loan with a coupon that was more generous than expected in order to put an end to a protracted period of rising uncertainty in the financial markets regarding the Treasury's ability to fund the budget deficit without taking recourse to foreign currency loans or other emergency measures. The Treasury made a stand, but it was a very expensive one. In order to guarantee a resounding reception for the new issue, the authorities erred on the safe side and offered a remarkably generous return. The taxpayers have to pay for such demonstrations of credit-worthiness, not only because of the high coupon on this particular issue but also because fear of future replays of the same scenario increases the perceived riskiness of nominal bonds. Of course, the other criticism of high-coupon long-term debt, namely that the authorities are betting against the success of their own anti-inflationary policies, applies also to all recent issues of long-term debt in Holland, including the 12¾% loan.

The leader writer of the Financial Times stresses that index-linked debt helps to impart stability to the financial markets. It is worth recalling that *all* long-term British government debt showed capital gains after the announcement on March 10th, 1982 that the restrictions on holding index-linked debt were abolished. Investors concluded that index-linked debt was going to play an enlarged role in the future, which reduced the risk that U.K. investors would find themselves in the position of their Dutch counterparts just prior to the announcement of the spectacular 12¾% loan in November 1981. As soon as the Treasury has the option of issuing indexed debt, holders of existing nominal long-term debt no longer have to fear that the authorities will combat an unfavourable market psychology by issuing a new loan with a higher-than-expected coupon which of course depresses the value of their current holdings. Indexation takes the showmanship out of debt management policy and thus reduces the required real rate of interest even on seasoned traditional long-term loans.

● *The pattern over time of the debt service corresponds better to the projected growth of tax revenues*

When nominal rates of interest incorporate a positive inflation premium, each interest payment includes a hidden repayment of part of the principal amount. The real average life of the loan is shorter than its official average life. Such 'front-loading' has often been mentioned as one reason why inflation could depress real business investment in a world of incomplete capital markets and significant transaction costs: a nominal rate of interest of 10%, composed of a real rate of 2% plus an inflation premium of 8% implies that after one year 8% of the principal has to be repaid. If the loan has been used to acquire a real asset that will only start to pay its way after some time, these hidden repayments put additional pressure on the cash-flow of the borrower.

Governments face similar problems when the inflation premium in the nominal rate of interest means that the state has to begin repayments immediately, but political emphasis on the actual current deficit precludes additional borrowings in order to service these implicit repayments.

A steady positive rate of inflation automatically reduces the real burden on all outstanding nominal loans, but stating the obvious may not help much if the political debate focuses on the current-year deficit, making it impossible to see through this form of money illusion.

Indexation makes the real burden of the interest payments constant over time, instead of shrinking at some unpredictable and variable rate as in the case of nominal long-term debt. As most of the government's sources of income are either inflation-proof or tied to the future growth in nominal national income, the matching of revenue and expenditure becomes much more successful if the debt service on the long-term debt is indexed against rises in the price level. There is no more 'front-loading' and the characteristics of the state's long-term obligations resemble more the projected proceeds from its power to tax.

● *The normative arguments: it also seems right that index retirement incomes should be available in the private sector at a realistic price*

Exactly: government creates inflationary uncertainty and has a duty to alleviate its consequences. A well-developed market for indexed long-term debt helps pension funds and life insurance companies to offer inflation-proof policies. Financial intermediaries – or the government itself as in the U.K. – can also offer savings schemes that allow the small saver to protect the real value of his savings in a risk-free way. The British government manages to fund part of its deficit at essentially a zero real after-tax rate of interest through selling savings deposits to individual savers. These citizens can protect the real value of their investments, and the authorities have a costless means of shifting expenditures forward in time.

● *Indexed debt can serve as a substitute for overseas investment by institutional investors*

Fixed-interest government debt issued by their own governments dominates the portfolios of many European institutional investors. Prudence requires substantial diversification into assets that have higher-than-expected real returns when the domestic rate of inflation turns out to be higher than was anticipated and capital losses are incurred on domestic debt. If higher domestic inflation tends to cause currency depreciation then overseas investments are a means of reducing the inflationary risks on the total portfolio. It follows that the optimal amount of overseas portfolio investment depends on the perceived degree of inflationary uncertainty in the domestic economy. Not only does the degree of inflationary uncertainty change over time – see chapter 5 – but the effectiveness of international diversification against inflationary uncertainty depends on the amount of covariation between national inflation rates which also varies over time. The optimal currency shares in the portfolio of an institutional investor thus may sometimes change rapidly and the ensuing attempts by managers to alter their portfolios may upset interest rates as well as exchange rates and contribute to a volatile and troubled financial climate. Political pressure may emerge for controls on capital movements which has further negative effects on financial stability (see for example, Dooley and Isard, 1979, for a careful analysis of what changing political uncertainty about capital controls did for interest rates in West-Germany during the first part of the 1970's).

'Indexed securities could in short be a source of stability in quite a broad sense' to quote the editorialist once again, and that is why Jevons, Marshall, Keynes, Fisher and other monetary economists, past and present, have advocated their issuance by sovereign borrowers.

One serious objection must be faced, however. Indexation of the government's long-term debt closes one escape route in case the budgetary problems become unsurmountable. Governments can print money, inflate the price level and shrink the real value of the outstanding debt; once the debt is inflation-proof they can't make a molehill out of a mountain anymore. Indexation of the government's long-term debt closes this particular emergency exit out of the budget bind. No longer will the authorities be able to resort to currency debasement as a means of alleviating the burden of the national debt.

Whether removing this temptation is a good or a bad thing depends on the alternatives. Sixty years ago when the economies of Western Europe were struggling under high burdens of debt incurred during World War I, J.M.Keynes set forth his views on the different policy options in 'A tract on monetary reform' (MacMillan, London, 1923). His opinions retain their force today and carry even more weight if we accept that monetary uncertainty puts a substantial risk premium into long-term interest rates. With the help of a few quotations from the 'Tract' we shall consider in the next section whether indexation should be avoided because it eliminates the option of currency debasement that otherwise remains available to governments in desperate budgetary straits, or whether indexation is more like a safety measure that reduces the risk of a financial disaster and forces the authorities to face their problems in a more sensible way.

7.4 Taxpayers and bondholders

Real national income in Holland decreased in 1980, 1981 and 1982, and the most recent forecasts for 1983 presage a paltry increase of 0.5 per cent in 1983. Rates of return on human and physical capital were considerably lower, therefore, than the returns on long-term financial assets, and 1983 may well prove to be no different. The difference is even more striking when we compare the yields on fixed-interest investments to the trend in real disposable incomes: the rewards for financial investment in fixed obligations of the state has risen far above the compensation for productive labour.

Similar situations exist in other developed economies and explosive growth in the ratio of outstanding government debt to national income will tend to prolong it, because investors will require additional compensation for absorbing fresh debt in their portfolios whilst the citizens will have to pay higher taxes to service the interest payments on the growing debt. Nobody can predict how long the potentially unstable situation of a long-term real rate of interest on government debt that exceeds the real rate of return on human and physical capital can persist, but is has become so much part of the current scene in many rich countries, that it pays to recall the political and economic judgement of Keynes in an earlier age of monetary and budgetary uncertainty. The chapter 'Public finance and the value of money' from 'A tract on monetary reform' (1923) takes as its point of departure that the taxpayers cannot become permanently enslaved to the bondholders. In other words: the ratio of debt service to national income cannot be maintained on a rising trend. If that threatens to happen, something has to give in and Keynes argues against systematic tinkering with the money supply as a remedy against a budgetary crisis:

'The active and working elements in no community, ancient or modern, will consent to hand over to the rentier or bond-holding class more than a certain proportion of the fruits of their work. When the piled-up debt demands more than a tolerable proportion, relief has usually been sought in one or other of two out of the three possible methods. The first is Repudiation. But, except as the accompaniment of Revolution, this method is too crude, too deliberate, and too obvious in its incidence. The victims are immediately aware and cry out too loud; so that, in the absence of Revolution, this solution may be ruled out at present, as regards internal debt, in Western Europe. The second method is Currency Depreciation ... Instead of dividing the burden between all classes of wealthowners..., it throws the whole burden on to the owners of fixed-interest bearing stocks... It follows the line of least resistance, and responsibility cannot be brought home to individuals. It is, so to speak, nature's remedy, which comes into silent operation when the body politic has shrunk from curing itself.

The remaining, the scientific, expedient, the Capital Levy, has never yet been tried on a large scale; and perhaps it never will be. It is the rational, the deliberate method. But it is difficult to explain, and it provokes violent prejudice by coming into conflict with the deep instincts by which the love of money protects itself. Unless the patient understands and approves its purpose, he will not submit to so severe a surgical operation.'

Keynes' preference was unequivocal:

'...it has become clear that the claims of the bond-holder are more than the tax-payer can support, and if there is still time to choose between the policies of a Levy and of further Depreciation, the Levy must surely be preferred on grounds both of expediency of justice.'

> J.M.Keynes: 'A tract on monetary reform', MacMillan, London, 1923, pp. 64–66.

The main argument against enforced currency depreciation as a means of reducing the burden of the national debt is that it is unjust: holders of fixed-interest claims suffer for putting too much trust in the value of paper money, whereas private debtors enjoy a free ride towards a healthier balance-sheet together with the government. The distributional effects entail economic costs also (see Garber, 1982, and Grossman, 1982), since unanticipated inflation on the scale necessary to significantly reduce the burden of the national debt shakes the economy. The booms and busts in the real estate markets in the U.K., the U.S. and many European nations during the 1970's examplify how upsetting an unpredictable rate of inflation can be;

imagine what prices of durable assets and interest rates would do and how orderly production decisions would be complicated and could turn out ex-post to have been fatally wrong if agents started to believe that their governments were seriously considering currency debasement as a solution to their budgetary problems.

Inflating the currency is unjust towards all creditors as well as to people who rent their accommodation or live on an earned retirement income, and imposes heavy costs on the economy, but how distasteful are the alternatives?

Special one-time taxes on wealth cause fewer distortions in the view of Keynes and are less unjust than currency debasement. If the politicians can agree, the case for issuing index-linked debt is even stronger than it was in his time. Monetary virtue begets its own reward and the real rate of interest on indexed debt will be lower than the expected real rate of return on ordinary long-term loans to the government. The savings can be very substantial, depending on one's estimate of the risk premium in the long-term nominal rate of interest. If 1 ½–2 per cent per annum is a reasonable estimate (see chapter 5) the government (and thus the taxpayers) will save this percentage of the outstanding national debt in each year.

Indexation would also imply substantial shifts over time of the interest obligations. The British indexed loan that was emitted on January 22, 1982 reduced the budget deficit for 1983 by almost 100 million pounds, according to a contemporaneous estimate (Financial Times, January 23, 1982).

Ehrbar estimates that 'the (U.S.) Treasury could save $ 28 billion on its 1984 interest expenses if it substituted indexed notes for all its scheduled borrowings and also refunded the 14% and 15% bonds it's been issuing lately' (1982, p. 54). Such estimates combine the gains from a permanently lower real rate of interest on indexed securities with the temporary advantages of shifting interest payments to future years. Under the circumstances of the early 1980's even the deferment of the interest payments that is accomplished by indexation would have made as much sense in the United States and in the countries of continental Europe as it did in the United Kingdom. Economic growth was low everywhere and many governments were engaged in anti-inflationary monetary policies that further increased budget deficits and added to the general climate of economic uncertainty created by the second oil price shock of 1970–80. It was a good time to streamline the management of the national debt through opting for a financial instrument that would be cheaper in the long run, less burdensome during the ongoing recession and would not punish the issuing governments if they were successful after all in eliminating inflation.

Strangely enough, the success of the index-linked issues in the United Kingdom was used sometimes as an argument against debt indexation in other countries. Some bankers were said to be afraid that index-linked schemes would prove so popular that private savers would run down their savings and term deposits to buy indexed instruments instead. The decrease in bank liabilities would then force the banks to reduce their earning assets according to this argument. But, even if we assume that an indexed bond issue is very popular, the authorities could use the additional proceeds to retire outstanding nominal debt. The previous holders of these seasoned issues will be more liquid and could be induced by the banking system to deposit their funds as time or savings deposits. As long as the money supply and the total volume of outstanding debt remain unaltered, portfolios of different groups of investors may change when the government decides to introduce indexed government debt, but it is myopic to argue that in the new equilibrium the banks necessarily will have fewer savings and term deposits.

A related concern is the possibility of substantial losses on outstanding nominal long-term bonds if the authorities switch to indexed debt. There may be a substitution effect that puts downward pressure on the price of existing bonds, but the act of issuing indexed debt shows that the issuers are serious in their anti-inflationary stance which by itself would be positive for nominal bonds. The net effect is unclear but assuming for the sake of argument that nominal bond prices fall, does that imply that the step to indexation should be avoided? Not often do firms decide against marketing a new product on the basis of the argument that the second-hand value of earlier products may fall. Even if indexed bonds are a superior product that makes more traditional government paper obsolete, their introduction does not mean that the authorities will no longer honour their obligation towards the holders of the nominal debt: government will continue to service its outstanding debt, and the real value of interest payments and principal value may well increase with indexation, since it shows seriousness of purpose in keeping inflation low.

Still, with one exception in the U.K., no steps towards indexation were taken. Keynes also offers some speculative thoughts on the question why Treasury officials and bankers often do not agree with his preference for one-time special taxes on wealth as an alternative to currency debasement:

> 'Many conservative bankers regard it as more consonant with their cloth, and also as economising thought, to shift public discussion of financial topics off the logical on to an alleged 'moral' plane, which means a realm of thought where vested interest can be triumphant over the common good without further debate. But it makes them untrustworthy guides in a perilous age of transition. The State must never neglect the importance of so acting in ordinary matters as to promote certainty and security in business. But when great decisions are to be made, the State is a sovereign body of which the purpose is to promote

the greatest good of the whole. When, therefore, we enter the realm of State action, everything is to be considered and weighed on its merits. Changes in Death Duties, Income Tax, Land Tenure, Licensing, Game Laws, Church Establishment, Feudal Rights, Slavery, and so on through all ages, have received the same denunciations from the absolutists of contract, who are the real parents of Revolution.'

Keynes (1923, p. 68)

My hope would be that his warnings are heeded and that more countries take steps in the direction shown by the United Kingdom:

- Conversion of a substantial amount of the outstanding government debt into index-linked form.
- Regular issue of new index-linked loans, so that a sufficiently deep market in index-linked bonds can develop, which will help pension funds to offer inflation-proof pensions, as in the U.K.
- A savings scheme for smaller savers that guarantees the purchasing power of their savings.

If it is necessary to make substantial cut-backs in the collective sectors of these countries, then this necessity remains even if management of the national debt is improved. However, a more rational debt policy would make it far easier for savings on collective expenditure to be translated into higher profit margins in the corporate sector and into additional investment, because the interest burden on the national debt would be both lower and spread out better over time. Also, governments could increase the credibility of their anti-inflationary policies and so reduce monetary uncertainty and help business investment.

Often enough tinpot schemes are proposed through which the financial sector shall assist in solving the problems of the real economy. In the case of indexation of long-term government debt, however, we have a proposal that has been underwritten by many great monetary economists and has proven successful in the U.K. in bringing down the real costs of servicing the national debt. And, in case the banks continue to the opposed, we have Keynes' word for it that conservative bankers may be 'untrustworthy guides in a perilous age of transition'.

chapter 8

Concluding comments 1983

"Flexibility is the great virtue of instruments of monetary and credit policy. Changes in the course of monetary policy can be made promptly and – if need be – frequently."

Arthur F. Burns, Chairman of the Federal Reserve, in a Speech at Bryant College, Rhode Island in May 1976, quoted in "The Fed", by Maxwell Newton, New York, Times Books, 1983, p. 190.

"Keynes directs us to examine the factors determining long-term expectations and to develop institutional arrangements that increase long-term stability. Perhaps those assignments are, at last, of major interest for economists."

Allan H. Meltzer, "On Keynes's General Theory", Journal of Economic Literature Volume XIX Number 1, March 1981, p. 63.

All the statistical estimates in this book have been computed in early 1983 with the most up-to-date numbers available at that time. Future research will decide whether monetary uncertainty was indeed as important a factor in keeping the interest rate high in the early 1980's as Mascaro-Meltzer and our research team in Rotterdam found it to be. A definitive judgment on the robustness of our research is better left to others ; I offer the following concluding comments to facilitate future evaluation. To begin, I enumerate some limitations in the analysis which may have affected both the theoretical arguments and the empirical equations. With these qualifications firmly in mind, I then review the principal conclusions in the light of the political debate on domestic monetary policy as it developed – if that is not too flattering an expression – during the first half of 1983.

The conclusions may be sensitive to one or more of the following restrictive features of the analysis:

- The theoretical analysis contains a simplifying short-cut in failing to derive a theory about the volume of consumption at each point in time from theoretical "first principles". In a more fundamental approach the choice between consumption or investment would follow logically from basic assumptions about the goals and preferences of different categories of economic agents.

- The empirical analysis looks at interest rates on long-term government bonds only. The different risk characteristics of private and public bonds have not been investigated here, because the theoretical analysis does not differentiate in the non-government sector between a financial sector, a non-financial business sector, and a personal sector.

- The statistical analysis focuses on short-term relationships between the different variables. The decision to employ first differences of the interest rates and their determinants means unavoidably that the "high-frequency" end of the spectrum is emphasized, whereas "low-frequency" connections may get lost. As explained in Chapter 5, the non-stationary behaviour of the unexplained parts of the real rates of interest plus our desire to apply standard statistical techniques to facilitate precise tests for statistical significance led to the choice for first-differenced data.

- Possible effects of taxes on interest rates have been neglected throughout. Whether tax regimes may have to be taken into account for the analysis of interest rates on government debt remains a matter of contention. We have followed the majority of studies cited in chapter 5 in omitting consideration of the tax system.

● The choice for a discrete-time model implies that uncertainty *between* periods can be analysed, but uncertainty within periods has to be neglected. The precautionary demand for money, for example, increases in the theoretical models of chapter 3 because economic agents are uncertain how many real balances they might require during the next quarterly period. In the real world, a scramble for money will occur also if a troublesome economic climate makes financial planning within each quarter more difficult.

● Macroeconomic factors have been investigated, but institutional changes in the financial sector and changes in the regulatory climate have been left out of the analysis. The unexplained parts of the interest rate regressions, therefore, must incorporate the net effects of changes in institutions and regulations. It may be hoped, however, that permanent changes in the institutional framework have one-time effects on the *changes* in interest rates, so that they may be subsumed under the residual errors.

● Some types of uncertainty are more amenable to statistical analyses than other sources of risk. Monetary and budgetary uncertainty can be defined as depending upon the estimated errors in predicting future rates of money growth and future budget deficits. By contrast, uncertainty about the tax regime or uncertainty about the regulatory climate are harder to compress into the margin of error in predicting a single number. Political uncertainties or perceived risks to the stability of the global financial system are still more difficult to quantify. Thus, the outcomes of the statistical analysis may suffer from bias in favour of those sources of *uncertainty* that can be distilled into the estimated *riskiness* of short-term predictions with respect to a single index variable.

I assume with confidence that the reader will discern other limitations to the research in addition to those listed above. Nevertheless, the research reported in this monograph makes it somewhat more difficult to dismiss the following statements :

Whatever one's impressions of the surrounding rhetoric, the factual re-cord of U.S. monetary policy between October 1979 and July 1983 dis-

proves the notion that America carried out an experiment with monetarist policies.

By definition a monetarist policy means adherence to a medium-term growth path for some monetary aggregate, allowing for infrequent adjustments to the target if there is strong evidence that the *trend* of velocity has changed. In no way did U.S. monetary policy after October 1979 obey this definition. Our index of monetary uncertainty, depicted in chapter 5, increased sharply, indicating that the quarter-to-quarter unpredictability of the growth rate of M1 became much higher than before. Under a monetarist regime the index should have declined, indicating that it was easier than before to predict future growth rates of the money supply. Recall that our index of monetary uncertainty is based on a sophisticated statistical technique which incorporates quick learning about any important changes to the level or the growth rate of the money supply. The Multi-State Kalman Filter guarantees that the increase in unpredictability was not caused by continued use of an inappropriate forecasting formula, but expresses the bewilderment of every forecaster.

The numbers on four-quarter rates of growth tell exactly the same story. The discrepancies between the announcements by the Federal Reserve and its achievements for the complete period to date in which it has announced targets for money growth are shown in table 8.1. Between October 1979 and mid-1982 the Federal Reserve has claimed to be more concerned about the growth rate of the money supply, but monetary control has been worse than before.

The annual errors have been larger, corroborating the evidence of increased variability on a quarterly basis: in retrospect it is clear that the Federal Reserve never adopted the monetarist proposal for a *gradual* and *planned* elimination of inflation, but opted instead for policies that were much more variable and unpredictable than before. Policy-makers found the "monetarist" label convenient, both because it absolved them from direct responsibility for the high interest rates that could be caused by a more restrictive policy, and because it would help to defuse any criticisms from Karl Brunner, Milton Friedman and Allan Meltzer, the three best-known independent experts on U.S. monetary policy and all three advocates of planned money growth.

Table 8.1 : Money Growth in the U.S. 1975-1983.

Percent Growth

Year Ending in 4th Quarter	Target Announced by Federal Reserve	Target Mid-point	Actual	Error
1976 (M-1)	4.5 - 7.5 %	6.0 %	5.8 %	− 0.2 %
1977 (M-1)	4.5 - 6.5	5.5	7.9	2.4
1978 (M-1)	4.0 - 6.5	5.2	7.2	1.9
1979 (M-1)	3.0 - 6.0	4.5	5.5	1.0
1980 (M-1B)	4.0 - 6.5	5.2	7.3	2.0
1981 (M-1B)	6.0 - 8.5	7.2	5.0	−2.2
1982 (M-1)	2.5 - 5.5	4.0	8.5	4.5
1983 (M-1)	4.0 - 8.0	6.0	14 *	4 **

* Estimated growth rate between 1982IV and 1983II at an annual rate.
** Estimated error in the level of 1983II, corresponding to an 8 percentage point error in the annualized growth rate.

Note : Revised targets for 1983 were announced on July 20, 1983 : a 5-9 % range for the growth rate between 1983II and 1983IV. The revised targets fully incorporate the excessive money growth between 1982IV and 1983II.

Monetary targets will have to be based on a forecast of the trend rate of growth of the income velocity of money. Macroeconomic uncertainty would increase, however, if the monetary targets were adjusted frequently on the basis of short-term movements in actual velocity.

Would any mariner fix the rudder angle of his ship instead of keeping the needle of his compass reading fixed and adjusting the rudder if necessary ? James Tobin of Yale University asked this rethorical question at the July 1983 Conference of U.S. academic and business economists in Seattle. Would it not be preferable indeed to replace a monetary target – a numerical goal for an intermediate variable of no intrinsic interest – with a target path for final sales or nominal gross national product ? Tobin answers this question in the affirmative and so do many other economists. Strongly advocated by Samuel Brittan of the "Financial Times" the proposal to target nominal gnp or a related variable has become especially popular with the staffs of supra-national bureaucracies. The director for macroeconomic analysis and policies of the Commission of the European Communities writes :

"In Europe as a whole one could envisage this proposal as being implemented in a coordinated way as follows. Countries would prepare together preliminary multi-year trajectories for nominal GDP growth and submit them for discussion both domestically to the social partners, and internationally, within the EC and a broader forum if other countries wished to participate. They would obtain feedback from both the social partners and the international discussions before deciding on their objectives. Countries participating in the European Monetary System, or informally associated with it, would choose their nominal GDP targets with a special eye on objectives for monetary and price convergence... For the medium-run it can be argued that the setting of nominal gdp targets is in principle similar to the setting of money supply targets, since over a period of two or three years or more the money supply/nominal GDP relationship is a close and faithful one. But in the shorter-run there would be important differences. Short-run money supply management is bedevilled by technical problems – changing institutional arrangements, instability of the demand for money, unexpected external shocks".

Michal Emerson, "The European stagflation disease in international perspective ; and some possible therapy", Paper presented at the Conference of the Centre for European Policy Studies on European policy priorities, Brussels, 1982, pp. 25-26.

In a similar vein, the July 1983 OECD "Economic Outlook" notes :

"Interest has developed in a number of countries in the possibility of setting policy in terms of, or at least paying closer attention to, the actual and prospective development of nominal GDP: there are perhaps two main reasons for this interest. First, policy making in the relatively low inflation era up to the late 1960s could afford to be concerned mainly with developments on the real side of the economy. But the inflationary upsurge of the 1970s compelled a greater concern with the nominal magnitudes. Secondly, the more recent experience with the consequences of adhering rigidly to a pre-specified growth target for the money aggregates has spurred the search for an approach that would permit greater responsiveness to events as they unfold, while at the same time not losing the financial discipline that money targets were intended to provide.

Whether an approach emphasising nominal income would be found more generally helpful is not yet clear. The approach might bring more information to bear on the conduct of monetary policy, while remaining applicable regardless of the short-run stability of the demand for money and the relative significance of fiscal and monetary policy instruments – empirical matters which differ from one country to another. As a *framework for policy discussion* in present circumstances, a focus on nominal GDP might serve to emphasise that as inflation falls sufficiently, room can appropriately be left for real growth. The authorities would make it clear that the extent to which nominal income growth would be reflected in output increases rather than inflation would in large part depend on decisions in the private sector. This might be particularly valuable in the context of wage bargaining.

An open question at present, however, is the extent to which the nominal income approach might be able to go beyond merely helping to frame policy discussion, and actually assist in the setting of policy. It is probably widely agreed that in the short to medium term macroeconomic policy has its predominant influence on the two components of nominal income – output and prices – jointly but not separately. At the same time, nominal income is not a variable that can be controlled in the short run in the same way as a monetary aggregate ; nor would the statistical base for this variable permit close monitoring in the short-term. The aim would have to be to bring about a steady course of nominal income over a run of years, whereby output could grow at potential provided inflation was held at a tolerable rate. Where there is a close relationship between money and nominal income there may be a presumption that if nominal income were an objective it would be controlled by money, a view having been taken on the likely course of velocity. In most countries, however, policy-makers would also probably see some role for fiscal policy ; one of the features of the nominal income framework is the scope it may offer for the joint consideration of the settings of monetary and fiscal policy".

OECD, "Economic Outlook", July 1983, pp. 12-13.

The research findings in this book bear on these proposals to consider "velocity-adjusted targets for money growth" or, more simply, targets for the rate of growth of nominal national income. Targets for nominal national expenditure would be preferable to targets for some monetary aggregate under the following conditions :

- *We would have to know how to do it.* Not only are the lags in the effects of monetary policy long and variable – this is Friedman's traditional argument against discretionary monetary policies – but the installation of systematic feedback rules may change the historical relationships between consumption, investment, national income and other macroeconomic variables. By contrast, substantial evidence has accumulated that targets for the narrow money supply can be implemented both in the U.S. and in small open economies (see, for example, Johannes and Rasche, 1979, Büttler et al., 1979 and Bomhoff, 1977).

- *Targeting of gnp should not destabilize inflationary expectations.* Although a target path for nominal gnp would be less dangerous for inflationary expectations than attempts at fixing nominal rates of interest, a real risk remains that over-optimistic assumptions about real growth drive up the underlying rate of inflation and leave the public at a loss whether this higher rate of inflation will be accommodated by the monetary authorities or whether next period's target for the growth rate of nominal gnp will be lowered. Presumably, if real growth turned out to be lower than expected, policy makers would not find it attractive to change to a more restrictive monetary policy. Note, that the feedback mechanism is much easier politically in the case of monetary targeting. If, for example, the rate of growth of velocity turns out to be higher than expected, inflation and real economic growth will usually both be higher than was anticipated which makes it easier for the monetary authorities to switch to a smaller rate of growth for the money supply in their next target period.

- *Targeting of nominal gnp requires the ability to specify all those temporary shocks to real output or prices to which the monetary authorities should not react.* Looking back on the 1970's and the failure of many advisory bodies to analyse the economic impact of the first energy price crisis, it appears ironic that a proposal becomes fashionable which requires instant judgments about the temporary or permanent character of all shocks that impinge on the economic system. Fewer hard decisions are needed, in my opinion, if the authorities adhere to a monetary target. Adjustments to the target during the target period would be necessary only in the case of significant permanent shifts in the income velocity of money, and I would maintain that the fall in velocity during 1982 was to a large extent the consequence of the extreme variability in U.S. monetary policy during 1980-1982 (see chapter 5 for the evidence). Financial innovations and changes in regulations can have important one-time effects on velocity, but such effects can be estimated and the definition of money be adjusted accordingly.

- *Targeting of gnp requires that greater monetary variability would have little impact on the economy.* Assuming that it could be done, that it would not destabilize inflationary expectations and that policy makers would be rather better at separating permanent from transitory shocks in the 1980's than they were during the 1970's, targeting of nominal gnp would be worthwhile only if the associated greater flexibility in money growth (now an instrument variable instead of an intermediate target of economic policy) would not harm the economy.
  Our findings confirm the conclusion by Mascaro-Meltzer that increased monetary variability is very damaging. Mascaro-Meltzer found that monetary uncertainty puts an important risk premium into U.S. interest rates, whereas uncertainty about the income velocity of money was generally irrelevant. Our research indicated that monetary uncertainty, defined as great variability in the growth rate of the money supply, did more damage to long-term interest rates than inflationary uncertainty, measured as quarter-to-quarter variability in the estimated underlying rate of inflation. These results suggest that economic agents know that many short-term changes in the growth of real income or prices have temporary causes that should not lead to major revisions in their assessment of long-term economic growth and inflation. By contrast, changes in the growth rate of the money supply are viewed as having an important permanent component and therefore as highly relevant to longer-term inflationary expectations. The additional risk premium which monetary uncertainty puts into long-term rates of interest means that for a given distribution of

national income between labour income and capital income, fewer investment projects will be undertaken. In this way great monetary uncertainty places an excess burden on the economy.

When this manuscript was completed, it was not yet clear whether targeting of nominal gnp would be applied in practice. Quite obvious, by contrast, was the damage done by the erratic monetary policies of the early 1980's in the U.S. and elsewhere. Instead of adhering to a systematic policy of disinflation, the Federal Reserve opted for extreme variability in the quarter-to-quarter rate of money growth and the resulting monetary uncertainty put an estimated 200 basis points into the long-term U.S. rate of interest. Until this risk premium has disappeared, some investment projects will remain infeasible even after the cyclical part of the 1981-1982 recession has disappeared. High risk premia in long-term interest rates mean that the equilibrium value of the capital stock will be lower than it otherwise would have been. For a given ratio of business profits to national income, the result is medium-term involuntary unemployment in the Keynesian sense. When Keynes wrote the "General Theory" he viewed the animal spirits as the basic source of uncertainty that reduced investment below its optimal level and thus led to medium-term involuntary unemployement. As pointed out by Meltzer (1981a), many types of uncertainty about the economic future can put an excess burden on the economy. Uncertainty in the early 1980's – and therefore part of the Keynesian unemployment in that period – was caused to a considerable extent by the rejection of a stable, systematic anti-inflation policy and the choice in favour of extreme variability in money growth and high monetary uncertainty.

appendix 1

Forecasts with
Multi-State Kalman Filters

with Clemens J.M. Kool

Introduction

We have described the Multi-State Kalman Filter method informally in chapter 4. The basic idea, developed by Harrison and Stevens (1971, 1976) consists of applying simultaneously a set of parallel filter models each using a different forecasting scheme. The final forecast is computed as a weighted average of the individual forecasts, where the relative weight of each separate forecast in the composite prediction is determined both by its general success over the past and its relevance to the most recent two observations.

In this way the method is capable of dealing with different types of disturbances both purely temporary shocks, fully permanent shifts in the level or in the growth rate and mixtures of temporary and permanent shocks. We have stressed in chapter 4 that this feature gives the MSKF-method an advantage over, for example, Box-Jenkins modelling, as Box-Jenkins time series models and similar techniques are designed only to cope with series where *each* disturbance is a mixture of temporary and permanent elements. We can deal both with such mixed shocks and with purely temporary and permanent disturbances.

A second advantageous feature of the MSKF-method is the incorporation of a learning mechanism which can cope with changes in the relative importance of the different types of shocks over time. The Bayesian approach of updating the prior probabilities of the individual forecast models on the basis of the most recent experience guarantees a sensible and intelligent learning process. By contrast, Box-Jenkins models, even if estimated recursively, will exhibit very slow adaptation to changes in the structure of the series because there is no un-learning or forgetting of previous experience. The dead weight of all earlier observations will continue to influence the parameters in a Box-Jenkins model, even if a permanent change in the characteristics of the series has made the old data irrelevant to forecasting.

In this Statistical Appendix we shall first present a mathematical exposition of the method, and subsequently illustrate its potential by applying it to an artificial series. Finally, we shall take up again the example of the Swiss money supply considered above in chapter 4, and present some additional materials on the way in which the MSKF-filter copes with data from the real world.

The Algorithm

Assume that the following model describes the behaviour of a time series:

$$x_t = \bar{x}_t + \varepsilon_t \qquad\qquad\qquad \varepsilon_t \sim N(0, V_\varepsilon) \qquad\qquad (A1)$$

$$\bar{x}_t = \bar{x}_{t-1} + \hat{\bar{x}}_t + \gamma_t \qquad\qquad \gamma_t \sim N(0, V_\gamma) \qquad\qquad (A2)$$

$$\hat{\bar{x}}_t = \hat{\bar{x}}_{t-1} + \rho_t \qquad\qquad\qquad \rho_t \sim N(0, V_\rho) \qquad\qquad (A3)$$

Here x_t is the observed value of a time series x, possibly after a logarithmic transformation to remove any exponential trends. $\bar{x}_t$ is the 'true' underlying level of x at time t and $\hat{\bar{x}}_t$ is the then prevailing 'true' underlying growth rate. ε_t, γ_t and ρ_t are serially uncorrelated, mutually independent, normally distributed disturbance terms with mean zero and variances V_ε, V_γ and V_ρ, respectively. As both the 'true' level and the 'true' growth rate are unobservable variables, the model has been designed to extract information from the observed values of x_t to form an optimal estimate of both $\bar{x}_t$ and $\hat{\bar{x}}_t$ at every point in time. We assume that the underlying 'true' level behaves like a random walk with stochastic drift $\hat{\bar{x}}_t$, while $\hat{\bar{x}}_t$ itself behaves like a random walk.

Another way of formulating the estimation problem is to say that we do not directly observe the underlying value of x_t, since three types of noise obscure the picture. The model's aim then is to distinguish between three different kinds of shocks, ε_t's representing observational errors which contaminate the series, γ_t's that cause once and for all shifts in the underlying level of the series and ρ_t's which produce permanent shocks to the underlying growth rate.

It follows from the structure of the model that in each period t, the prevailing estimates $\bar{x}_t$ and $\hat{\bar{x}}_t$ are sufficient statistics for predicting x in all subsequent periods, since all future shifts in the underlying level and growth rate are unpredictable. The optimal k-period prediction for x, conditional on all information up to and including period t equals $(\bar{x}_t + k.\hat{\bar{x}}_t)$.

We now assume that $\bar{x}_{t-1}$ and $\hat{\bar{x}}_{t-1}$ have a bivariate normal prior density with mean vector (m_{t-1}, b_{t-1}) and covariance matrix:

$$V_{t-1} = \begin{pmatrix} V_{mm} & V_{mb} \\ V_{mb} & V_{bb} \end{pmatrix}_{t-1}$$

$$(\bar{x}_{t-1}, \hat{\bar{x}}_{t-1}) \sim N\left(\begin{pmatrix} m_{t-1} \\ b_{t-1} \end{pmatrix}, V_{t-1} \right) \qquad\qquad (A4)$$

Then the statevector $(\bar{x}_t, \hat{x}_t)$ conditional on observation x_t has a bivariate normal distribution also with mean vector (m_t, b_t) and covariance matrix V_t. The mean vector and covariance matrix may be calculated recursively using the Kalman filter equations as follows:

$$e_t = x_t - m_{t-1} - b_{t-1} \tag{A5}$$

$$m_t = m_{t-1} + b_{t-1} + A_1 e_t \tag{A6}$$

$$b_t = b_{t-1} + A_2 e_t \tag{A7}$$

where

$$A_1 = r_{11}/V_e \tag{A8}$$

$$A_2 = r_{12}/V_e \tag{A9}$$

$$V_e = r_{11} + V_\varepsilon \text{ is the one step ahead error variance.} \tag{A10}$$

The r_{ij} are defined as:

$$R = \begin{pmatrix} r_{11} & r_{12} \\ r_{12} & r_{22} \end{pmatrix}$$

$$r_{11} = V_{mm_{t-1}} + 2.V_{mb_{t-1}} + V_{bb_{t-1}} + V_\gamma + V_\rho \tag{A11}$$

$$r_{12} = V_{mb_{t-1}} + V_{bb_{t-1}} + V_\rho \tag{A12}$$

$$r_{22} = V_{bb_{t-1}} + V_\rho \tag{A13}$$

The new covariance matrix V_t then may be written as:

$$V_{mm_t} = r_{11} - A_1^2.V_e \tag{A14}$$

$$V_{mb_t} = r_{12} - A_1.A_2.V_e \tag{A15}$$

$$V_{bb_t} = r_{22} - A_2^2.V_e \tag{A16}$$

From the equations above it is obvious that specification of the variances of ε, γ and ρ combined with the information on the past of the series as expressed by m_{t-1}, b_{t-1} and V_{t-1} completely determines the expected values of $\bar{x}_t$ and $\hat{\bar{x}}_t$ and their covariance matrix. Extending the argument into the future this means that the complete path of the expected underlying 'true' level $\bar{x}_t$ and the expected underlying 'true' growth rate $\hat{\bar{x}}_t$ is determined by subsequent actual data only conditional on the variances of the various disturbance terms.

Once the variances of the disturbances have been fixed, the stochastic properties of the series are fixed also: the contribution of the data is to determine the underlying level of the series and its growth rate, but there is no feed back from the data to the structure of the model. In other words: the state variables are functions of the data, but the model parameters are not, and the adequacy of the assumed model is not tested.

Two avenues exist to create a channel from the data to the structure of the model. On the one hand we could try to estimate both the unobservable state variables and the variance terms simultaneously in a recursive manner. Our statistical implementation of the Recursive Prediction Error Method in Statistical Appendix II examplifies this approach. For the univariate forecasts discussed in this Statistical Appendix we have chosen another approach in which the different variances are not estimated simultaneously with the unobservable state variables. Instead we use not one but a number of models of the type represented by equations (A1) - (A3), differing from each other only in the specification of the variances of ε_t, γ_t and ρ_t. Forecasts of the time series are computed as weighted averages of the forecasts from the individual models. As time goes by, the weights of the separate forecasts are adjusted according to the success of each model over the recent past. In this way a feedback channel from the data to the model is created.

In the Multi-State approach, with six different models to describe the behaviour of each time series x, we again assume that $(\bar{x}_{t-1}, \hat{\bar{x}}_{t-1})$ has a bivariate normal prior distribution, but now it is a weighted average of the six normal distributions of $(\bar{x}_{t-1}^{(i)}, \hat{\bar{x}}_{t-1}^{(i)})$ corresponding to the separate models:

$$(\bar{x}_{t-1}, \hat{\bar{x}}_{t-1}) \sim \sum_{i=1}^{6} q_{t-1}^{(i)} \cdot N \left(\begin{pmatrix} m_{t-1}^{(i)} \\ b_{t-1}^{(i)} \end{pmatrix}, V_{t-1}^{(i)} \right) \tag{A17}$$

where $q_{t-1}^{(i)}$ is the posterior probability with respect to observation x_{t-1} that the process was in state (model) i in period t-1. Assuming that the process was in state i in period t-1 and is in state j in period t, we may rewrite equations (A5) - (A6) for all i and j:

$$e_t^{(i)} = x_t - \underset{t-1}{E} (x_t \mid (i), x_{t-1}, \ldots) = x_t - (\bar{x}_{t-1}^{(i)} + \hat{\bar{x}}_{t-1}^{(i)}) \tag{A18}$$

$$m_t^{(i,j)} = m_{t-1}^{(i)} + b_{t-1}^{(i)} + A_1 \, e_t^{(i)} \tag{A19}$$

$$b_t^{(i,j)} = b_{t-1}^{(i)} + A_2 \, e_t^{(i)} \tag{A20}$$

$$A_1 = r_{11}/V_e^{(i,j)} \tag{A21}$$

$$A_2 = r_{12}/V_e^{(i,j)} \tag{A22}$$

$$V_e^{(i,j)} = r_{11} + V_\varepsilon^{(j)} \tag{A23}$$

$$r_{11} = V_{mm_{t-1}}^{(i)} + 2\,V_{mb_{t-1}}^{(i)} + V_{bb_{t-1}}^{(i)} + V_\gamma^{(j)} + V_\rho^{(j)} \tag{A24}$$

$$r_{12} = V_{mb_{t-1}}^{(i)} + V_{bb_{t-1}}^{(i)} + V_\rho^{(j)} \tag{A25}$$

$$r_{22} = V_{bb_{t-1}}^{(i)} + V_\rho^{(j)} \tag{A26}$$

$$V_{mm_t}^{(i,j)} = r_{11} - A_1^2 \cdot V_e^{(i,j)} \tag{A27}$$

$$V_{mb_t}^{(i,j)} = r_{12} - A_1 \cdot A_2 \cdot V_e^{(i,j)} \tag{A28}$$

$$V_{bb_t}^{(i,j)} = r_{22} - A_2^2 \cdot V_e^{(i,j)} \tag{A29}$$

The result is that $(\bar{x}_t, \hat{\bar{x}}_t)$ has a bivariate normal density with mean vector $(m_t^{(i,j)}, b_t^{(i,j)})$ and covariance matrix $V_t^{(i,j)}$, conditional on observation x_t and on state j prevailing at period t and state i at period t-1:

$$(\bar{x}_t, \hat{\bar{x}}_t \mid x_t, S_t = j, S_{t-1} = i) \sim N\left(\begin{pmatrix} m_t^{(i,j)} \\ b_t^{(i,j)} \end{pmatrix}, V_t^{(i,j)} \right) \tag{A30}$$

The complete posterior density of $(\bar{x}_t, \hat{\bar{x}}_t)$ conditional on observation x_t only, can be written as:

$$(\bar{x}_t, \hat{\bar{x}}_t \mid x_t) \sim \sum_{i,j} p_t^{(i,j)} \cdot N\left(\begin{pmatrix} m_t^{(i,j)} \\ b_t^{(i,j)} \end{pmatrix}, V_t^{(i,j)} \right) \tag{A31}$$

where $p_t^{(i,j)}$ = Probability $[S_t = j, S_{t-1} = i \mid x(t)]$

$x(t) = (x_t, x_{t-1}, x_{t-2} \ldots)$

Now $p_t^{(i,j)}$ can be written as:

$$p_t^{(i,j)} = \Pr [x_t \mid S_t = j, S_{t-1} = i, x(t-1)] \ . \tag{A32}$$

$$\Pr [S_t = j \mid S_{t-1} = i, x(t-1)] \ .$$

$$\Pr [S_{t-1} = i \mid x(t-1)]/\Pr [x_t \mid x(t-1)]$$

The first factor on the right-hand side of equation (A32) represents the conditional likelihood function of x_t which has the form:

$$(2\pi V_e^{(i,j)})^{-1/2} \ . \ \exp \left(- (x_t - m_{t-1}^{(i)} - b_{t-1}^{(i)})^2/2V_e^{(i,j)}\right) \tag{A33}$$

The second factor shows the probability, prior to observation x_t and conditional on all information up to period t-1, that the process will be in state j at period t: $_{t-1}\pi_t^{(j)}$. The third factor on the right-hand side of equation (A32) is the posterior probability $q_{t-1}^{(i)}$ defined above that the process was in state i in period t-1 given observation x_{t-1}. The final factor is a normalization constant, independent of both the indices i and j. This results in the following formula for $p_t^{(i,j)}$:

$$p_t^{(i,j)} = k \ . \ (2\pi V_e^{(i,j)})^{-1/2} \ .$$

$$\exp \left(-(x_t - m_{t-1}^{(i)} - b_{t-1}^{(i)})^2/2V_e^{(i,j)}\right) \ . \ _{t-1}\pi_t^{(j)} \ . \ q_{t-1}^{(i)} \tag{A34}$$

Equation (A34) shows that the probability $p_t^{(i,j)}$ conditional on all information up till period t depends on three sources. Both $_{t-1}\pi_t^{(j)}$ and $q_{t-1}^{(i)}$ contain information from the past and no current information at all. They may be calculated already before observation x_t comes available. It is easy to see that $p_t^{(i,j)}$ will be higher for a certain combination (i,j) the higher $q_{t-1}^{(i)}$ relative to the other models' posterior probabilities and the higher $_{t-1}\pi_t^{(j)}$ relative to the other models' prior probabilities. However, this is a partial analysis only, depending on the value of the current observation x_t. In general, if observation x_t fits poorly the assumptions as specified by the indices i and j, the forecast error will be large and the likelihood function small, resulting in a low value for $p_t^{(i,j)}$.

In other words, $p_t^{(i,j)}$ is a combination of past and current information.

If these two sources reinforce each other for some combination of i and j, that $p_t^{(i,j)}$ will be quite large. However, if the evidence from present and past conflicts a smaller $p_t^{(i,j)}$ will result, indicating increased uncertainty about the process.

Starting with a prior density for $(\bar{x}_{t-1}, \hat{\bar{x}}_{t-1})$ composed of $N(=6)$ components (cf. equation (A17)) and a current observation x_t, a posterior density for $(\bar{x}_t, \hat{\bar{x}}_t)$ is calculated using $V_\varepsilon^{(j)}$, $V_y^{(j)}$, $V_\rho^{(j)}$ and $_{t-1}\pi_t^{(j)}$ $\forall_j$, which contains N^2 components. This posterior density can serve in turn as prior density with respect to observation $t + 1$. In this way, we would generate further posterior densities with N^3, N^4, ... components as new observations x_{t+1}, x_{t+2}, ... become available. To avoid computational problems, we assume in the algorithm that it is not too inaccurate to compress the posterior densities in the following way:

$$q_t^{(j)} = \sum_i p_t^{(i,j)} \tag{A35}$$

$$m_t^{(j)} = \sum_i p_t^{(i,j)} \cdot m_t^{(i,j)}/q_t^{(j)} \tag{A36}$$

$$b_t^{(j)} = \sum_i p_t^{(i,j)} \cdot b_t^{(i,j)}/q_t^{(j)} \tag{A37}$$

$$V_{mm_t}^{(j)} = \sum_i p_t^{(i,j)} \cdot (V_{mm_t}^{(i,j)} + (m_t^{(i,j)} - m_t^{(j)})^2)/q_t^{(j)} \tag{A38}$$

$$V_{mb_t}^{(j)} = \sum_i p_t^{(i,j)} \cdot (V_{mb_t}^{(i,j)} + (m_t^{(i,j)} - m_t^{(j)})(b_t^{(i,j)} - b_t^{(j)}))/q_t^{(j)} \tag{A39}$$

$$V_{bb_t}^{(j)} = \sum_i p_t^{(i,j)} \cdot (V_{bb_t}^{(i,j)} + (b_t^{(i,j)} - b_t^{(j)})^2)/q_t^{(j)} \tag{A40}$$

The approximated posterior density of $(\bar{x}_t, \hat{\bar{x}}_t)$ then becomes

$$(\bar{x}_t, \hat{\bar{x}}_t) \sim \sum_{j=1}^{6} q_t^{(j)} \cdot N\left(\begin{pmatrix} m_t^{(j)} \\ b_t^{(j)} \end{pmatrix}, V_t^{(j)} \right) \tag{A41}$$

A final note on the condensation procedure as described above concerns the inclusion of terms such as $(m_t^{(i,j)} - m_t^{(j)})^2$. To understand this decision let us examine more closely the way the condensation procedure works. Suppose for example that the estimated variances $V_{mm_t}^{(i,j)}$ for a given j are all very small and further that the estimates $m_t^{(i,j)}$ for the six different models differ considerably. In that case neglecting the term $(m_t^{(i,j)} - m_t^{(j)})^2$ would result in a very low value for $V_{mm_t}^{(j)}$. This low value of $V_{mm_t}^{(j)}$ would reflect the fact that each model is quite certain about its own point estimate of the 'true' underlying level of the series. However, it would not reflect the uncertainty arising from the combination of the diverging point estimates of the 'true' underlying level into one aggregated estimate. To capture this uncertainty we have included the term $(m_t^{(i,j)} - m_t^{(j)})^2$ in equation (A38). Equations (A39) and (A40) are treated analogously.

Specification of the different models

We have used the equivalence between the model as presented in equations (A1) - (A3) and the well known ARIMA (0,2,2) model:

$$\Delta^2 x_t = (1 - \theta_1 B - \theta_2 B^2) a_t \qquad a_t \sim N(0, V_a) \qquad (A42)$$

to specify the six individual models which together make up the MSKF-system. Eliminating $\bar{x}_t$ and $\hat{x}_t$ from equations (A1) - (A3) results in

$$\Delta^2 x_t = \varepsilon_t - 2\varepsilon_{t-1} + \varepsilon_{t-2} + \gamma_t - \gamma_{t-1} + \rho_t \qquad (A43)$$

By writing out the autocorrelation fucntions of equations (A42) and (A43) it is easy to show that the following restrictions hold between θ_1, θ_2 and V_a on the one hand and V_ε, V_γ and V_ρ on the other hand:

$$V_\varepsilon = -\theta_2 . V_a \qquad (A44)$$

$$4V_\varepsilon + V_\gamma = \theta_1 (1 - \theta_2) . V_a \qquad (A45)$$

$$6V_\varepsilon + 2V_\gamma + V_\rho = (1 + \theta_1^2 + \theta_2^2) . V_a \qquad (A46)$$

Writing $V_\varepsilon = R_\varepsilon . V_0$, $V_\gamma = R_\gamma . V_0$, $V_\rho = R_\rho . V_0$ and $V_a = R_a . V_0$, (A44) - (A46) may be simplified to:

$$R_\varepsilon = -\theta_2 . R_a \qquad (A47)$$

$$4R_\varepsilon + R_\gamma = \theta_1 (1 - \theta_2) . R_a \qquad (A48)$$

$$6R_\varepsilon + 2R_y + R_\rho = (1 + \theta_1^2 + \theta_2^2) \cdot R_a \qquad (A49)$$

where V_0 is the basic variance of the process. Specification of V_ε, V_y and V_ρ determines the stochastic properties of model (A1) - (A3). As there is a one-to-one link from these three variances to θ_1, θ_2 and V_a, we may equivalently choose θ_1, θ_2 and V_a to specify our models. From (A42) we derive the following equation:

$$x_t^e = x_{t-1}^e + (x_{t-1}^e - x_{t-2}^e) + (2 - \theta_1)(x_{t-1} - x_{t-1}^e) \qquad (A50)$$

$$- (1 + \theta_2)(x_{t-2} - x_{t-2}^e)$$

Suppose all deviations of actual observations from predicted values are of a temporary nature. In that case we don't want our prediction errors $(x_{t-1} - x_{t-1}^e)$ and $(x_{t-2} - x_{t-2}^e)$ to affect next period's prediction. This would require values for θ_1 and θ_2 of about 2.0 and -1.0, respectively. Our prediction rule then would not depend on actual data and would reduce to:

$$x_t^e = x_{t-1}^e + (x_{t-1}^e - x_{t-2}^e) \qquad (A51)$$

A process which is characterized by permanent changes in the level however, should be predicted quite differently. Now values of 1.0 and 0.0 are appropriate for θ_1 and θ_2. The prediction rule can be written as

$$x_t^e = x_{t-1} + (x_{t-1}^e - x_{t-2}) \qquad (A52)$$

From (A52) it's clear that the observed value of x at period t-1 is the base for next period's prediction in contrast with (A51) where the expected value of x_{t-1} is used. The permanent increment in the series is represented by $(x_{t-1}^e - x_{t-2})$.

A series where every prediction error indicates a permanent change in the growth rate is best represented by the following prediction rule:

$$x_t^e = x_{t-1} + (x_{t-1} - x_{t-2}) \qquad (A53)$$

In this case θ_1 and θ_2 are both equal to zero. Next period's expectation is an extrapolation purely based on the last two observations.

In our empirical work we have used this distinction between three types of shocks. First we split up our six models in two groups, each consisting of three models. Within each group, one model is specified so as to be able to take account of transient shocks, one is designed to deal with permanent changes in the level and one can cope with permanent slope changes. The difference between the two groups is the level of the variances. A low variance group is meant to deal with small shocks, while a high variance group is designed for outlier shocks.

Table A1

State	θ_1	θ_2	R_ε	R_y	R_ρ	R_a
1. small temporary change	1.85	−0.86	0.86	0.001	0.0001	1
2. small permanent step change	1.10	−0.11	0.11	0.781	0.0001	1
3. small permanent slope change	0.10	−0.025	0.025	0.025	0.855625	1
4. large temporary change	1.99	−0.99002	15.84032	0.9568×10^{-3}	6×10^{-9}	16
5. large permanent step change	1.01	−0.011	0.176	15.63376	1.6×10^{-5}	16
6. large permanent slope change	0.01	−0.001	0.016	0.09616	15.715216	16

Table A1 displays the specification of the six models, both in terms of the ARIMA (0,2,2) model and of the MSKF-method. In table A1 R_a is set equal to 1.0, the numeraire of the system. Given the way we want the various models to predict a series, we choose the parameters θ_1 and θ_2. This immediately determines the ratio's between R_ε, R_y and R_ρ. Normalizing R_a to 1.0, also fixes the absolute levels. We restrict R_a to be constant within each group of the models. A final restriction links the variance of the outlier models to that of the small-change models. We choose the standard deviation of the outlier models four times as large as the standard deviation of the small-change models, so that its variance will be sixteen times as large.

Adaptive updating of the variance level

To calculate the variance levels for the different models an estimate of V_0

is required. As we have no prior information on the variability of the series x, we use the first 10 observations of x to calculate two approximate measures of that variability:

1. the median of $(x_t - x_{t-1})$ $\quad t = 2, \ldots, 10$

2. the median of $(x_t - \bar{x})$ $\quad t = 2, \ldots, 10$ where $\bar{x} = \dfrac{1}{9} \displaystyle\sum_{t=2}^{10} x_t$

The initial V_0 is calculated by taking the smaller of these medians, dividing it by 0.6745 and taking the square of this expression (see Huber, 1981). For the first ten periods V_0 is fixed. Afterwards it is adjusted each period by the following formula:

$$V_{0_t} = V_{0_{t-1}} + 0.25 \left(\frac{VF_t}{MVBAR_t} - 1.0 \right) V_{0_{t-1}} \tag{A54}$$

Here, VF_t is a robust measure of the realized variance of the forecast errors of the last 19 periods; the procedure to calculate VF_t is to take the absolute value of the last 19 forecast errors. Deleting the two smallest and the two largest absolute errors, we calculate the mean of the remaining fifteen absolute values. Dividing this mean by 0.6745 and taking the square of the ratio determines VF_t. The factor 0.25 in equation (A54) is arbitrary. MVBAR is a robust approximation of the theoretically variance of the forecast errors of the last 19 periods and is calculated by means of VBAR, which is the theoretical variance of the unconditional forecast m_{t+1}^f:

$$m_{t+1}^f \quad = \sum_{j=1}^{6} q_t^{(j)} (m_t^{(j)} + b_t^{(j)}) \tag{A55}$$

$$VBAR_{t+1} = \sum_{j=1}^{6} q_t^{(j)} (X_t^{(j)} + (m_{t+1}^f - m_t^{(j)} - b_t^{(j)})^2) \tag{A56}$$

$$X_t^{(j)} \quad = \sum_{i=1}^{6} p_t^{(i,j)} [V_e^{(i,j)} + (m_t^{(i,j)} - m_t^{(j)})^2 + (b_t^{(i,j)} - b_t^{(j)})^2 \tag{A57}$$

$$+ 2(m_t^{(i,j)} - m_t^{(j)}) (b_t^{(i,j)} - b_t^{(j)})]/q_t^{(j)}$$

where $x_t^{(j)}$ is the uncertainty associated with next period's prediction, conditional on the use of model j. Using the last 19 estimates of VBAR, we again delete the two smallest and the two largest values. The mean of the remaining observations is denoted by $MVBAR_t$. An intuitive interpretation of (A54) is that as soon as the forecast errors start rising in absolute value without an increase in MVBAR, probably V_0 should be adjusted upward. If MVBAR stays relatively small, indicating a fair degree of agreement between the various models and no increased uncertainty about their relative weights, rising forecast errors are likely to signal an increase in the variance of the process. Thus, V_0 should adapt.

In equation (A54) a practical change has to be made at the beginning of the process. For t less than 21 we replace the ratio $VF_t/MVBAR_t$ by

$$\frac{(t\text{-}1)VF_t + (20\text{-}t)V_{0_{t=1}}}{(t\text{-}1)MVBAR_t + (20\text{-}t)V_{0_{t=1}}}$$

Learning about the prior probabilities

Changes in the prior probabilities of the different models constitute the feedback channel from the data to the composite model. We assign to each of the small-change models an initial prior probability of $31\frac{2}{3}\%$, as it is not possible to decide which of them is better suited to the series x without further information; we constrain the prior probabilities of these three models to sum to 95% at all times. The remaining 5% probability is divided between the three outlier models. Initially each model is allotted a chance of $1\frac{2}{3}\%$.

The updating of the prior probabilities is as follows:

$$_t\pi^{(j)}_{t+1} = \frac{_{t\text{-}1}\pi^{(j)} + \bar{p}^{(j)}_{t\text{-}1}}{\sum_j (_{t\text{-}1}\pi^{(j)} + \bar{p}^{(j)}_{t\text{-}1})}$$

where $\bar{p}^{(j)}_{t\text{-}1} = \sum_i p^{(j,i)}_t$ = the probability, conditional on observation x_t that the process was in state j at period t-1.

Thus, in updating the priors we use the data a second time. Since it is impossible to assess the nature of a shock at the moment of its occurrence, we wait until the next observation to determine whether last period's shock was temporary or permanent. This evaluation serves as learning mechanism about changes in the characteristics of the series.

A stylized example

In figure A1 an artificial series is presented to demonstrate the characteristics of the MSKF-method. We have designed the series in such a way that the first part suffers from temporary outliers only, while permanent changes in the level dominate the second part and large slope changes occur in the final part. The continued line in the figure indicates the level of the artificial series; the dotted line indicates the forecasts, which are located on the same vertical line as the observations which they try to predict. Thus, the forecasts have been computed one period earlier.

Take, for example, the forecast that has to be formed at point A. It is clear from the last two observations of the series that an outlier occurred at A, but it is still impossible to determine which type of outlier. Accordingly, the only thing the method can do is to trust its information from the past and to rely almost completely on the prevailing prior probabilities of the different outlier models. The posterior weights of the small-change models are zero of course, so that the composite forecast is a weighted average of the forecasts of the three outlier models, whereby the weight on the permanent step change model is almost 60%, the weight on the transitory model is almost 30%, leaving 13% for the slope change model. These priors are a legacy from the series' history up to time A.

The result is a forecast for next period in which this period's forecast error is almost completely incorporated. However, at that moment it becomes clear that the outlier at point A was temporary. This leads to a reshuffling of the prior probabilities as is demonstrated by the forecasts when subsequent outliers occur. At point B the outlier is already considered to be temporary with a 93% probability when it occurs, so that next period's forecast deviates only slightly from the permanent level at B. The third transient outlier at C is deemed to be 98% temporary and does not significantly affect next period's forecast. We conclude therefore that after three outlier shocks with a temporary character the method has learnt to ignore these shocks.

When outlier D occurs, the MSKF-method still forecasts on the assumption that large shocks are transient. Therefore, next period's prediction remains at the previously estimated permanent level of the series. However, the outlier proves to be of a permanent nature and the method only slowly adjusts to the new permanent level. It takes about four periods before reasonably accurate predictions are made again. Meanwhile the priors have been adjusted too. Before outlier D the 5% chance on the outlier models was almost wholly concentrated on the transitory model, which had a prior of 4.98%. Afterwards the priors have shifted away from the transitory outlier model to the step change model. The respective probabilities now are 3.3% and 1.7%. When further permanent outliers occur the priors change further which causes the method to adjust more rapidly to each new shift. At point G for example, the prior probability of the permanent step change model is 4.98% leading to an immediate incorporation of the error into next period's forecast. It is noteworthy to see that when outlier H occurs, the shift is less rapidly recognized as when outlier G occurred. This is caused

Figure A1   The Multi-State Kalman filter

A forecasting technique which incorporates automatic learning about the difference between temporary and permanent changes

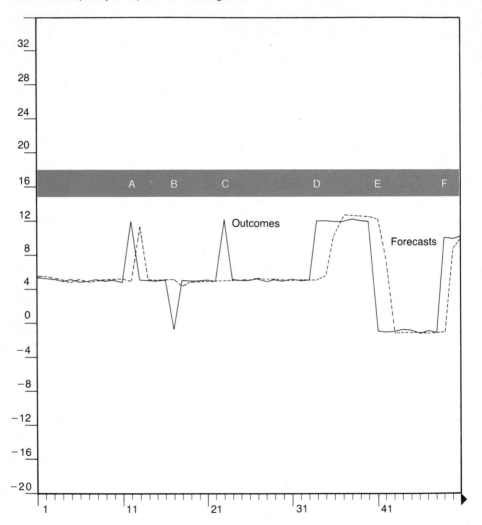

The forecasting scheme has to cope with large temporary outliers, large permanent shocks to the level of a series, and important permanent changes in its growth rate. The figure shows how the algorithm learns the optimal reponse after the second or third occurrence of a new type of disturbance.

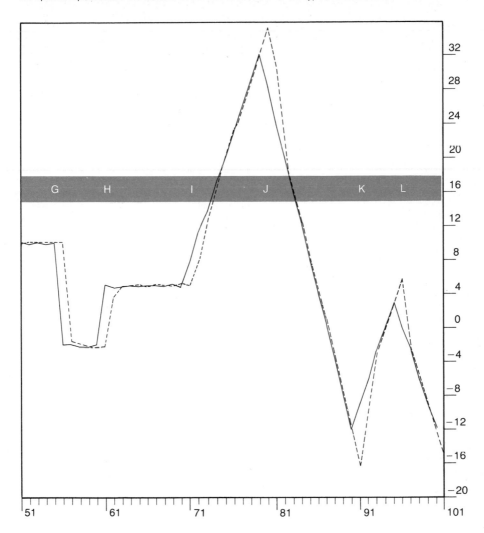

by two reasons. First the shift at H is of a smaller magnitude, second the basic variance of the process has been rising steadily because of the large number of shifts and associated forecast errors in the series. Both reasons cause the method to revise its evaluation of outliers and small shocks. At point H, the method hesitates between these two possibilities and assigns a probability of 46% to the large step change model, but also a 26% probability to the transitory small change model and a 23% probability to the small step change model.

After outlier H the stochastic nature of the artificial series changes again. Now only slope changes occur. It is clear that the first slope change is recognized very slowly. The series is underpredicted for four periods. As time goes by however, the method is learning again and is able to catch up with slope changes as soon as they ocur, which is proved by the predictions after outlier L. Thus, the method is capable of recognizing different values for the drift parameter and adjusts its behaviour accordingly.

The Swiss money supply: a real world example

Table A2 shows the prior probabilities of the six forecast models in the MSKF-method for the episode in the history of the Swiss money supply which was discussed in chapter 4. Contrary to the experience of the model before 1973, in the first three quarters of 1973 a slop change occurs, reducing the permanent growth rate to about zero. As the priors are biased in favour of level changes at that moment, it takes a few periods before the method has adjusted itself, leading to consistent overpredictions in these three quarters. Also, there is a shift in the priors. Starting with a 4.92% probability on a large level change and a 0.03% chance on a slope change in 1973I, these probabilities are 3.11% and 1.81% respectively in 1973III. The old situation returns again however, when a new shock in 1973IV raises the level permanently by an amount of 0.03. Then in 1974III the money supply starts declining unexpectedly, causing a series of positively correlated errors due to the fact that not a slope change, but a level change is assumed to have occurred. Of course the priors are adjusted again though only with a small amount, leading to an average prior of approximately 3.5% for the large step change model and of 1.2% for the slope change through 1975. A new slope change in 1975IV upsets the priors, and the large slope change model becomes dominant from then on until 1978I. This seems contradictory at first sight with the observation in chapter 4 that in 1976 and 1977 predicted changes in the slope are very smooth when compared with the actual growth rates. A closer look however reveals that these changes are of a minor magnitude, leading to small prediction errors, which are deemed to be transitory to a large extent as is confirmed by the prior probability on the transitory small change model of around 65% during 1977. Table A2

Table A2: Prior probabilities for the six different models (%)[1]

Period	Model 1	Model 2	Model 3	Model 4	Model 5	Model 6
1973I	49.6	26.3	19.2	0.0	4.9	0.0
II	47.5	26.8	20.8	0.8	3.4	0.7
III	42.9	25.1	27.0	0.1	3.1	1.8
IV	43.3	25.2	26.6	1.6	3.3	0.1
1974I	43.7	24.8	26.6	0.2	4.8	0.1
II	53.6	22.4	19.1	0.3	4.6	0.1
III	62.4	17.5	15.1	0.3	4.7	0.0
IV	63.8	16.7	14.5	0.2	3.7	1.1
1975I	50.5	16.9	27.7	0.1	4.3	0.6
II	48.4	18.0	28.6	0.1	3.7	1.2
III	40.3	13.8	40.9	0.1	3.4	1.6
IV	65.8	7.9	21.3	0.4	3.7	0.9
1976I	51.4	10.9	32.7	0.1	2.0	2.9
II	49.0	10.2	35.9	0.0	0.3	4.7
III	65.5	7.2	22.3	0.0	0.3	4.7
IV	59.9	6.9	28.1	0.0	0.0	5.0
1977I	65.7	7.7	21.6	0.0	0.4	4.6
II	74.4	5.5	15.1	0.0	0.3	4.7
III	63.8	8.7	22.5	0.0	0.4	4.6
IV	69.6	7.0	18.4	0.0	0.4	4.6
1978I	69.9	7.2	18.2	0.0	3.4	1.6
II	78.9	5.2	10.9	0.0	1.6	3.4
III	84.2	3.5	7.2	0.0	4.5	0.5
IV	87.3	3.2	4.4	0.0	4.3	0.7
1979I	84.3	4.0	6.8	0.0	4.4	0.6
II	88.6	2.4	4.0	0.0	4.2	0.8
III	62.4	4.1	28.5	0.0	3.4	1.6
IV	72.3	3.7	19.0	0.0	3.4	1.6
1980I	69.6	4.3	21.1	0.0	3.6	1.4
II	71.7	4.2	19.1	0.0	3.6	1.4
III	68.2	4.7	22.1	0.0	3.6	1.4
IV	70.0	4.7	20.3	0.0	3.7	1.3

[1] It's possible that the probabilities don't sum to 100% because of rounding errors. Further we note that in practice all prior probabilities are restricted to be at least 0.01% to avoid computational problems.

immediately clarifies what happened in 1977IV: a step change occurred, which was misinterpreted as a slope change because of the then prevailing priors. This causes some large forecast errors and subsequent revision of the priors, giving a larger weight again to changes in the level. Therefore the next large outlier in 1979I is considered in first place to consist of a large change in the level. However, large errors are made as this shock turns out to be a slope change.

This real world example shows how the method attempts to distinguish between different types of shocks and to update its prior probabilities regarding the upcoming disturbances to the series. If the major shocks are separated in time, as in our artificial example, the learning mechanism can be illustrated easily. When the importance of different categories of shocks changes rapidly over time, as in the case of the Swiss money supply, learning becomes harder and the algorithm has greater difficulty in interpreting new information. However, the flexible approach should guarantee that the forecast errors will not cumulate longer than is necessary.

appendix 2

On-line forecasts
with the RPE-method

with Clemens J.M. Kool

This Statistical Appendix will be much more concise than Statistical Appendix 1, since an excellent paper by Moore and Weiss (1979) sets forth the general features of the method. Moreover, we have less practical experience with the recursive prediction error (RPE) method than with the MSKF-method of Statistical Appendix 1, and we reckon that further experiments by others and ourselves will lead to deeper insights into the best ways of using this powerful technique.

Kalman filters are meant in the first place to 'filter' incoming data and produce estimates of 'state variables'. Noisy signals about the location of a space satellite, for example, could be filtered to generate estimates of its velocity. The laws of motion are known, and the Kalman filter technique applies a fixed known model to each period's fresh observations. In economic applications we would like both estimates of the 'state variables', such as the rate of inflation, the rate of economic growth etc. and estimates of the coefficients in the equations describing the economy, since so much less is known about economic 'laws' than about the laws of nature.

The Multi-State Kalman filter technique solved the problem of simultaneous uncertainty about the state variables and the model parameters by applying a battery of fixed models to the incoming data. Shifts in the relative importance of the different separate filters provided a means of adjusting the composite forecasts to changing characteristics of the data. As each of the separate filters corresponded to a Box-Jenkins model with two parameters, we were able to 'cover' the parameter space by a very small number of filters. If, however, the forecasts have to be based on several input variables, many more parameters will be required to describe the economic structure, and an impractically large number of separate models would be required to 'cover' the full parameter space. Thus, we have applied a different extension of Kalman filtering to the multivariate forecasting problem of chapter 4. The RPE-method developed by Moore and Weiss (1979) allows for simultaneous estimation of the unobservable state variables and the unknown parameters of the model. Although the model has to be linear in its variables, estimation is a highly nonlinear problem since both parameters and state variables are unknown. An approximate solution of the estimation problem is obtained by updating the estimated parameters each period, given the state variables, and by subsequently adjusting the state variables using the updated parameters. The derived RPE-method, inspired by the excellent article of Moore and Weiss (1979), is based on approximated minimization of index $J_{t\theta}$ for each t to achieve a recursive update of a parameter estimate θ_t. $J_{t\theta}$ is expressed in terms of the prediction error $\tilde{z}_{k\theta} = z_k - z_{k|k-1,\,\theta}, k = 1, 2, \ldots$ for a one-step-ahead prediction estimate $z_{k|k-1,\,\theta}$

$$J_{t\theta} = \frac{1}{2}\left[\sum_{k=1}^{t} \tilde{z}_{k\theta}^T \Lambda_{k\theta}^{-1} \tilde{z}_{k\theta} + \log \det \Lambda_{k\theta} \right] \tag{B1}$$

where $\Lambda_{k\theta}$ is a positive definite weighting matrix.

The model

Let us consider a linear innovations model described by

$$x_{t+1} = A(\theta)x_t + B(\theta)u_t + K(\theta)\varepsilon_t \tag{B2}$$

$$z_t = C(\theta)x_t + \varepsilon_t \tag{B3}$$

where x_t, z_t and u_t are vectors of dimensions n, m, and p, respectively, u_t is an input vector, x_t is a vector of state variables, z_t is an output vector, and the sequence ε_t consists of independent random vectors with zero mean and covariance matrix:

$$E(\varepsilon_t\varepsilon_s{}^T) = \Lambda_{ts}\delta_{ts} \tag{B4}$$

The prediction error $\hat{\varepsilon}_t = \tilde{z}_t$ is given from

$$\hat{x}_{t+1} = A(\hat{\theta})\hat{x}_t + B(\hat{\theta})u_t + K(\hat{\theta})\hat{\varepsilon}_t \tag{B5}$$

$$\hat{\varepsilon}_t = z_t - C(\hat{\theta})\hat{x}_t \tag{B6}$$

We define:

$$M_t = M(\hat{\theta}_t, \hat{x}_t, u_t, \hat{\varepsilon}_t) \tag{B7}$$

$$= \frac{\partial}{\partial\theta}[A(\theta)\hat{x}_t + B(\theta)u_t + K(\theta)\hat{\varepsilon}_t]_{\theta=\hat{\theta}_t}$$

$$D_t = D[\hat{\theta}_t, \hat{x}_t] \tag{B8}$$

$$= \frac{\partial}{\partial\theta}[C(\theta)\hat{x}_t]_{\theta=\hat{\theta}_t}$$

$$W_t = \frac{\partial\hat{x}_t}{\partial\hat{\theta}_t} \tag{B9}$$

$$\psi_t = -\left(\frac{\partial \varepsilon_t}{\partial \hat{\theta}_t}\right)^T = [C(\hat{\theta}_t) W_t + D_t]^T \tag{B10}$$

$$\varphi_t^T = \left\{ tr\left(\Lambda_t^{-1} \frac{\partial \Lambda_t}{\partial \theta_1}\right), \ldots \ldots, tr\left(\Lambda_t^{-1} \frac{\partial \Lambda_t}{\partial \theta_v}\right)\right\} \tag{B11}$$

where θ_j is the j-th element of the v dimensional vector θ

$$\mu_t = \hat{\varepsilon}_t^T \Lambda_t^{-1} \left\{ \frac{\partial \Lambda_t}{\partial \theta_1} \Lambda_t^{-1} \hat{\varepsilon}_t, \ldots \ldots, \frac{\partial \Lambda_t}{\partial \theta^m} \Lambda_t^{-1} \hat{\varepsilon}_t \right\} \tag{B12}$$

then

$$\hat{\theta}_t = \hat{\theta}_{t-1} - P_t \left\{ -\psi_t \Lambda_t^{-1} \hat{\varepsilon}_t + \frac{1}{2} \varphi_t - \frac{1}{2} \mu_t^T \right\} \tag{B13}$$

$$P_t^* = P_{t-1} - P_{t-1} \psi_t S_t^{-1} \psi_t^T P_{t-1} \tag{B14}$$

$$S_t = \Lambda_t + \psi_t^T P_{t-1} \psi_t \tag{B15}$$

$$P_t = P_t^* - P_t^* \varphi_t (2 + \varphi_t^T P_t \varphi_t)^{-1} \varphi_t^T P_t^* \tag{B16}$$

$$W_{t+1} = (A(\hat{\theta}_t) - K(\hat{\theta}_t) C(\hat{\theta}_t)) W_t + (M_t - K(\hat{\theta}_t) D_t) \tag{B17}$$

$$\Lambda_t = \frac{t}{t+1} \Lambda_{t-1} + \frac{1}{t+1} \hat{\varepsilon}_t \hat{\varepsilon}_t^t \tag{B18}$$

$$t \leqslant t_0 + 15$$

$$\Lambda_t = c_0 \cdot \sum_{k=0}^{15} \lambda^k \hat{\varepsilon}_{t-k} \cdot \hat{\varepsilon}_{t-k}^T \tag{B19}$$

$$. t \geqslant t_0 + 15$$

Equations (B5) - (B6) and (B13) - (B19) constitute the recursive algorithm used for the multivariate forecasting problem of chapter 4. P_t is the currently estimated covariance matrix of the estimated parameter vector θ_t and Λ_t is the estimate of the covariance matrix of the vector of prediction errors $\hat{\varepsilon}_t$.

Estimation starts in period t_0. The initial value θ_0 of the parameter vector θ is set at zero, while P_0 is a diagonal matrix with all diagonal elements equal to 0.25.

A starting value for Λ_0, the covariance matrix of $\hat{\varepsilon}_t$, is derived by calculating two measures of dispersion and transforming them into a robust variance estimate, in a way similar to that described in Statistical Appendix 1 above. During the first 16 periods Λ_t is adjusted gradually using all forecast errors starting from period t_0. After these 16 periods Λ_t is adjusted each period using the computed prediction errors over the 16 most recent periods with a weighting factor λ (decay parameter) equal to 0.9 and a normalization constant c_0 equal to $(1 - \lambda)/(1 - \lambda^{16})$.

In the algorithm the estimate $\hat{\theta}_t$ is constrained such that:
$| \lambda_i [A(\hat{\theta}_t) - K(\hat{\theta}_t) . C(\hat{\theta}_t)] | < 1$ for all i,t
where $\lambda_i (x)$ denotes the i-th eigenvalue of x. In case the constraint is violated the stepsize P_t of the updating is reduced to half its previous size. This procedure is repeated until an estimate $\hat{\theta}_t$ is found for which the restriction does hold. The rationale behind these restrictions is to guarantee the stability of W_{t+1} and thus the stability of the algorithm.

The particular form of the general model in chapter 4 is as follows:

state equations:

$$y^e_{t+1} = y^e_t + \eta^e_{t+1} + \theta_1\gamma^e_{t+1} + \theta_9\varepsilon_{p_t} + \theta_2\varepsilon_{y_t} \tag{B20}$$

$$\eta^e_{t+1} = \eta^e_t + \theta_{11}\Delta\hat{M}^e_{t+1} + \theta_{12}\Delta\hat{M}^e_t + \theta_3\varepsilon_{p_t} + \theta_4\varepsilon_{y_t} \tag{B21}$$

$$V^e_{t+1} = V^e_t + \gamma^e_{t+1} + \theta_5\eta^e_{t+1} + \theta_6\varepsilon_{p_t} + \theta_{10}\varepsilon_{y_t} \tag{B22}$$

$$\gamma^e_{t+1} = \gamma^e_t + \theta_{13}\Delta\hat{M}^e_{t+1} + \theta_{14}\Delta\hat{M}^e_t + \theta_7\varepsilon_{p_t} + \theta_8\varepsilon_{y_t} \tag{B23}$$

$$p^e_{t+1} = M^e_{t+1} + V^e_{t+1} - y^e_{t+1} \tag{B24}$$

output equations:

$$p_t = p^e_t + \varepsilon_{p_t} \tag{B25}$$

$$y_t = y^e_t + \varepsilon_{y_t} \tag{B26}$$

By substituting for the state variables with index $(t+1)$ on the right-hand side of the system of state equations, the model may be written as:

$$
\begin{bmatrix} y^e_{t+1} \\ \eta^e_{t+1} \\ V^e_{t+1} \\ \gamma^e_{t+1} \\ p^e_{t+1} \end{bmatrix}
=
\begin{bmatrix}
1 & 1 & 0 & \theta_1 & 0 \\
0 & 1 & 0 & 0 & 0 \\
0 & \theta_5 & 1 & 1 & 0 \\
0 & 0 & 0 & 1 & 0 \\
-1 & (\theta_5\text{-}1) & 1 & (1\text{-}\theta_1) & 0
\end{bmatrix}
\begin{bmatrix} y^e_t \\ \eta^e_t \\ V^e_t \\ \gamma^e_t \\ p^e_t \end{bmatrix}
+
\begin{bmatrix}
0 & \theta_{11}+\theta_1\theta_{13} & \theta_{12}+\theta_1\theta_{14} \\
0 & \theta_{11} & \theta_{12} \\
0 & \theta_{13}+\theta_5\theta_{11} & \theta_{14}+\theta_5\theta_{12} \\
0 & \theta_{13} & \theta_{14} \\
1 & \theta_{13}(1\text{-}\theta_1)+ & \theta_{14}(1\text{-}\theta_1)+ \\
 & \theta_{11}(\theta_5\text{-}1) & \theta_{12}(\theta_5\text{-}1)
\end{bmatrix}
\begin{bmatrix} M^e_{t+1} \\ \Delta\hat{M}^e_{t+1} \\ \Delta\hat{M}^e_t \end{bmatrix}
$$

$$
\begin{bmatrix}
\theta_3 + \theta_1\theta_7 + \theta_9 & \theta_4 + \theta_1\theta_8 + \theta_2 \\
\theta_3 & \theta_4 \\
\theta_7 + \theta_3\theta_5 + \theta_6 & \theta_8 + \theta_4\theta_5 + \theta_{10} \\
\theta_7 & \theta_8 \\
\theta_6 - \theta_9 + \theta_7(1\text{-}\theta_1) + & \theta_{10} - \theta_2 + \theta_8(1\text{-}\theta_1) + \\
+ \theta_3\,(\theta_5\text{-}1) & + \theta_4\,(\theta_5\text{-}1)
\end{bmatrix}
\begin{bmatrix} \varepsilon_{p_t} \\ \varepsilon_{y_t} \end{bmatrix}
\qquad \text{(B27)}
$$

In the notation of the algorithm above this means

$$ x_t \quad = (y^e_t,\ \eta^e_t,\ V^e_t,\ \gamma^e_t,\ p^e_t)' \qquad\qquad \text{(B28)} $$

$$ z_t \quad = (p_t,\ y_t)' \qquad\qquad \text{(B29)} $$

$$
A(\hat{\theta}_t) \quad =
\begin{bmatrix}
1 & 1 & 0 & \theta_1 & 0 \\
0 & 1 & 0 & 0 & 0 \\
0 & \theta_5 & 1 & 1 & 0 \\
0 & 0 & 0 & 1 & 0 \\
-1 & (\theta_5-1) & 1 & (1-\theta_1) & 0
\end{bmatrix}
\qquad \text{(B30)}
$$

$$B(\hat{\theta}_t) = \begin{bmatrix} 0 & \theta_{11} + \theta_1\theta_{13} & \theta_{12} + \theta_1\theta_{14} \\ 0 & \theta_{11} & \theta_{12} \\ 0 & \theta_{13} + \theta_5\theta_{11} & \theta_{14} + \theta_5\theta_{12} \\ 0 & \theta_{13} & \theta_{14} \\ 1 & \theta_{13}(1-\theta_1) + \theta_{11}(\theta_5-1) & \theta_{14}(1-\theta_1) + \theta_{12}(\theta_5-1) \end{bmatrix} \tag{B31}$$

$$u_t = (M^e_{t+1}, \Delta\hat{M}^e_{t+1}, \Delta\hat{M}^e_t)' \tag{B32}$$

$$K(\hat{\theta}_t) = \begin{bmatrix} \theta_3 + \theta_1\theta_7 + \theta_9 & \theta_4 + \theta_1\theta_8 + \theta_2 \\ \theta_3 & \theta_4 \\ \theta_7 + \theta_3\theta_5 + \theta_6 & \theta_8 + \theta_4\theta_5 + \theta_{10} \\ \theta_7 & \theta_8 \\ \theta_6 - \theta_9 + \theta_7(1-\theta_1) + \theta_3(\theta_5-1) & \theta_{10} - \theta_2 + \theta_8(1-\theta_1) + \theta_4(\theta_5-1) \end{bmatrix} \tag{B33}$$

$$C(\hat{\theta}_t) = \begin{bmatrix} 0 & 0 & 0 & 0 & 1 \\ 1 & 0 & 0 & 0 & 0 \end{bmatrix} \tag{B34}$$

$$\varepsilon_t = (\varepsilon_{p_t}, \varepsilon_{y_t})' \tag{B35}$$

$$\theta = (\theta_1, \theta_2, \ldots\ldots, \theta_{13}, \theta_{14})' \tag{B36}$$

Partial derivatives are as defined in (B7) - (B11). We refer to the article by Moore and Weiss (1979) for further details.

appendix 3

Data used

This appendix lists the definitions and sources of all data used in the analysis. The principal source of data has been 'International Financial Statistics', a monthly publication of the International Monetary Fund, Washington D.C. Most data have been transferred directly from the December 1982 IFS data tape. We have indicated the IFS line number corresponding to each variable. The symbols I, II, III and IV refer to the four quarters of a year. The meaning of the abbrevations of the countries is as follows:

U.S.	=	United States
D	=	Germany
NL	=	The Netherlands
CH	=	Switzerland
B	=	Belgium
A	=	Austria
DK	=	Denmark

List of variables

M   *Money stock*, according to the narrow (M1) definition (currency and demand deposits), seasonally adjusted.

      U.S.:   Quarterly average of daily figures.

              Source: Federal Reserve Bank of St. Louis.

      Other countries: Quarterly averages of end-of-month figures.

              Source: International Financial Statistics, line 34.b.

      Austria: An institutional change (Kreditwesengesetz) in March 1979 providing for the free determination of interest rates as well as permitting banks to agree on interest rates on deposits, had spectacular consequences for the rates of growth of the monetary aggregates. The end-of-month numbers for Austrian M1 during the first nine months of 1979 show a sharp decline, followed by a stabilization during the summer months:

Jan.	Feb.	March	April	May	June	July
136.95	141.75	131.98	122.04	123.30	123.26	122.12

August	Sept.
121.88	122.68

We have decided not to construct artificial data to put in the place of the true numbers for the Austrian money supply in 1979. We would have felt more comfortable to do this if there had been a uniform pattern in at least some other monetary aggregates. But, the two measures that should be least affected by this regulatory upheaval, the adjusted monetary base on the one hand and the broadest measure of liquidity (M3) on the other hand, show quite divergent behaviour during 1979 and the first half of 1980. Thus, we have omitted part of 1979 in the regressions of chapter 2, and put the time series for monetary accelerations equal to 0 for 1979II and III in chapter 5.

Y   *Gross national product or gross domestic product in current prices*, seasonally adjusted, measured on an annual basis.

y   *gnp or gdp in constant prices*, seasonally adjusted, measured on an annual basis.

p   *Implicit price deflator of gnp or gdp.*

Description and source of these three variables:

U.S.:   gnp, 1975 = 100.
Source: International Financial Statistics, lines 99a and 99a.r.

D: gnp, 1975 = 100.
Source: International Financial Statistics, lines 99a and 99a.r.

NL: gnp, 1977 = 100.
Source: De Nederlandsche Bank, Quarterly Statistics, 1982-3, and De Nederlandsche Bank, Kwartaalconfrontatie van middelen en bestedingen 1957-1980, Augustus 1982.

CH: gnp, 1970 = 100.
Series constructed by Basler Arbeitsgruppe für Konjunkturforschung; kindly provided by Dr. Wolfgang Fautz, Schweizerischer Bankverein.

B: gnp, 1975 = 100.
Volume index constructed by interpolation using an index of industrial production (International Financial Statistics line 66 b), a trend variable and a trend squared variable.
Price index proxied by consumer price index (International Financial Statistics, line 64).
The time series have been adjusted to make sure that the yearly totals of quarterly data are equal to the annual figures (International Financial Statistics, lines 99a and 99a.p).

A: gdp, 1975 = 100.
Source: International Financial Statistics, lines 99b and 99b.p.

DK: gdp, 1975 = 100.

Volume index computed by interpolation using an index of manufacturing production (International Financial Statistics, line 66ey), a trend variable and a trend squared variable.

Price index proxied by consumer price index (International Financial Statistics, line 64).

The time series have been adjusted to make sure that the yearly totals of quarterly data are equal to the annual figures (International Financial Statistics, lines 99b and 99b.p).

fp   *Forward premium* (three-month forward exchange rate less spot rate as a proportion of the spot rate vis-à-vis the US dollar (the price of the dollar in national currencies). Quarterly averages of end-of-month figures.

Source:
D:	OECD, Main Economic Indicators
NL:	OECD, Main Economic Indicators
CH:	OECD, Main Economic Indicators
B:	OECD, Main Economic Indicators.
A:	International Financial Statistics, starting 1967III.
DK:	International Financial Statistics, starting 1973I.

i_T: *Interest rate on three-month time deposits.*

Quarterly averages of end-of-month figures.

D:	Three-month deposits larger than DM5 million.
	Source: Monthly Bulletin, Deutsche Bundesbank.
NL:	Three-month loans to local government.
	Source: Quarterly Statistics, De Nederlandsche Bank.
CH:	Three-month deposits with major banks.
B:	Three-months deposits with commercial banks.
A:	Treasury bill rate.
DK:	Central government bonds.
	Source for the last four countries: OECD Interest Rates 1960-1974 and OECD Financial Statistics.

i_S: *Interest rate on three-month savings deposits.*

Quarterly averages of end-of-month figures.

D:	Savings deposits with legal period of notice.
.NL:	Three-month savings deposits.
CH:	Savings deposits with cantonal banks.
B:	Three-month treasury certificates.
A:	Savings deposits with legal period of notice.

DK: Three-months deposits with commercial and savings banks.
Source: as i_T.

i_b *Yield on long-term government bonds.*
Quarterly averages.
U.S.:   Long-term government bonds with 20-year constant maturity.
D: All public authorities' bonds with an average remaining life to maturity of more than three years.
NL: Three latest long-term government bond issues.
CH: Ten government bonds with at least five years to maturity.
B: All five to eight per cent government bonds issued after December 1962 with more than five years to maturity.
A: All government bonds not yet redeemed.
DK: 3.5% Perpetual government bond 1886.
Source: IFS, line 61.

Def: *Government budget deficit.*
Corresponding to International Financial Statistics, line 80, but computed by separate seasonal adjustment of revenues and expenditures.
CH: Starting in 1971I.
DK: Central government's net financing requirement.
Source: Monetary Review, Danmarks National Bank. Quarterly data from 1976I onwards. Before 1976 quarterly data have been obtained by interpolation. Four-quarter differences have been used in the regressions of chapter 5, because normal seasonal adjustment is ruled out.

Trade: *Volume of world exports*, constant prices of 1975.
Source: International Financial Statistics, lines 001 70d and 74d.

p_{oil} *Spot price of oil* (1% fuel oil, US$ per metric ton).
Source: Platt's Oilgram Price Service, kindly provided by NOVOK, Rotterdam.

Relative rates of growth have been computed throughout as first differences of natural logarithms, multiplied by a factor 100, to make the resulting growth rates directly comparable to percentage rates of increase. A caret '^' has been used to indicate a relative rate of growth. Rates of growth have been annualized (multiplied by 4) in all the regression work, but not in the

Kalman filter programs of chapters 2 and 4. We have used ordinary first differences, indicated by Δ, for all interest rate variables including the forward premia used in chapter 2. All interest rate variables have been expressed as percentages per annum, i.e. 6 instead of 0.06 for a rate of 6% per year.

Acknowledgements

In the Autumn of 1981, the Directors of Bank Mendes Gans in Amsterdam decided to sponsor a book on a topical issue in macroeconomics in order to mark their Jubilee in August 1983. On a previous occasion in 1962, the Bank sponsored an essay on the theory of economic growth, written by J.E. Andriessen. Andriessen discussed the theory of balanced economic growth under the then usual assumptions of perfect foresight and no uncertainty. Twenty years have since passed and the 1983 Centennial of the Bank is marked with this study on the relations between the absence of economic growth and the high uncertainty and economic opacity that characterized the beginning of the 1980's.

I wish to thank Mr. M. Ligtenstein, Managing Director of Bank Mendes Gans and his colleague Mr. A. J. Ch. van der Noordaa, Director of the Bank, for a generous research grant that enabled me to keep up an intensive working relationship with some of the professional colleagues mentioned below. The Bank consented also to my request for extensive graphical support of the argument. It is a pleasure to acknowledge the collaboration of Hans den Hollander who supplied all the graphics and designed this book.

To a considerable extent, the book is a joint product. Clemens J.M. Kool and Paul T.W.M. Veugelers co-authored the empirical chapters and the two Statistical Appendices. I am very grateful to both of them. Valuable research assistance was provided by Fred M. Bär, Victor de Jonge, K. Geert Rouwenhorst, Isolde B. Woittiez en Eduard A. van Zuijlen.

Initial drafts of many chapters were presented at Seminars or Conferences at Carnegie-Mellon University, the University of Chicago, Siegen University, the University of Siena, and at the Konstanz Seminar on Monetary Theory and Monetary Policy as well as several Dutch Universities. I am grateful to all these professional audiences for their patience and their suggestions.

Many conversations with Allan H. Meltzer of Carnegie-Mellon University helped me to clarify my thinking on the economic implications of uncertainty about permanent and transitory changes in the economic environment. I should be glad if this book could be regarded as a first step to implementing empirically some of the fruitful ideas that were developed jointly by Karl Brunner of the University of Rochester, Alex Cukierman of Tel-Aviv University and Allan Meltzer. Helpful comments and suggestions on the complete manuscript were received from Scott E. Hein of the St. Louis Fed and from my colleague Peter D. van Loo. With so many knowledgeable friends there is not much of an excuse left for any remaining errors in the analysis, but I take all responsibility.

Erna Zwaanswijk-ten Cate produced all successive versions of the manuscript. I truly appreciate her extremely competent contribution.

Since Janneke did so much more than just allow me to write a second book so shortly after the first, my deepest gratitude goes – once again – to her.

Eduard J. Bomhoff
June 1983

References

Andersen, L.C. and J.L. Jordan (1968), Monetary and fiscal actions : a test of their relative importance in economic stabilization, *Review Federal Reserve Bank of St. Louis*, 50, Nov., 11-24.

Bank of England (1982), *Bank of England Quarterly Bulletin*, 22, no. 4 (Dec.).

Barro, R.J. (1977), Unanticipated money growth and unemployment in the United States, *American Economic Review*, 67, no. 2 (March), 101-115.

Barro, R.J. (1978), Unanticipated money, output, and the price level in the United States, *Journal of Political Economy*, 86, no. 4 (Aug.), 549-580.

Blejer, M.J. (1978), The demand for money and the variability of the rate of inflation : some empirical results, *International Economic Review*, 20, no. 2, 545-549.

Bomhoff, E.J. (1977), Predicting the money multiplier : A case study for the U.S. and the Netherlands, *Journal of Monetary Economics*, 3, no. 3 (July), 325-346.

Bomhoff, E.J. (1980), *Inflation, the quantity theory and rational expectations*, North-Holland, Amsterdam.

Bomhoff, E.J. (1981), The attractions of index-linked government debt, *Kempen's economic monitor*, no. 2 (Sept.).

Bomhoff, E.J., (1982), Predicting the price level in a world that changes all the time, in : K. Brunner and A.H. Meltzer (eds.), Economic policy in a world of change, *Carnegie-Rochester Conference Series on Public Policy*, 17, Autumn, 7-56.

Bomhoff, E.J. and P. Korteweg (1983), Exchange rate variability and monetary policy under rational expectations : some Euro-American experience 1973-1979, *Journal of Monetary policy Economics*, 11, no. 2 (March), 169-206.

Box, G.E.P. and G.M. Jenkins (1970), *Time series analysis, forecasting and control*, Holden-Day, San Francisco.

Breeden, D.T. (1979), An intertemporal asset pricing model with stochastic consumption and investment opportunities, *Journal of Financial Economics*, 7, no. 3 (Sept.), 265-296.

Brunner, K. (ed.) (1972), *Problems and issues in current econometric practice*, The Ohio State University, Columbus.

Brunner, K. (1982), The voices of "failure" and the failure of monetary policy-making, in : Shadow Open Market Committee, *Policy Statement and Position Papers*, Graduate School of Management, University of Rochester, September 12-13.

Brunner, K., A. Cukierman and A.H. Meltzer (1980), Stagflation, persistent unemployment and the permanence of economic shocks, *Journal of Monetary Economics*, 6, no. 4 (Oct.), 467-492.

Brunner, K. and A.H. Meltzer (eds.) (1978), The problem of inflation, *Carnegie-Rochester Conference Series on Public Policy*, 8.

Butter, F.A.G. den, and M.M.G. Fase (1981), The demand for money in EEC countries, *Journal of Monetary Economics*, 8, no. 2 (Sept.), 201-230.

Büttler, H.-J., et al. (1979), A multiplier model for controlling the money stock, *Journal of Monetary Economics*, 5, no. 3 (July), 327-341.

Büttler, H.-J. and K. Schiltknecht (1983), Transitory changes in monetary policy and their implications on money-stock control, in : K. Brunner and A.H. Meltzer (eds.), *Carnegie-Rochester Conference Series on Public Policy*, 19, Autumn, forthcoming.

Carlson, J.A. (1977), A study of price forecasts, *Annals of Economic and Social Measurement*, 6, no. 1 (Winter), 27-56.

Central Planning Bureau (1977), *Een macro model voor de Nederlandse economie op middellange termijn (VINTAF II)*, Occasional Paper no. 12, The Hague.

Commission of the European Communities (1983), *European Economy*, Supplement C, no. 1 (March).

Cukierman, A. (1983), Relative price variability and inflation. A survey and further results, in : K. Brunner and A.H. Meltzer (eds.), *Carnegie-Rochester Conference Series on Public Policy*, 19, Autumn, forthcoming.

Cukierman, A. and P. Wachtel (1979), Differential inflationary expectations and the variability of the rate of inflation : theory and evidence, *American Economic Review*, 69, no. 4 (Sept.), 595-609.

Davis, R.G. (1971), How much does money matter ? A look at some recent evidence, in : W.E. Gibson and G.G. Kaufman (eds.), *Monetary economics, Readings on current issues*, McGraw Hill, New York, 132-147. Originally published in : *Monthly Review Federal Reserve Bank of New York*, 51, June, 1969, 119-131.

Dooley, M.P. and P. Isard (1980), Capital controls, political risk, and deviations from interest-rate parity, *Journal of Political Economy*, 88, no. 2 (April), 370-384.

Ehrbar, A.F. (1982), How to cut those deficits – and why, *Fortune*, February 22, 50-55.

Emerson, M. (1982), *The European stagflation disease in international perspective, and some possible therapy*, Paper presented at the Conference of the Centre for European Policy Studies on European policy priorities, December 15-17, Brussels.

Fama, E.F. and G.W. Schwert (1977), Human capital and capital market equilibrium, *Journal of Financial Economics*, 4, no. 1 (Jan.), 95-125.

Friedman, B.M. (1979), Substitution and expectation effects on long-term borrowing behavior and long-term interest rates, *Journal of Money, Credit and Banking*, 11, no. 2 (May), 131-150.

Friedman, M. (1948), A monetary and fiscal framework for economic stability, *American Economic Review*, 38, no. 3 (June), 245-264.

Friedman, M. (1968), The role of monetary policy, *American Economic Review*, 58, no. 1 (March), 1-17.

Friedman, M. and A.J. Schwartz (1982), *Monetary trends in the United States and the United Kingdom : their relation to income, prices, and interest rates, 1867-1975*, University of Chicago Press for the National Bureau, Chicago.

Garber, P.M. (1982), Transition from inflation to price stability, in : K. Brunner and A.H. Meltzer (eds.), Monetary regimes and protectionism, *Carnegie-Rochester Conference Series on Public Policy*, 16, Spring, 11-46.

Gordon, M.J. and P.J. Halpern (1976), Bond share yield spreads under uncertain inflation, *American Economic Review*, 66, no. 4 (Sept.), 559-565.

Gramlich, E.M. (1983), Models of inflation expectations formation : a comparison of household and economic forecasts, *Journal of Money, Credit and Banking*, 15, no. 2 (May), 155-173.

Granger, C.W.J. and P. Newbold (1977), *Forecasting economic time series*, Academic Press, New York.

Grossman, H.I. (1982), Comment on the Garber paper, in : K. Brunner and A.H. Meltzer (eds.), Monetary regimes and protectionism, *Carnegie-Rochester Conference Series on Public Policy*, 16, Spring, 43-46.

Hall, R.E. (1978), Stochastic implications of the life cycle-permanent income hypothesis : theory and evidence, *Journal of Political Economy*, 86, no. 6 (Dec.), 971-987.

Hansen, L.P. and K.J. Singleton (1983), Stochastic consumption, risk aversion, and the temporal behavior of asset returns, *Journal of Political Economy*, 91, no. 2 (April), 249-265.

Harrison, P.J. and C.F. Stevens (1971), A Bayesian approach to short-term forecasting, *Operational Research Quarterly*, 22, no. 4, 341-362.

Harrison, P.J. and C.F. Stevens (1976), Bayesian forecasting, *Journal of the Royal Statistical Society*, Series B, 38, no. 3, 205-247.

Huber, P.J. (1981), *Robust statistics*, Wiley and Sons, New York.

Indexed Linked Mortgage and Investment Company Ltd. (1982), *The low start flexible repayment mortgage for commercial loans*,London.

International Mathematical and Statistical Libraries (1980), *The IMSL library*, volume 2, Houston.

Johannes, J.M. and R.H. Rasche (1979), Predicting the money multiplier, *Journal of Monetary Economics*, 5, no. 3 (July), 301-325.

Karnosky, D.S. (1976), The link between money and prices, 1971-1976, *Review Federal Reserve Bank of St. Louis*, 58, no. 6 (June), 17-23.

Keynes, J.M. (1923), *A tract on monetary reform*, Macmillan, London.

Klein, B. (1977), The demand for quality-adjusted cash-balances : price uncertainty in the U.S. demand for money function, *Journal of Political Economy*, 85, no. 4 (Aug.), 691-715.

Kool, C.J.M. (1982), The Multi-State-Kalman Filter method, in : K. Brunner and A.H. Meltzer (eds.), Economic policy in a world of change, *Carnegie-Rochester Conference Series on Public Policy*, 17, Autumn, 39-46.

Krasker, W.S. (1980), The "peso problem" in testing the efficiency of forward exchange markets, *Journal of Monetary Economics*, 6, no. 2 (April), 269-276.

Lazard Index Linked Mortgage Unit Trust (1982), *Interim report and accounts*, London.

Leeuw, F. de and E.M. Gramlich (1971), The channels of monetary policy, in : W.E. Gibson and G.G. Kaufman (eds.), *Monetary economics, Readings on current issues*, Mc Graw-Hill, New York, 148-168. Originally published in : Federal Reserve Bulletin, 55, June, 1969, 472-491.

Levi, M.D. and J.H. Makin (1979), Fisher, Phillips, Friedman and the measured impact of inflation on interest, *Journal of Finance*, 34, no. 1 (March), 35-52.

Lintner, J. (1965), Security prices, risk, and maximum gains from diversification, *Journal of Finance*, 20, no. 5 (Dec.), 587-616.

Lucas, R.E. (1972), Expectations and the neutrality of money, *Journal of Economic Theory*, 4, no. 2 (April), 103-124.

Lucas, R.E. (1975), An equilibrium model of the business cycle, *Journal of Political Economy*, 83, no. 6 (Dec.), 1113-1144.

Lucas, R.E. (1977), Understanding business cycles, in : K. Brunner and A.H. Meltzer (eds.), Stabilization of the domestic and international economy, *Carnegie-Rochester Conference Series on Public Policy*, 5, 7-29.

Lucas, R.E. (1981), *Studies in business-cycle theory*, The MIT Press, Cambridge (Mass.).

Lucas, R.E. (1982a), The death of Keynes, in : T.J. Hailstones (ed.), *Viewpoints on supply-side economics*, R.F. Dame, Inc., Richmond, 3-5.

Lucas, R.E. (1982b), Interest rates and currency prices in a two-country world, *Journal of Monetary Economics*, 10, no. 3 (Nov.), 335-359.

Makin, J.H. (1982), Effects of inflation control programs on expected real interest rates, *IMF Staff Papers*, 29, no. 2 (June), 204-232.

Mascaro, A. and A.H. Meltzer (1983), Long- and short-term interest rates in a risky world, *Journal of Monetary Economics*, 12, no. 3 (Nov.), forthcoming.

Mayers, D. (1972), Nonmarketable assets and capital market equilibrium under uncertainty, in : M.C. Jensen (ed.), *Studies in the theory of capital markets*, Praeger, New York, 223-248.

McNees, S.K. (1981), The recent record of thirteen forecasters, *New England Economic Review*, Sept./Oct., 5-21.

Meigs, A.J. (1972), *Money matters*, Harper and Row, New York.

Meltzer, A.H. (1981a), On Keynes's General Theory, *Journal of Economic Literature*, 19, no. 1 (March), 34-64.

Meltzer, A.H. (1981b), Speaking at a *Hearing for the Joint Economic Committee*, Congress of the United States, October 6.

Merton, R.C. (1973), An intertemporal capital asset pricing model, *Econometrica*, 41, no. 5 (Sept.), 867-887.

Mishkin, F.S. (1976), Illiquidity, consumer durable expenditure and monetary policy, *American Economic Review*, 66, no. 4 (Sept.), 642-654.

Mishkin, F.S. (1978a), Monetary policy and liquidity : simulation results, *Economic Inquiry*, 16, no. 1 (Jan.), 16-36.

Mishkin, F.S. (1978b), The household balance sheet and the Great Depression, *Journal of Economic History*, 38, no. 4 (Dec.), 918-937.

Moore, J.B. and H.J. Weiss (1979), Recursive error methods for adaptive estimation, *IEEE Transactions on systems, man and cybernetics*, 9, no. 4, 197-205.

Mullineaux, D.J. (1978), On testing for rationality : another look at the Livingston price expectations data, *Journal of Political Economy*, 86, no. 2, part 1 (April), 329-336.

Mullineaux, D.J. (1980), Unemployment, industrial production and inflation uncertainty in the United States, *Review of Economics and Statistics*, 62, no. 2 (May), 163-169.

Newton, M. (1983), *The Fed. Inside the Federal Reserve, the secret power center that controls the American economy*, Times Books, New York.

North, D.C. (1981), *Structure and change in economic history*, W.W. Norton & Company, New York and London.

OECD (1983), *Economic Outlook,* July, Paris.

Olson, M. and M.J. Bailey (1981), Positive time preference, *Journal of Political Economy*, 89, no. 1 (Febr.), 1-25.

Parkin, J.M. (1975), The politics of inflation, *Government and opposition*, 10, no. 2 (Spring), 189-202.

Parkin, M. (1981), *Oil push inflation ?* Paper prepared for the Conference "The price of oil and the economy", Erasmus University Rotterdam, April 3.

Pearce, D.K. (1979), Comparing survey and rational measures of expected inflation : forecast performance and interest rate effects, *Journal of Money, Credit and Banking*, 11, no. 4 (Nov.), 447-456.

Phelps, E.S. (1968), Money-wage dynamics and labor-market equilibrium, *Journal of Political Economy*, 76, no. 4, part II (July/Aug.), 678-711.

Phelps, E.S. et al. (1970), *Micro-economic foundations of employment and inflation theory*, Macmillan, London.

Rasche, R.H. and J.A. Tatom (1977), Energy resources and potential GNP, *Review Federal Reserve Bank of St. Louis*, 59, no. 6 (June), 10-23.

Schwert, G.W. (1979), Tests of causality : the message in the innovations, in : K. Brunner and A.H. Meltzer (eds.), Three aspects of policy and policymaking : knowledge, data and institutions, *Carnegie-Rochester Conference Series on Public Policy*, 10, 55-96.

Sharpe, W.F. (1964), Capital asset prices : a theory of market equilibrium under conditions of risk, *Journal of Finance*, 19, no. 4 (Sept.), 425-442.

Shiller, R.J. (1982), Consumption, asset markets and macroeconomic fluctuations, in : K. Brunner and A.H. Meltzer (eds.), Economic policy in a world of change, *Carnegie Rochester Conference Series on Public Policy*, 17, Autumn, 203-238.

Siegel, J.J. and J.B. Warner (1977), Indexation, the risk-free asset, and capital market equilibrium, *Journal of Finance*, 32, no. 4 (Sept.), 1101-1107.

Sims, C.A. (1972), Money, income, and causality, *American Economic Review*, 62, no. 4 (Sept.), 540-552.

Sweeney, R.J. (1982), *Some macro implications of risk*, Paper, Claremont Graduate School.

Tatom, J.A. (1979), The meaning and measurement of potential output : a comment on the Perloff and Wachter results, in : K. Brunner and A.H. Meltzer (eds.), Three aspects of policy and policymaking : Knowledge, data and institutions, *Carnegie-Rochester Conference Series on Public Policy*, 10, 165-178.

Webb, R.H. (1983), Forecasts 1983, *Economic Review, Federal Reserve Bank of Richmond*, 69, no. 1 (Jan./Febr.), 3-6.

Wilcox, J.A. (1983), Why real interest rates were so low in the 1970's, *American Economic Review*, 73, no. 1 (March), 44-53.

Working, H. (1960), Note on the correlation of first differences of averages in a random chain, *Econometrica*, 28, Oct., 916-918.

Zellner, A. (1979), Causality and econometrics, in : K. Brunner and A.H. Meltzer (eds.), Three aspects of policy and policymaking : knowledge, data and institutions, *Carnegie-Rochester Conference Series on Public Policy*, 10, 9-54.

Index